UNDER THE SIGN OF NATURE
Explorations in Ecocriticism

Editors
Michael P. Branch, SueEllen Campbell, John Tallmadge

Series Consultants
Lawrence Buell, John Elder, Scott Slovic

Series Advisory Board
Michael P. Cohen, Richard Kerridge, Gretchen Legler,
Ian Marshall, Dan Peck, Jennifer Price, Kent Ryden,
Rebecca Solnit, Anne Whiston Spirn,
Hertha D. Sweet Wong

JOHN ELDER

PILGRIMAGE TO
VALLOMBROSA

From Vermont to Italy in the Footsteps
of George Perkins Marsh

University of Virginia Press

Charlottesville & London

. . .

University of Virginia Press

© 2006 by the Rector and Visitors
of the University of Virginia

All rights reserved

Printed in the United States of America
on acid-free paper

First published 2006

I 3 5 7 9 8 6 4 2

Library of Congress Cataloging-in-Publication Data

Elder, John, 1947–

Pilgrimage to Vallombrosa : from Vermont to Italy in the footsteps
of George Perkins Marsh / John Elder.

p.   cm. — (Under the sign of nature)

Includes bibliographical references (p.) and index.

ISBN-13: 978-0-8139-2576-9 (cloth : acid-free paper)

1. Human ecology—Philosophy. 2. Nature—Effect of human
beings on. 3. Philosophy of nature. 4. Geographical perception.
5. Elder, John, 1947– —Travel. 6. Marsh, George Perkins,
1801–1882—Travel.

I. Title. II. Series.

GF21.E53 2006

304.2—dc22   2006004723

To Scott Russell Sanders and Jefferson Hunter,
two friends who've been like brothers to me

CONTENTS

FOREWORD

by David Lowenthal

How, wonders John Elder, can we begin to feel at home in the universe? By telling "the story of a place through the narrative of our individual lives," as he does so superbly here. His enchanting book recounts two lives, that of George Perkins Marsh and his own. It is framed by two unforgettable formative places, Woodstock, Vermont, and Vallombrosa, Italy. Inspired by a "passionate compulsion to reinscribe the world," Elder emulates Dante in compelling those who travel with him to "see and change."

For over thirty years, says Elder, he has been on his way to Woodstock's once denuded and since reforested Mount Tom, which looms over Marsh's birthplace. I owe the pleasure of prefacing this book to having been en route there for twice as long. Ever since I found Marsh's prophetic *Man and Nature* in 1947, my life has been entwined with his. Two Marsh biographies later, whatever I know of nature and history mirrors Elder's debt to this incomparable "looker and rememberer." It was Marsh, wrote Wallace Stegner, who in 1864 gave blind American faith in nature's boundless cornucopia "the rudest kick in the face" it had ever received.

His prescient insights are acclaimed today by many along with Elder. At Piòbesi, the Po village where Marsh penned *Man and Nature* in 1863, a *cena* and *conversazione* in September 2005 commemorated the fete at his home for the Union victory at Vicksburg; the ceremonial inaugurated a local *Sagra del pane*—an apt coda to the local olive festival Elder describes in this book. In Woodstock and Florence, Marsh's transatlantic partnerships were acknowledged in bicentenaries for his lifelong friend, the famed neoclassical sculptor Hiram Powers. At Vallombrosa, the abbey-cum-forestry reserve of Marsh's last days, an international symposium celebrated his diplomatic acumen and stewardship in the Risorgimento Italy he served as American envoy over two decades.

Elder's book exalts two opposed aspects of being: immersion and transcendence. As stewards of our denizened Earth we need to feel embedded within, yet also buoyed up beyond, our own immediate time and ken. Of this dual vision both Elder and his mentor Marsh are past masters. Magnanimous love of place stems from knowing and caring for many places; indeed, having a concern for the entire cosmos. The tympanum of European experience, in Elder's overarching medieval metaphor, matured Marsh's visionary Vermont perceptions. In like fashion, the olive groves of Elder's own Italian pilgrimage inform his Vermont scything and sawing and syrup making, larding his labors with chastened and calloused devotion.

Travel makes us "at once more patriotic and more philanthropic—cosmopolitan in the right sense," wrote Marsh. Being abroad shows us how to improve "the prosperity or morality of our own" country, and also to repay our foreign hosts for these gains—as with his own gifts of sorghum and okra to Tuscan farmers, of laurel to reforest Portugal, and of walnut and sugar maple to Vallombrosa. Back home in Vermont, John Elder repays not only Italy but all of us everywhere. For this book rekindles modes of rural life that speak to our hunger for community, sustenance, durability, and sheer sensuous earthiness. We "must all remember," Elder enjoins us, "from time to time, to go to grass."

Elder like Marsh twins ecology with etymology, the saga of woods with the story of words. For the latter Marsh required "real live books," not grammatical abstractions. "You may feed the human intellect on roots, stems, and endings, as you may keep a horse on saw-dust, but you must add a little literature in the one case, a little meal in the other." For Elder art likewise adorns nature in this "real live book." Just as the poet Jones Very's lyrics webbed the world for Marsh, so Robert Frost's "The land was ours before we were the land's" fructifies Elder's vision.

To grasp the reforms, physical, social, above all moral, that animate *Man and Nature* and this book alike requires not just mourning ecological loss but accepting and learning from that loss. Elder shows what Aldo

Leopold and Rachel Carson gleaned from the landscape losses they witnessed. Equally poignant was Marsh's recall of his Woodstock boyhood, when "the flocks of wild geese which formerly passed, every spring and autumn, were very frequently lost, and I often heard their screams in the night as they flew wildly about in perplexity as to the proper course," their anserine map deranged by the clearing of woods and by the village lights. Two centuries later, Elder finds us similarly disoriented by the loss of darkness that deprives us of nightly contact with the stars, those "bright stones cast together in the sky" that formerly reminded earthlings of their smallness and warned them against taking nature for granted.

History like ecology humbles Earth's stewards. I do not mean lessons of past folly only, but the capacity to see our own lifetime as but a brief moment in the far lengthier sagas of society and nature. Outliving the self is a uniquely human enterprise. It ennobles awareness of mortality with life-enhancing links to those who came before and will come after us. And conservation is the crux of the fellowship that unites the living and the dead and those who are to be born. As Marsh and Elder alike avow, stewardship is the duty we owe our descendants on behalf of our ancestors.

Elder's most memorable "ancestor in the land" is the Marsh-Billings-Rockefeller National Historical Park in Woodstock, created to tell the story of American despoliation and conservation. Like many of Elder's eloquent stewards, Marsh left no other progeny (two sons were tragically lost) than that park—his birthplace—and his enduring words and thoughts. Marsh deplored American mobility, the flitting transience that scorned rooted sentiment, past respect, and future protection. But he thought it unstoppable. And because few Americans inhabited parental lands, few would care for them. Self-interest defeated stewardship.

Elder revives hope in self-interest. He is cheered that his own children, unlike their immigrant forebears, may continue to cherish his own "providential" Vermont. But even if his sons and daughter go elsewhere, this book attests Elder as the best of ancestors. The greater family of his readers inherit an exemplary legacy of civic participation. Elder's impassioned pilgrimage shows us how to delight in messy wilderness, to secure a curative habitation of the world, and, with Marsh, to lend ecological nous to our gravest task: knowing ourselves and respecting one another. Let the maple seeds and olive stones of Elder's visionary harvest restore to us a reflective and redemptory future.

ACKNOWLEDGMENTS

I am grateful to the many people who helped me with this project. I was introduced to the life and work of George Perkins Marsh by Rolf Diamant, Superintendent of the Marsh-Billings-Rockefeller National Historical Park in Woodstock, Vermont, and Nora Mitchell, Director of the National Park System's Conservation Study Center, also housed in Woodstock. Among their many thoughtful acts was introducing me to David Lowenthal, the authority on Marsh and a scholar both generous and profound. Following my interest in Marsh to Italy became possible because of a Fulbright Senior Research Fellowship supporting my wife, Rita, and me during our sojourn in Florence; I truly appreciate this help. While in Italy, I had the good fortune to meet a number of individuals who freely offered me their time and expertise. Professor Antonio Gabrielli at the Institute for Forest Science in Fiesole opened the doors for me at the forestry school and arboretum at Vallombrosa and gave a day to driving Rita and me up there for our second visit. Professor Mauro Agnoletti at the University of Florence pointed me toward essential literature both about the forest history at Vallombrosa and about parallels between the Vermont and Tuscan landscapes. Franco Tassi, Director of the Abruzzo National Park, invited us to a conference at Abruzzo where we were fortunate to meet many authorities on Italian conservation and environmental history. Two of these were American scholars living and working in Europe, Marcus Hall and James Sievert, who kindly shared both their own research and writing and their guidance on a memorable outing to the forests and park at Casentino. In Florence we profited both during the sabbatical and on subsequent visits from the help and hospitality of Claudia Mastrangelo, Fabrizio Fiumi, Terry Fowler, Stefano Magazzini, and Janet Shapiro. Through opening up the world of traditional Tuscan olive culture to us, Stefano and Janet provided one of the catalytic experiences of our travels.

Since returning to Vermont I have benefited in many ways from the support of my home institution, Middlebury College, while finishing up my research and writing and preparing this manuscript. The special collections that were most valuable for me at this stage were the rare book collection at the University of Vermont's Bailey-Howe Library, the Crane Family Papers at the New York Public Library, and the archives at the Arnold Arboretum. Chris McGrory Klyza of Middlebury's Environmental Studies Program was an excellent resource on the political and cultural context of environmental policy. Natasha Chang of our Italian Department helped me translate an archaic passage about the forest of Vallombrosa. Forest ecologists Eric Sorenson and Tom Wessels, visionary forester David Brynn, and ace birders Warren and Barry King taught me about the landscape and wildlife around Maggie Brook. Eric Freyfogle was invaluable in giving me an overview of Aldo Leopold's evolving philosophy of conservation. A number of friends and colleagues offered wonderfully discerning readings of my book at various stages. In this connection I want to convey my warm thanks to the following: Marion Wells, Scott Russell Sanders, Jefferson Hunter, Bill McKibben, and David Lowenthal. I am honored to have Professor Lowenthal provide the foreword for *Pilgrimage to Vallombrosa*. Rita, in addition to being my companion on the European pilgrimage, was a perceptive reader and encouraging brainstormer throughout the whole process of composition. And shortly before I proceeded to publication, John Tallmadge stepped forward to offer a thorough and pointed assessment of the manuscript; he helped me in many crucial ways to bring this diverse project into focus. Boyd Zenner and Ellen Satrom at the University of Virginia Press have been a joy to work with, and Ruth Melville did an extraordinarily fine job with the copyediting.

Finally, having acknowledged all this essential help, I want to acknowledge that whatever errors or omissions remain are of course my own responsibility.

. . .

I would also like to express my sincere thanks for permission to quote from these copyrighted materials: "Dust of Snow" and excerpt from "Directive" from *The Poetry of Robert Frost,* edited by Edward Connery Lathem. Copyright 1923, 1947, 1969 by Henry Holt and Company. Copyright 1951 by Robert Frost, copyright 1975 by Lesley Francis Ballantine. Reprinted by permission of Henry Holt and Company, LLC. The tale of Gluskabe's creation of people from the ash trees, in Joseph Bruchac, *The Faithful Hunter: Abenaki Stories* (Greenfield Center, NY: Greenfield Review Press, 1988), 9, 10. Reprinted by permission of Joseph Bruchac. Portions of several chapters of the present book previously appeared in periodical form: "Inheriting Mt. Tom," *Orion* (Spring 1997); "A Conversation at the Edge of Wilderness," *Wild Earth* (Winter 1999); "The Poetry of Experience," *New Literary History* (Summer 1999); "Darkness and Memory," *Wild Earth* (Fall 2002); "George Perkins Marsh and the Headwaters of Conservation," *Wild Earth* (Winter 2003); "Unfolding the Map: The Champion Lands and the Future of Vermont," *Vermont Life* (Autumn 2003); "A Dust of Snow: Awakening to Conservation," *Tricycle* (Fall 2003); "After Olive Picking," *Orion* (Fall 2003).

PILGRIMAGE TO
VALLOMBROSA

PROLOGUE
SPIRAL HOME

In March, when the sun drops behind our southwest ridge, cold cruises up this hollow like a mile of ice. That's when the slender, budded maple twigs begin to suck in sap. Their only chance as temperatures fall is to engorge themselves. Furred with frost, they'll hold their breath all night and keep on doing so until the morning light has shone on them for several hours. Then they can finally give it up again, sap trickling down a thousand springs into the river of the trunk. Then the lidded buckets, still half filled with ice, can start to tick on every tree. Under the sugar bush's slump of snow, the soil is stirring too. Last fall's leaf meal starts to thaw and clot. Tiny embedded stars of ice detach, winking down into the O-horizon's deep black sky. A maple seed, dormant since it whirled to earth six months ago on wings veined like the wings of a dragonfly, opens now at the touch of water. It will give everything it has for one pale root to slide into a loosening world, for a tender stem and two round leaves.

Each sugar maple makes a watershed of its own in the larger circulation of the land. As sap wells out to the branches' tips, descends with the new day's thaw, and lifts again at dusk, it echoes the pulse of tidal rivers and the respiration of the sea. The life of our own family, too, sways with the seasonal ebb and flow of this sugar bush in the hills of Starksboro, Vermont—close to the village of Bristol, where we have our house. For seven years, we have worked to become good stewards of the land. We have put in water bars and culverts to forestall erosion on recklessly laid out old logging roads. We have studied the principles of sustainable forestry, carefully thinning the crowded, third-growth woods in order to release the canopy. Using the small amounts of merchantable sawtimber from such cuts, we have collaborated with our neighbors to produce batches of hardwood flooring and other value-adding ventures. Our biggest commitment of all, though, has been to sugaring. In collaboration with our sons, Matthew and Caleb, and our daughter, Rachel, my wife, Rita, and I built a sugarhouse and began to orient our calendar to the March-and-April ritual of collecting sap and distilling it into maple syrup. Our connection with the sugar bush feels like the culmination of a relationship that began when Rita and I moved to Addison County, Vermont, in 1973. Though neither of us had grown up in this state, the wooded beauty of its mountains and the vitality of its villages made us want to put down roots and raise our children here. And that decision led in turn to a wish to participate in the living rural traditions of our chosen landscape through practical measures of stewardship.

Photographs in the upstairs hallway of our Bristol house tell the story of a typically mobile American family. A picture of my self-possessed Cajun grandmother, Thérèse Richard, taken against the painted backdrop in a Biloxi, Mississippi, studio, hangs beside one of Rita's mother's family, the Cianfonis. Margarita was a girl of six in that solemn family portrait taken with her immigrant parents, Cesare and Federica, and her siblings, Oreste and Maria. They had entered the United States through Ellis Island just a few years before. Nearby are photographs of my Scotch-Irish mother, Lois, who grew up in northern Louisiana, of my father, Lyn, as a fifteen-year-old in Biloxi, and of Rita's dad, Roy Pinkston, whose family moved to California from Tennessee when he was a young man.

We frequently pause in the hallway to inspect the faces of these ancestors, and to muse on the convergences that have made our family what it is. Rita and I have now spent almost our entire adult lives in Vermont, where none of those predecessors had ever set foot before our parents began to visit us here. For over three decades, we have been learning to identify with the landscape, history, and culture of this chosen place. As we work in the woods now with our grown children, we have also begun to harbor a hope that, for the first time in almost a century, at least two generations in a row of our family may end up making their homes in the same locale. The challenge of sustainable forestry in a transient society is summed up by the fact that the life span of a sugar maple can be as much as three times longer than the halest human being's. The health of the woods and the family will both be served if they are identified with one another and grow alongside each other for much longer than three score years and ten.

· · ·

In ways that we never anticipated, though, our sense of affiliation with Vermont was also deepened by an excursion that Rita and I took between the end of one sugaring season and the beginning of the next. *Pilgrimage to Vallombrosa* tells the story of that journey and of the changes it brought to our life and work at home. We had conceived of this time away as a temporary interruption of our seasonal commitments in the woods—framed by my year's leave from teaching English and environmental studies at Middlebury College and Rita's sabbatical from her work as a special educator at Lincoln School. But just as crown and root pursue their tidal dialogue beneath the maple's bark, in the life of a family, too, departures and returns may contribute to a larger process of growth. Thus it happened one year, after we'd pulled the taps, washed out the evaporator pans, and stacked the buckets upside down in the sugarhouse loft, that Rita and I found ourselves traveling to Italy on a dual quest.

Rita was intent on reconnecting with her Italian relatives. Her bilingual mother had taken responsibility for maintaining the cross-Atlantic bonds through correspondence and visits. But after her mom's passing, Rita began brushing up her own Italian. Her goal was for us to travel back to Artena, the ancient hill town east of Rome from which her grandparents emigrated, and introduce ourselves to the remaining family members there. The fact that Caleb, the youngest of our three, had just left home for college heightened our sense of this as a watershed year in the life of our family. Throughout our months in Italy we made trips to Artena to spend time with the Cianfonis, Vendettas, and Corsettis there. We found them just as eager as we were to consolidate an extended family that also included Elders and Pinkstons. At Christmas, when our three children flew over to join us, along with Matthew's girlfriend, Becca, we celebrated the season with a series of parties that sometimes saw over thirty of us gathered around a room-filling table. Among the highlights of those meals were homemade wine, mushrooms gathered from the nearby woods, and smoky lasagna carried in from the *forno al legno* in the backyard.

My simultaneous project was to pursue the footsteps of the pioneering conservationist George Perkins Marsh. Marsh was born in Woodstock, Vermont, in 1801 and died at Vallombrosa, in the mountains of eastern Tuscany, in 1882. His masterpiece, *Man and Nature*—published in 1864 while Marsh was serving as Lincoln's minister plenipotentiary to the new Kingdom of Italy—has been described by Lewis Mumford as "the fountainhead of the conservation movement."[1] Stocked with an extraordinary wealth of information about the environmental history of the Mediterranean region, it also drew extensively on the human and natural history of the author's native Vermont. Since this is the state where our own family is also rooted, such a connection made me eager to know more about the evolution of Marsh's environmental thought and practice. While some of our weekends were spent in Artena or taking a trip to the beach with Rita's cousin Gloria and her family, our other outings often found us hiking through the ancient chestnut and beech forests of Tuscany or visiting monasteries, villas, and other landmarks from Marsh's eventful life in Italy. In both endeavors, though, Rita and I were undertaking a pilgrimage during an interval between the seasonal runs of sap. We were determined, in these complementary projects, to broaden our perspective on the wholeness of family and home.

A pilgrimage might be defined as a purposeful journey, undertaken to reconnect with the sources of life's meaning and strength. Such a quest necessarily involves indirection and discovery, rather than a foray for a single purpose. Even though we each had strong reasons to make this journey, for much of it Rita and I were uncertain, and a bit apprehensive, about exactly what the outcome would be. She was going to see cousins she'd last met as a little girl, and to meet their children, whom she didn't know at all. None of these relatives were pictured on our wall in Bristol, and the degree to which they would feel a reciprocal interest in us was still unclear. For my part, I wanted to reflect on the life and achievement of a Vermont ancestor by revisiting sites from the final decades of his life. But being neither an environmental historian nor a professional forester, I would be walking into a story rather than undertaking anything that resembled systematic research.

Another way to put this is that I was hoping for a personal dialogue with Marsh, stimulated by rereading his book in the landscape where he wrote it. But my reflections also turned out to be colored in many important ways by the experience of traveling with Rita and sharing in her effort to forge a connection with the wider circle of her Italian relatives. Increasingly, I understood my exploration of Marsh's life within this familial context, and specifically with relation to the issue of generational inheritance. If Marsh was a catalyst for me, in other words, the crystallization to which he contributed included a range of personal and emotional associations that were specific to our family.

I also undertook the trip with a sense that *Man and Nature* would be a bridge between my decades of teaching environmental literature at Middlebury and our family's newer endeavors in sugaring and sustainable forestry. But I learned, during our sojourn abroad, that this was a bridge that could be crossed in both directions. Marsh's vision, and the era that he brought into focus for me, made both the earlier poets of earth and the nature essayists of our own day available in a new way. In returning to our sugar bush at the conclusion of this year away, I was thus surprised to discover that my sense of vocation at Middlebury College had also been renewed. Teaching and writing came to feel like an outgrowth of our family's work in the woods, as well as a preparation for it.

. . .

Even though we had only eight months between the end of one school year and the beginning of a new sugaring season in March, we decided to devote our first two months to a walk toward Italy. Allotting about two weeks to cross England on the Coast to Coast Walk and another six weeks to traverse southern France between La Rochelle and the Mediterranean village of Cassis, we'd have a chance to reflect on the connections between this long excursion and our ordinary lives. What we found, as generations of pilgrims before us have done, was that the journey and the destination became inseparable.

A river registers the countryside's bedrock and tectonic history every time it bends its course around an obstacle. It recalls the passage of a glacier when winding down through a broad, U-shaped pass to cross the gravels of an ancient shore. Pilgrimage too is a journey of recapitulation. It brings a dawning recognition that the landscape through which we walk, as well as the sites toward which we journey, is hallowed ground. In "Walking," Thoreau justifies his preference for "sauntering" by the fact that a river's meandering course is "all the while sedulously seeking the

shortest course to the sea."[2] Such purposeful sauntering is often motivated, its accidents and contingencies organized into a story, by an inspiring example. My own main landmark on this journey was that book published by George Perkins Marsh over 150 years ago. Though Marsh made
me want to go to Italy, what I eventually found there—and on the way
there—also helped me in unexpected ways to integrate both his story
and the landscapes through which we passed into our family's relationship with the sugar bush in Starksboro.

Just as, throughout that long walk, Rita was anticipating our arrival
at the hill town of Artena, there was a particular sugar maple tree—
planted in Tuscany over a century ago—that I wanted to see and stand
beside. Just three days before his death on July 23, 1882, Marsh wrote a
letter to Charles Sprague Sargent of Harvard's Arnold Arboretum. He
told Sargent that he was "disappointed at not seeing a single *compatriot*
among the forest growths" of Italy's first forestry school at Vallombrosa,
and asked him to send over the seeds of several New England trees, including the sugar maple.[3] I was drawn to this tree as an intersection
between our home landscape and the mountainous region of eastern
Tuscany that was so important to Marsh. I hoped that the maple of Vallombrosa would help me trace the dialogue between our Vermont pre-
cursor and the environmental challenges and opportunities of the present. This relic would be a link not only with an inspiring figure from
Vermont but also with our sugar bush at home. An equally important
but unanticipated connection was made when we became acquainted
with the olive trees of Impruneta, near Florence. Having picked olives
there with friends who make traditional Tuscan olive oil continues to enrich our experience of producing maple syrup in Vermont, and our perspective on its meaning for the culture and future of our home landscape.

. . .

Pilgrimage is a journey motivated by the power of old stories, a path
along which ordinary citizens may pursue the traces of saints, heroes, or
prophets. Those setting out on such a path are spurred both by a sense of
connection with their grand models and by the discrepancy between
their own lives and those more galvanic ones. Such has been my experience, as a college teacher and woodlot owner from Vermont, in following
the footsteps of George Perkins Marsh and the prophetic tradition of

conservation that he inaugurated. A story that is too big for us may by the same token offer a landscape in which we can lose, and find, ourselves.

Man and Nature was the first book to describe and document the drastic, long-term impact of human actions on living systems. People had of course always recognized the local damage caused by certain behavior. The earth seemed so vast, though, and our powers so relatively puny, that such effects were assumed to be no more than minor disturbances in the scheme of things. But with his archaeological bent and his wide travels, Marsh was able to assess the cumulative damage of deforestation in particular. Each generation saw only its own cutting, yet century by century the forest kept disappearing. No society has ever intended to deplete its source of fuel, wash away the topsoil on which farmers depend, disturb its region's climate and rainfall, or render its harbors useless by filling them with silt. But Marsh found evidence of exactly that pattern at ancient, abandoned settlements around the Mediterranean. Such social and ecological failures brought to mind the rapacious deforestation he had observed in boyhood around Woodstock, Vermont. It was through connecting the environmental history of Europe in the classical and medieval eras with that of his own time and place that Marsh recognized the urgency for restraint in our private practices and public policies alike.

Writing as he did in an era when steam power and railroads were greatly accelerating the human capacity to alter the landscape, Marsh declared that we must now either change our ways or destroy the natural fabric supporting our own survival: "The earth is fast becoming an unfit home for its noblest inhabitant, and another era of equal human crime and human improvidence, and of like duration with that through which traces of that crime and that improvidence extend, would reduce it to such a condition of impoverished productiveness, of shattered surface, of climactic excess, as to threaten the depravation, barbarism, and perhaps even extinction of the species."4 With this voice, he inaugurated a lineage that has extended through Aldo Leopold and Rachel Carson and that includes contemporaries like Bill McKibben and Stephanie Mills.

If Marsh and his successors ask that we look steadfastly at the disasters confronting us, they do so in order that we may find the resolve for necessary changes. In this way, their writing is both shadowed and hopeful. Thus, in order to give a balanced view of Marsh's vision, the apocalyptic passage quoted above needs to be linked with one in which his emphasis is on restoration and reform. Marsh saw awareness of ecological disasters as the first step toward social and economic changes that could realign our culture with the larger cycles of nature.

> All human institutions, associate arrangements, modes of life, have their characteristic imperfections. The natural, perhaps the necessary defect of ours, is their instability, their want of fixedness, not in form only, but even in spirit. The face of physical nature in the United States shares this incessant fluctuation, and the landscape is as variable as the habits of the population. It is time for some abatement in the restless love of change which characterizes us, and makes us almost a nomade rather than a sedentary people. We have now felled forest enough everywhere, in many districts far too much. Let us restore this one element of material life to its normal proportions, and devise means for maintaining the permanence of its relations to the fields, the meadows, and the pastures, to the rain and the dews of heaven, to the springs and rivulets with which it waters the earth.[5]

Just as the deforestation of Vermont in Marsh's boyhood prompted *Man and Nature's* admonitions, our present-day reforestation and conservation efforts respond to his calls for restoration and sustainability. His book inscribes a broad arc in our history.

With all the historical and ecological breadth of his vision, Marsh never forgot his boyhood experiences in a Green Mountain village ravaged by logging and suffering from the related problems of erosion, clogged streams, and uncontrolled forest fires. His way of telling these stories engaged me as a householder in Bristol, just up the mountains' spine from his town of Woodstock. Marsh's admonition about the need for people to become "co-workers with nature" spoke to the value of stewardship in wounded and recovering landscapes like Vermont and the Mediterranean alike. Traveling on foot through Europe transformed my perspective, though, just as it had affected his views 140 years earlier. It located his story within a much longer pilgrimage toward environmental mindfulness, and helped me see as joined within one journey the efforts of our own family and neighbors in Vermont and those of Italian farmers and conservationists we met. No single generation, much less any one person, can adequately register all the gifts and losses flowing out of the past. This book offers my own cupful from those braided currents.

Wendell Berry writes, in an essay that critiques prevailing environmental terminology, "The real names of the environment are the names
of rivers and river valleys; creeks, ridges, and mountains; towns and
cities; lakes, woodlands, lanes, roads, creatures, and people."[6] Working
in the sugar bush, like walking through some of the byways of English or
French or Italian history, offers an immediate physical model for such
specificity, mutuality, and affiliation. Activities of this sort may give rise
to enhanced experiences of community. A more grounded sense of identity may, by the same token, make our personal relationships more stable
and promote a successful transition from one generation to the next.
This does not, however, imply a nostalgic look backward toward earlier
social structures.

The ideal of environmental stewardship, originally associated with
lordly structures of authority, has today modulated to a tragic key: a
chastened and participatory concern for the larger cycles of health that
our own projects have disrupted. Vallombrosa, the name of the Tuscan
forest where Marsh died, might be translated as "the shadowed vale."
This is a reverberant image for the pattern of insights emerging from disasters, or wholeness following separations, to which this book continuously returns. I find hope in such a shadowed beauty. Family and community, like environmental stewardship, might now be understood in
less assertive and more inclusive ways. My readings of Marsh have done
much to shape this perspective. But so too has the long meander though
sites charged with history that Rita and I undertook together. And returning to our home in the Green Mountains has offered the best chance
of all to grasp the meaning of what we saw and did on our excursion.

. . .

Pilgrimage to Vallombrosa describes a personal path through three landscapes connected in their different ways to George Perkins Marsh's stern
but hopeful vision of conservation. The sections into which the book is
organized each correspond to one of these landscapes, with the first section being framed by our journeys to and within Tuscany. The terrain
that encompasses Florence, its surrounding hill towns, and the celebrated forests to their east is filled with locales important in Marsh's life.
Coming to know present-day Italians who practice the values of conservation, stewardship, and sustainability brought *Man and Nature* into this
landscape all the more vividly.

The second landscape grounding this book is that of literature. I had appreciated Marsh as the initiator of a prophetic tradition in conservation but had not been inclined to place him very firmly in a literary lineage. A couple of aspects of our travels made me think differently about him, however. One of these was keeping a journal along the way in which several authors repeatedly came to mind with reference to Marsh and to the countryside through which we were passing. Specifically, Wordsworth, Bashō, and Frost were the poets mapping this literary landscape for me, and helping me see the terrain we traversed as also being a receptacle of aesthetic, spiritual, and familial values. Such insights also related closely for me to a particular essay by our contemporary Leslie Marmon Silko. A further catalyst for such connections was the presence of standing stones and other ancient monuments along our route. They were both physical and cultural facts. It dawned on me that these stone witnesses all spoke to the human desire to find, if not permanence, at least longevity in our relation to natural processes and to our own mortality. Marsh, too, was strongly motivated by a longing for durable values in our relations with nature. He wanted to identify in human history the basis for wisdom and health, not just a self-devouring appetite.

The Ottauquechee River, from which the third section receives its name, flows through George Perkins Marsh's native Woodstock. *Pilgrimage to Vallombrosa* concludes by taking its own meander through the mountains of Vermont in order to register Marsh's continuing influence in a local and immediate way. The ravages of the early nineteenth century have been significantly repaired in this region, partly through the efforts of Vermonters like Frederick Billings who were themselves inspired by reading *Man and Nature*. Other initiatives have reinforced such early efforts; they have extended Marsh's legacy into the present. In 1977 the Vermont Land Trust (originally the Ottauquechee Land Trust) was founded in Woodstock. It has played a decisive role in protecting Vermont's rural landscape, setting a standard of effectiveness and creativity for the land-trust movement nationwide. In 1998 Vermont's first national park also opened there—the Marsh-Billings-Rockefeller National Historical Park. It both celebrates a specific history of environmental stewardship and provides a home for the Conservation Study Institute, a new organization devoted to furthering discussion of conservation and stewardship in the entire National Park System.

The old-fashioned and genteel village of Woodstock offers an appropriate place to meditate on what might have seemed the archaic concept of *stewardship*. That term's association with aristocratic structures of power has sometimes made it less attractive for conservationists in our democratic society. The concept of stewardship is now regaining currency, however, not as a mode of service to either human or transcendent authorities, but rather as a way of affirming such values as biodiversity and sustainability. It identifies deeply with beloved landscapes and takes responsibility, from within, for the webs of intimate relationship they support. Having learned, from Marsh and his successors, the extent to which human actions have damaged and continue to damage natural systems, we must now set out to correct those mistakes. This calls for a civic and participatory commitment to stewardship rather than a hierarchical one. As stewardship continues to evolve, it will do so under a shadow of ecological disaster, and it will also enter into a confluence with social and intellectual currents never anticipated by Marsh. But his adventurous example can still remind us of the advantage of travel, both personal and intellectual, in grasping the dangers of local carelessness and in considering alternatives to such practices.

This book's third section juxtaposes the values of stewardship, as manifest in Woodstock, with more-controversial conservation initiatives in Vermont. I explore the tensions and promise both of current proposals for expanded wilderness in the Green Mountain National Forest and of the Champion Lands project in Vermont's Northeast Kingdom. "Maggie Brook," the chapter concluding both the third section and the book as a whole, returns to the sugar bush where this prologue began. Cartographers speak of "ground-truthing" as the test of a map by walking the land it is supposed to depict. The question for our family is how our future practices in the woods will register the three landscapes of our Italian pilgrimage. After following in Marsh's footsteps it is time for us to come home again, through the shadows that marked his path and ours, and set to work.

. . .

When sugaring season ends each year, Rita and I find ourselves returning in the evenings to the meadow below our sugarhouse. From late May till the start of June, woodcocks stage their courtship ritual here. As the male struts around the clearing he sounds a nasal tone like the reiterated note of an oboe. The female watches from out of sight. Aldo Leopold, who called this spectacle "the sky dance," also pointed out that it occurs fractionally later each evening. The woodcock is as much a perfectionist as the maple seed. He struts and flies each night when the light is exactly 0.05 foot-candles,[7] just as that seed germinates (earlier than any other hardwood seed) at precisely 34 degrees Fahrenheit.

We try to get here half an hour early or so. We sit on a tattered foam pad from our camping box, lean back against the concrete footings of a long-gone barn, and wrap a blanket around our shoulders in preparation for the show. When the bird finally begins, he struts around the meadow for a few minutes "peenting," then launches into a powerful climb. The ascent traces an outward spiral, like the unfurling of fiddlehead ferns in the nearby woods. Higher and higher he ascends, until we can't see him anymore in the dimness. Then he plunges into a power dive that makes his primary feathers throb and whistle in the wind of his descent. Just before hitting the ground, he pulls himself out of the dive, lands nonchalantly, and begins to circle again.

We spiral outward to return enriched with stories. We meander to the sea. We bear the living currents as far into the crown as they can reach, then let them surge back down to earth, flooding us to our roots.

PART I
VALLOMBROSA

1

MARRYING
THE MAP

Although we knew our destination from the start, we were happy to take our time in getting there. Rita and I were traveling toward Florence, and the start of my leave devoted to the Italian career of George Perkins Marsh. We decided to allow ourselves the adventure of eight weeks walking across Europe before settling in Italy, though. First we would follow England's Coast to Coast Walk from St. Bees, on the Irish Sea, to Robin Hood's Bay, on the North Sea. Then we would improvise a path through southern France on that country's magnificent Grande Randonnée trail network. We hoped that we could get pretty far toward the Italian border by the time August 15 came, and with it the official start of my fellowship. When we first planned this summer's itinerary, it seemed a holiday before the serious work of the year began. The historically rich terrain through which we passed, though, and the meaning that accrued to our walk at this juncture of our marriage, made it feel increasingly like a personal quest, and a pilgrimage, for both of us. Marsh gained a new significance for me in such a context, not only as an influential historical figure but also as the initiator of a continuing, multigenerational effort of mindfulness and restoration with which we felt affiliated.

The summer Rita and I undertook the trek toward Italy would also bring our thirtieth wedding anniversary, at the end of August. As the youngest of our three children entered college, this felt like a watershed year in our marriage—a time, with Rachel, Matthew, and Caleb all launched, to reflect on the past two and a half decades of parenting. Our long walk also seemed a good chance to consider the next chapters in our vocations as teachers, Rita at Lincoln School and I at Middlebury College, as well as in our life together. We wanted, if not exactly to kick up our heels, at least to lift them off the ground more regularly. We would step resolutely out of householder mode and into day after day of living out of backpacks. Because we planned to stay in hostels or bed-and-breakfasts in England, in *gîtes* or *chambres d'hôtes* in France, we didn't need to carry tents, stoves, or sleeping bags. A change of clothes and shoes, rain gear, a kit for toiletries, and a short stack of maps, books, and journals were augmented each day on the trail by a couple of water bottles and a lunch. In France, we would discover a new use for those little straps on the sides of our packs, attaching fresh baguettes in the morning as we strode off through the vineyards, sunflower fields, or oak forests of the Charente. Our weeks of walking felt like a second honey-moon. Rita and I were no longer twenty-two and twenty-three, but we still felt healthy and fit enough to take to the open road together. Grant-ed, we weren't sure how long such a state of affairs would continue. All the more reason to spring for such a strenuous holiday now. We even brought along a paperback copy of *The Wind in the Willows*, which we'd read on our first honeymoon on the Mendocino coast.

In addition to reading, we both devoted a good bit of time to our jour-nals during afternoon breaks in the shade, and again after checking into our rooms for the night and washing off the day's dust. I was surprised to discover, with each passing day, how thoroughly this long hike with Rita was reframing my project for the sabbatical. I had gone into the year intending to learn more about the biography and insights of George Perkins Marsh and to pursue a dialogue between the landscapes of Tus-cany and Vermont. But all those journal entries and conversations on the trail, as Rita and I recalled the years of a marriage whose richness had grown through shared loss and grief as well as through joys, helped me to glimpse another implication of Marsh's thought. During the same years when our children were beginning their own lives outside the home, all three of our remaining parents had died. Walking with these loved ones in mind encouraged me to think about conservation also within the frameworks of marriage, family, inheritance, and commu-nity. It drew me increasingly to the old-fashioned word stewardship, with its local and participatory connotations. And it made me want to map the experiences and values of our own family more specifically in the terrain through which we were passing—to understand the central stories of our lives as also being stories written in the land.

Our intimate human relationships offer compelling models for such specificity, mutuality, and affiliation. They may give rise in the natural realm, as they do in the human order, to enhanced experiences of community. A more grounded sense of identity may, by the same token, make our personal relationships more stable and promote a successful transition from one generation to the next. This does not imply a nostalgic look backward toward earlier social structures, any more than I would ever wish to affirm environmental stewardship as a mode of hierarchical authority. As the ecofeminist theologian Joan Chittister writes, "What the world needs are more circles and fewer pyramids."[1] But stewardship, beginning with the impetus of Marsh's book, has modulated to a chastened and participatory concern for the larger cycles of health that our human actions have disrupted. I find hope in this shift. Family and inheritance, too, must now be understood in more flexible and inclusive ways. We need to proceed experimentally toward a renewed sense of relationship within the larger community of life. In this book I have followed a long meander through landscapes charged by history—an outing undertaken with my life's companion and framed by the beloved place from which we set out and to which we have now returned.

Marsh's story, too, when considered while walking along such a path, reverberated with the themes of loss and memory, marriage and inheritance. And it would also have been much less accessible without the efforts of Caroline Crane Marsh. Marsh's first wife, Harriet, and their small son Charles both died in 1833. Looking back from Italy at the years that followed these losses, Marsh wrote, "Every night was one long wail of the deepest sorrow, for even my dreams were full of death."[2] But in 1839, at the age of thirty-eight, Marsh was married again, to Caroline Crane. This twenty-two-year-old woman, who would be in poor health for much of their life together and in fact often bedridden, became his confidante and intellectual companion. Like him, she was a gifted linguist, translating poetry from several languages as well as composing poems of her own and maintaining a wide correspondence. As her letters make clear, she was also a remarkably high-spirited and positive person, despite her physical challenges. She took special pains to facilitate the extended visits they received from American relatives, including the nieces and nephews who became so important to her husband following the estrangement and premature death of his son George.

The most important source of original documents by and about George Perkins Marsh is in the Special Collections of the University of Vermont's Bailey-Howe Library. Patrons who have submitted a slip with their requests and taken their places at a long reading table have numbered cardboard cartons wheeled out to them on a trolley. Carton XVII in the Marsh Papers is one that I've gone up to UVM several times to inspect, both before and after our trip to Italy. It contains Caroline Crane Marsh's compendium "Life and Letters of George Perkins Marsh," two volumes, of which only the first was ever published. In her careful script, she transcribed all the letters Marsh had written that she could recover. When I contacted the Arnold Arboretum to see whether there was any record of Charles Sprague Sargent's having sent the seeds Marsh asked for in his final letter, officials in the archives there could come up with no such documentation. But they did find a letter of September 18, 1884, from Sargent to Caroline Marsh. It began, "In compliance with your request I enclose the letters received from Mr. Marsh during the few years I enjoyed the advantage of his correspondence. You will notice that the last of the series was written only a few days before his death, and after his arrival at Vallombrosa."[3] In addition to locating, transcribing, and ordering such letters, Caroline Marsh added notes that placed them in context. The most striking of these is an extended account of her husband's final days. This eloquent narrative helped me imagine more clearly the circumstances of the Marshes and their entourage at Vallombrosa. I will return to it in the next chapters.

. . .

Our fifteen days on the Coast to Coast Walk began at St. Bees. The cobbled streets of this Cumbrian village rise steeply from the sea, beside a bay whose northern sweep is bounded by the massive bluff of St. Bees Head. On top of the head is a bird sanctuary for breeding populations of gulls, cormorants, kittiwakes, guillemots, and puffins. We arrived on the afternoon train from Carlisle and checked into our bed-and-breakfast, Stone House Farm. This far north, and in mid-June, daylight promised to last well past ten o'clock. So after a supper of curry and a pint at the

Queens Hotel, we set off for a walk to the bay and the ritual dipping of feet in the Irish Sea. Our path wound by the lovely Norman Church of St. Mary, with its weathered, reddish portico. St. Bega, an Irish princess, founded a priory here in 650. It was subsequently destroyed by those naughty Danes, but then reconstituted as a Benedictine abbey in 1120. A beautiful grammar school—also called St. Bees—was built across the road from the church, and of the same ruddy stone, four centuries ago.

Foxgloves and ferns crowded our track to the bay. A flock of sheep grazed in the meadow to our left, vocalizing their sheepishness more or less constantly. After we eventually arrived in Italy, Rita would characterize our summer's walk as having been a progression from the bleating of flocks, all across the Lake District and Yorkshire, to the thunderous chirring of cicadas in Provence. But now, commencing at that shore, we photographed each other grinning as the cold foam swirled around our ankles. Then we laced on our boots and climbed the head for a better view of Cumbria's coast. To our north, fern hills undulated through the luminous haze, while the cove to our south was dominated by the massive, curved silhouette of a nuclear power plant's cooling tower. When we retraced this ascent of the head next morning, at the actual start of our 190-mile crossing of England, we found ourselves in a driving rain. We plodded up the trail seeing nothing but our own muddy feet. Whereas the night before we'd stood amid choruses of wheeling kittiwakes and gulls, today we heard only the flapping of our hoods and the rattling of our nylon pack covers in the wind.

Fifteen miles later, with a glow in our legs from the final steep and slippery descent through Nannycatch Gate, we arrived at our second bed-and-breakfast—the Old Vicarage at Ennerdale Bridge. After hot baths in one of those magnificent long English tubs we strolled to a nearby pub, the Fox and Hound, for dinner. That's where we met three Englishmen, also staying at the Old Vicarage, who ended up being our companions at many points during the first week. Bob, Alan, and Chris had been friends, and fellow cricketers, during their years together in the Royal Air Force. Bob was now a fireman in Nottingham, while Alan and Chris had both taken early retirement from the RAF and were living on their pensions in Spain.

Our rhythm on the Coast to Coast Walk was now firmly established. Days of twelve to eighteen miles left us feeling shaky and tired, especially

in the craggy Lake District. If we'd known in advance about the possibility of having one's bags carried from stop to stop by a company called
Sherpa Van, we'd probably have planned on that. As it was, once we'd
started carrying our own belongings, and knowing there'd be no such
option in France, we stubbornly continued strapping on our packs each
morning. Though often staggering at the end of a stage, after a hot meal
and a bath we generally felt much restored. We also found that we frequently ran into the same people, like Chris, Alan, and Bob, both on the
trail and at our stopping points each night. Since we were all walking at
about the same pace, and since most people also followed the path from
west to east, we encountered only a handful of hikers in our Coast to
Coast world. The social dimension of the crossing became increasingly
important as the level of exertion and fatigue rose. Our third day on the
trail found us climbing steeply out of Rosthwaite on the way to Gras-
mere. We were just pulling ourselves up with hands and feet, trying not
to topple backward from the weight of our packs, when we heard "Hello,
Vermont!" shouted out from high up on the ridge. It was the ebullient
Chris, swinging his legs atop a scarp as his own little band took a break
after their early start.

For a number of the other hikers we got to know on this late June and
early July hike, a similar impulse of knitting together a life and celebrating long relationships seemed to lie behind their commitment to such an
outing. The three friends we met at Ennerdale were taking this walk not
just to celebrate their time together in the RAF and reminisce about
cricket (a game Alan tried to explain to me whenever we ended up walking together). They also manifested the introspective mood that comes
on the cusp of a change. Bob was planning to retire from the fire department fairly soon, while the other two had only recently taken their own
early retirement. Chris and Alan enjoyed the climate in Spain, where
they had small villas with swimming pools. But this trip was also about
reconnecting with their native North of England. At the end of our
crossing Rita and I fell in for a couple of days with Peter and Sheila Smith
from Brisbane, and found that they too were walking as a sort of personal ritual. Peter, a rugged tugboat captain, had broken his neck in an
accident in Brisbane Harbor. Recovering from such an injury had made
this taciturn but amiable man and his hilariously talkative wife Sheila
eager to enjoy their health and good fortune together. We were interested to find out that, despite their marked Australian accents and strong

sense of pride in their country, they had emigrated separately from England almost forty years earlier. Sheila had just finished closing up the home where her aged mother had died near London. So she and Peter, too, were undertaking a process of grieving and consolidation.

Our growing sense that we, and those we befriended on the trail, were pursuing pilgrimages was reinforced by the markers left by earlier wayfarers in this exposed landscape. Though villages, and a few sizable towns, are scattered through the countryside, much of the zone south of Hadrian's Wall feels less populous or developed even than northern Vermont. Human artifacts thus take on a special impressiveness. Aqueducts and other Roman remains are surprisingly well represented up here, as are massive Norman churches even in some of the smaller villages. More ancient than these, though, and more mysterious are the standing stones we encountered in North Yorkshire. Near Blakey Ridge, in the final week of our walk, we stopped to inspect three imposing stones, which were indicated on the map with the unaccounted-for but memorable names of Marjery, Fat Betty, and Young Ralph. The last of these, with its cruciform top, has been taken as the symbol of England's national parks.

When we had finished up the Coast to Coast and dipped our feet in the North Sea, Rita and I made the crossing to France and took a train down to St. Rochelle. After a night there, we stepped into the Grande Randonnée network at Rochefort. The French trails are magnificent, with their *balisage*, or blazes, marked on trees, walls, and power poles in neat stripes of red and white. Often they led us through farms and forests rather than along roads, and in fact we never saw another hiker on the trails during our five weeks in France. Perhaps the locals preferred to travel in organized clubs. Or maybe everyone but us knew it would be too crowded in southern France during July and August and stayed away. We navigated with a series of maps in three scales. There was one for the entire national network of trails, a second for each region we traversed, and a third, highly localized set. These last, which we purchased every several days at bars and tobacconists, showed each barn, bridge, and creek along the way and also listed local *chambres d'hôtes*. While my French is serviceable, Rita's is excellent. So it became her job, once or twice each week, to call up and arrange for our next accommodations. Our route took us first through the province of Charente-Maritime, then through Charente, the Dordogne, and Provence. Walking through fields of wheat and sunflowers and through vineyards spangled with white and blue wildflowers, we felt what a garden France is. But in this lush region, too— such a contrast to the austere expanses of Yorkshire—we constantly found stone witnesses testifying to earlier pilgrims on our path.

For one thing, southern France is filled with vestiges of the Knights Templar, who were such a powerful influence around the Mediterranean region in the twelfth and thirteenth centuries. They funded the Crusades, established hospitals and hostels for pilgrims, and, while trying in various ways to reform church and state, established a parallel social order of their own. They were crushed in the early years of the fourteenth century, but their story lingers in the stone granaries, pilgrimage churches, and fortresses standing, often in spectacular isolation, beside narrow dirt tracks or on the grassy brows of hills. These are the ruins of an ancient vision of renewal. Even more impressive relics on this portion of our walk were the signs for various routes to the pilgrimage church of Santiago de Compostela in Spain. The Way of St. James was, along with the journey to Jerusalem, one of the two chief pilgrimages of medieval Christendom. But since the devout came from all over Europe, many different paths branched down from the north and east before converging in one main path through Spain. We repeatedly crossed or paralleled these devotional tributaries. Sometimes they were announced by grand pilgrimage churches like the ones at Saintes and Conques. But often their only indications, apart from legends on our maps, were the carved or painted scallop shells we found on stone posts or ancient trees. Often enough, these appeared beside our own red-and-white *balisage* for the Grande Randonnée. Walking along with our staffs and backpacks, we got asked more than a few times if we were following the Chemin de St. Jacques. This reinforced our sense that we were in fact on a sort of pilgrimage, in part to celebrate our life together, in part to foster the wholeness of a family divided by immigration, and in part to seek inspiration from the journey, a century and a half ago, of George Perkins Marsh.

Early on in the French portion of our walk, we spent an afternoon and night in the ancient pilgrimage site of Saintes. While I sat in the park and caught up with my journal, Rita set off to explore the town, returning after several hours with a small woodblock print she had picked up in the cathedral. Just about half the size of a piece of typing paper, it rode on to Italy in our packs, protected in its manilla envelope. Pictures of a walking staff (looking remarkably like ours) and the traditional pilgrim's emblem of a scallop shell framed a greeting from the bishop of Saintes, Georges Pontier, to all those passing through on the path to Spain. It began, "Se mettre en marche sur les chemins de Saint Jacques, n'est-ce pas accepter de se 'mettre en marche' dans sa vie, de regarder comment sa propre vie marche?" Such a sense of taking to the path so that one's whole life, too, might forge forward captured our experience of these weeks on foot together. Walking turned out to be not just a means of travel to our destination but a way of entering into our goal more immediately, of giving ourselves to it day by day.

In her book *The Resurgence of the Real*, Charlene Spretnak discusses the need to go beyond the mind-body split by affirming the wholeness and wisdom of "the knowing body." For her, such a direction accords with a view of the cosmos as organic and creative and with a renewed awareness of place as essential to cultural and spiritual values. These perspectives all represent revolts against modernist or scientific worldviews that see "the body as nothing but a biological machine, the biosphere and cosmos as nothing but a predictable, mechanistic clockwork, and place as nothing but background scenery for human projects."[4] I recognize both the peripatetic method of this book and the meaning of Rita's and my journey in the rationale Spretnak describes here. Because walking is such a slow way to proceed, it can allow for heightened receptiveness to the world's movement all around you—first of all, to the always changing sky, with its massing clouds that may mean rain, its darkness that gathers as you check your watches and lengthen your strides toward a roof for the night. But it also brings a gradual opening to the particularity of each place through which you pass—to the way in which certain villages' locations are so clearly determined by soils, waterways, and woodlands, the way the color and texture of churches and homes disclose the shifting country rock of a region. Slowing down can be a way to remember that nature is more than a set of resources to be mined. It is both our long home and our companion on a walk.

In an important sense, Marsh inaugurated a pilgrimage to environmental mindfulness that continues today. He combined ecological insight with a willingness to face certain deeply ingrained errors in our treatment of nature. While his worldview had germinated in Vermont, it flowered after Marsh moved to the Old World. Americans have always needed, as our environmental movement definitely does today, to cultivate a broader sense of history. Walking across the blossoming French countryside in high summer, Rita and I followed routes traveled by our human ancestors over thousands of years. This recognition increasingly occupied our minds.

On July 26 we decided to interrupt our walk and rent a car for a week. We wanted to visit a number of pilgrimage sites—including the celebrated painted caves as well as the churches at Conques and Rocamadour—that were scattered through the Dordogne area. No single walking route would have allowed us to see more than a couple of these.

In addition to the churches and caves, we visited an amazing site called La Rocque Saint-Christophe. Rita has become susceptible to claustrophobia in recent years, just as I have to fear of heights. (These new sensitivities seem to be on the same timetable as our intensified reaction to caffeine and need for reading glasses.) At Rita's preference, then, we had flown from England to France instead of taking the Chunnel, and I descended into the caverns at Lascaux II and Pech-Merle alone while she sought out shade trees to read and relax above ground. But Rocque Saint-Christophe is a terraced system of deep ledges cut into a cliff face. Since the terraces, though receding deep into the rock, are not completely enclosed, this was a site we had the pleasure of exploring together over the course of a long day. The habitable part of the cliff face rises over a hundred meters above the lovely valley of the Vézère River. Few places on earth show as long and continuous a record of human habitation. By 72,000 years ago there were Neanderthals living here (or "Mousterians," to give them a name more pleasing to Gallic pride), replaced about 40,000 years ago by Cro-Magnons. There's also ample archaeological evidence of occupation here during the Neolithic period (9,000 BP), the Bronze Age (4,500 BP), and the Iron Age (3,000 BP). This site subsequently held a Gallo-Roman furnace, then supported a fortress defended by locals against, in sequence, the Vikings, Normans, English, and Catholics. Henry III was so angry about the Huguenots' successes in holding out against him here that when he finally captured it in 1588 he had both the fortress and the associated town destroyed.

La Rocque Saint-Christophe thus holds a story of human inhabitation extending over 72,000 or 40,000 years (depending on one's view of Neanderthals' humanity). And an endless spectacle—at least during the "historical" era—of warfare. Looking across the broad valley, with its lovely, pale gray cliffs rising above mature hardwood groves, we could see another ancient fortification at just about the same elevation as the ledges where we stood. It was one of a sequence of twenty-two *relais* where blown horns could pass along the news of invading armies—say, just to sharpen the point, a horde of Vikings. In three to five minutes, such a message could cover a distance of over 180 kilometers, allowing workers in the fertile fields along the river to ascend into the relative safety of the Rocque, pulling their ladders and ropes up behind them before the enemy's arrival.

Today, its houses and catapults alike eradicated by a pissed-off king, Rocque Saint-Christophe is an airy platform from which to view the valley where early humans learned to dream and paint. But it is also a vantage point from which to reflect about the centuries of conflict and suffering of which this site is such a beautiful, stripped-down vestige. Every village we passed in southern France seemed to have a stone monument "aux enfants," with the names of local youths slain in World War I listed on a tablet encircled by carven soldiers and angels and laurel wreaths. So picturesque, these small-town memorials—at least to those of us arriving all these decades later. They made me think of Frost's reference in the poem "Directive" to "a time made simple by the loss / Of detail, burned, dissolved, and broken off / Like graveyard marble sculpture in the weather."⁵

During our walk in southern France I also often thought of the manicured fields, planted with groves of headstones, near Normandy Beach. They commemorate the site where, over half a century earlier, on D day, so many of my father's comrades were killed in the space of a single day. He served in the 82nd Airborne Division as one of the first army chaplains to be trained as a paratrooper during the war. Following D day, since the Catholic chaplain and the graves registration officer had both been killed, he was assigned to walk Omaha Beach identifying the slain. Weeks later, after completing his task, he suffered an emotional breakdown and was consigned briefly to a field hospital. But he was back in action soon enough to be seriously wounded by shrapnel at the Battle of the Bulge. As a boy on family expeditions to the ocean, I often noticed the wide scar where a flattened scrap of steel had entered his back and exited his side. But only toward the end of his life, in 1994, and through conversations with my mother afterward, did I realize how deliberate a choice had been his cheerful patience throughout my childhood. He had decided to live, notwithstanding the nightmares that, as my mother reported, awoke him screaming for years after the war. Loving-kindness was reinforced, for him, by steady recollection of the horrors.

. . .

Walking toward Italy through the storied landscapes of northern England and southern France amplified the connection between George Perkins Marsh's environmental vision and the venerable impulse and rhythms of pilgrimage. Both might be seen as a return to origins and a commitment to personal and social renewal. Freud once wrote that the neurotic repeats instead of remembering. Pilgrimage enacts, in the body, a healing effort of memory. It seeks out the wellsprings of culture and belief and, in Marsh's case, of ecological health; it pursues renewal in company with other seekers. Along this path, we listen to each other's stories and come to understand the cyclical and collective nature of our passage through the map. In the well-trodden terrain under our feet, we discover and chart the topography of a more inclusive sympathy. By reflecting on the insights of George Perkins Marsh within a medium of personal stories and landscape description, I also hope to open up and walk around in certain key passages from his book. Marsh's dense, formal prose and copious documentation have made him much less read than the power of his ideas deserves. Taking some of his passages back out into specific landscapes that were important to Marsh, and considering them within the context of a grounded story, is an attempt to make them more accessible. To put this another way, my purpose is to cultivate the soil *around* Marsh's insights, in order to see how they might grow in our own day.

The concept of stewardship, despite its anthropocentric connotations and its aristocratic history, can similarly flower in new ways within the democratic, feminist, and ecological discourses of our own day. Marsh's title, with its now outmoded use of "man" as an inclusive term for humanity, has been a stumbling block for some readers. But his insights in fact prepare for and anticipate Aldo Leopold's "land ethic," with its call for ever-widening circles of inclusion and enfranchisement. We need to appreciate Marsh as a vital initiator, not ask him to walk our stretch of the road as well as his own. Our urgent challenge today is to find an approach to conservation that emphasizes participation and community rather than either domination or separation. A respectful and energetic dialogue with the author of *Man and Nature* might do much to help us progress in such a direction.

Marsh formulated his fundamental insights from observing the deforestation around his boyhood home. But he needed to travel to the Mediterranean region—serving initially as a diplomat in Turkey, then being appointed America's first minister plenipotentiary to Italy—before grasping the full implications of what he had seen in Vermont. My own Italian journey was similarly motivated by a desire to see our state's natural and cultural environment within a more global perspective, as well as within a broader historical context. Doing so in the company of Rita, and with a heightened emphasis on extended family because of her personal goals for the year, helped me see the landscape of history as also being a field of relationships and inheritance.

2
HEADWATERS

The path toward conservation and stewardship leads through a land-scape shadowed by disasters. Ignorance and mistakes may become more than errors, however, when we find the courage to learn from them. They may open broader vistas on both the wholeness of nature and culture and the historical implications of our immediate, local decisions. For the past thirty years, our family has lived in the wounded and recovering terrain of Vermont. Over the course of these decades I have become more and more impressed by the power, for conservation thought, of what might be called creative grieving. By this term I mean the potential for new ecological insight and social resolve to grow out of catastrophe.

The environmental history of Vermont has fostered such growth. During the early decades of the nineteenth century, the Green Mountains were deforested with a rapaciousness equal to any on this continent. Zadock Thompson's 1853 *Natural History of Vermont* described a wasteland of stumps and gullies.[1] Whole communities of farmers failed and emigrated, and large mammals became extinct in most of the state. Today, Vermont is more heavily forested than at any time in the past two centuries and also supports an increasing diversity of wildlife. Not just beaver and deer but also viable populations of fishers, otters, bears, and bobcats have been reestablished here. Catamounts have been spotted in a number of sites, and the possibility for reintroducing wolves has become a topic for discussion among biologists and politicians. Such re-

wilding has been accompanied by a host of state and local conservation
initiatives. Several of the most notable of these have been centered in
Woodstock, the town where George Perkins Marsh was born in 1801,
and they can be related directly to his vision and accomplishments.

While growing up, Marsh saw the slopes of Mount Tom denuded. The
resultant slash burned in a series of uncontrollable fires, from which the
woods were long in recovering. Throughout his boyhood, he watched as
unchecked erosion ruined fishing in the streams and drove many local
farmers off their land. Marsh carried these images with him for the rest
of his life. Years later, when he was sent first to Turkey and then to Italy
as a diplomat, he began to investigate the centuries of deforestation in
the Mediterranean world. Generally considered the most gifted American linguist of his generation, he was able to carry out his research in
biblical and classical languages and in many of the modern European
tongues. His studies confirmed that a number of the exposed, arid, and
depopulated expanses he visited had once sustained rich civilizations.
The pattern he observed was one in which the incremental cutting of
trees over generations eradicated a resource that had seemed inexhaust-
ible to people. He also noted that modern industrial society, around the
world, was accelerating such destructiveness at an alarming rate.

After his 1861 appointment as Lincoln's representative to the new
Kingdom of Italy, Marsh shifted his operations as the capital was relo-
cated, first from Turin to Florence and then to Rome. But until his death
in 1882 he always retained a home in Florence. The connections between deforestation and recovery in Tuscany and Vermont intrigued
him for the rest of his life. At Vallombrosa, one of the most ancient,
beautiful, and culturally prestigious forests in Italy, his final letters rev-
eled in the beauty of that landscape and in the local legacy of stewardship, both ancient and modern, on behalf of the forest. The dialogue between Tuscany and Vermont may offer to us today, as it did to Marsh, a
more international and comparative perspective on conservation. In beginning my book at Vallombrosa and concluding it in the mountains
near Woodstock, I seek to round out the circle of his life and to pursue
the specific contributions of these two landscapes to emerging models of
stewardship.

George Perkins Marsh never doubted that it was right for human beings to cultivate the soil or extract natural resources. Nor was he oriented toward any vision of a Golden Age. But his belief in the possibility

of scientific progress was balanced by a grim sense of the ignorance and destructiveness in his own era's land use. In the introductory chapter of *Man and Nature*, he writes,

[A] certain measure of transformation of terrestrial surface, of suppression of natural, and stimulation of artificially modified productivity becomes necessary. This measure man has unfortunately exceeded. He has felled the forests whose network of fibrous roots bound the mould to the rocky skeleton of the earth; but had he allowed here and there a belt of woodland to reproduce itself by spontaneous propagation, most of the mischiefs which his reckless destruction of the natural protection of the soil has occasioned would have been averted. He has broken up the mountain reservoirs, the percolation of whose waters through unseen channels supplied the fountains that refreshed his cattle and fertilized his fields; but he has neglected to maintain the cisterns and the canals of irrigation which a wise antiquity had constructed to neutralize the consequences of its own imprudence. While he has torn the thin glebe which confined the light earth of extensive plains, and has destroyed the fringe of semi-aquatic plants which skirted the coast and checked the drifting of the sea sand, he has failed to prevent the spreading of the dunes by clothing them with artificially propagated vegetation. He has ruthlessly warred on all the tribes of animated nature whose spoil he could convert to his own uses, and he has not protected the birds which prey on the insects most destructive to his own harvests.[2]

Marsh does not have a problem with either forestry or agriculture per se. For him, the grievous error is a long-continued lack of restraint, which comes from ignorance of what a forest is really like. A woods is not just a sort of lumber warehouse from which timber can be removed at our will or even cleared off altogether with impunity. Rather, it is an intricate community of life, on which the health of the whole landscape depends.

Marsh's prose is sometimes hard to focus on, as in the passage cited above. In part, this is because of his heavy use of Ciceronian parallelism, the constant qualifications within his statements, and the abstract tendencies of his vocabulary. He could use more short sentences. Another reason that *Man and Nature* is sometimes daunting to a reader is the profuseness of its documentation. The dense paragraph from which I've just quoted gives rise to a footnote over three times as long. This note interweaves references to Norwegian folktales, an Icelandic saga, a traveler's narrative of the court of Morocco, a geographical account of coastal France, and observations from the author's New England childhood.[3] Marsh does not wear his learning lightly. But the power and impressiveness of his argument derive from these same attributes: he has an astounding capacity to see parallels between different eras and landscapes, to understand the implications of natural and social facts, and to marshall a wealth of scientific, historical, and economic information. He was for many years a practicing attorney, and he always retained an appetite for evidence. It is often in fact easiest to feel the sweep of Marsh's argument by dwelling on just a passage at a time, I believe, rather than trying to take in all his nuances and examples at once. He is a microcosmic writer or, as Hugh Kenner has said of authors like Shakespeare and Joyce, a "fractal" one. Thus, although *Man and Nature* is rarely lyrical, it repays the sort of attention one brings to a poem—reading a passage aloud, slowly and reflectively, and frequently pausing over suggestive phrases. Marsh's writing is also clarified through connection to our own concrete situations on the land and in history. My intention in this book is to pursue such a dialogue with him in some of the landscapes he was most inspired by. Taking a cue from that long footnote, I have found that parallel narratives of travel and conversations with a wide range of voices both offer ways to pause over and appreciate Marsh's insights.

Man and Nature continually draws attention, as in the quotation, to the "network of fibrous roots [which bind] the mould to the rocky skeleton of the earth." Marsh thus focuses on a crucial fact that loggers, builders, and governmental policy makers are frequently in danger of forgetting. At least half the biomass of a tree is below the ground, and much of that is in the intergrafted fabric of root hairs that rise up from the larger roots and hold the soil. When a forest is cleared, massive erosion is the predictable consequence, especially if it stood on land with any significant slope. The surface of the land, the microclimate in the forest's shade, and the general climate of the region are drastically affected by such clear-cuts. Thus, both "the mountain reservoirs" and the "percolation" of those waters "through unseen channels" are ruptured by the rending of the forest's subterranean "network." These are unintended consequences, resulting from blindness to the dynamic unity of ecological and social health.

Marsh, like the prophetic lineage of conservationist writers who succeed him, wants above all to help us see. In the final sentence of the cited passage, when he calls on us to remember the birds that protect our crops against destructive insects, he in fact directly anticipates arguments by Aldo Leopold and Rachel Carson. The point for all these writers is that we need to bear in mind the whole cycle of life, including but not limited to what we can perceive around us in our limited visual and temporal range. Once we can more adequately envision the fullness of a forest's life, and grasp its contributions to our farms and cities, we can make more-informed choices. We can begin to understand stewardship as a form of civic participation rather than a model of hierarchy, dominion, or altruism. Both the disasters and the ecological insights of our own day reinforce this aspect of Marsh's argument.

Man and Nature was a major force behind the 1873 Timber Culture Act, the 1885 founding of Adirondack State Park, and the 1891 Forest Reserves Act. The last of these, in William Cronon's words, "created national forests as we know them today."[4] Marsh's carefully documented examples and forceful writing had earlier played a crucial role in the development of our national parks, during the years between the protection of Yosemite Valley (originally as a state park) in 1864 and the establishment of Yellowstone in 1872 as the first national park in the world. In *The Brown Decades*, Lewis Mumford writes, "For the pioneer, the land existed to be acquired, to be devoured, to be gutted out, to serve for a hasty turnover of profit. The conception that each man had a legal right to do as he would with his own far outbalanced any sense of the common weal. George Perkins Marsh was the first man to sense the destruction that was being wrought, to weigh its appalling losses, and to point out an intelligent course of action."[5] As Mumford discusses, Marsh's work exists within a larger progression. Before him was Thoreau, who in *Walden* "advocated the preservation of the wild spaces, as a habitat for man's soul as well as for the wild creatures themselves." After him came the remarkable landscape planner and park founder Frederick Law Olmsted. But Marsh's writings provided a crucial hinge, with their economic, geographical, and historical analysis. Paying closer attention to his achievements will enhance our sense of a redemptive continuity in American thought and practice. The environmental movement of our own day is thus not simply a reaction against all that has gone before, in American history or in the tradition of the West. If it were, we would have little hope of changing our social policies and practices. In fact, though, Marsh stands in a powerful tradition in our culture, one for which he was also a catalyst. A pilgrimage to his life and thought can clarify and encourage our efforts in the present.

Another enduring aspect of Marsh's achievement is the chastened hopefulness of his voice, which remains a powerful model for mindfulness and reform. He looks steadfastly at the gravity of our collective errors over the centuries, and at the darkness of the prospect to which they have brought us, and he insists that we regard this terrifying spectacle along with him. Grounded, thus, in the dangers, he can also look forward (in the title of one of his book's subheadings) to a "restoration of disturbed harmonies." He can envision humanity becoming "a coworker with nature in the reconstruction of the damaged fabric which the negligence or the wantonness of former lodgers has rendered untenantable. He must aid her in reclothing the mountain slopes with forests and vegetable mould, thereby restoring the fountains which she provided to water them."[6] David Lowenthal's biography *George Perkins Marsh* is subtitled *Prophet of Conservation.* If Marsh is a prophet, he is one who echoes Jeremiah and Isaiah alike. By this I mean that he both harshly condemns the wastefulness and selfishness characterizing so much of our history and at the same time envisions a new era of balanced wisdom. His complex tone in this regard anticipates the ecological insight and rhetorical power so essential to the American conservation movement.

. . .

Rita and I settled in Florence primarily because of that city's proximity to sites important in Marsh's life and thought. A further reason to choose the Tuscan capital as our base was that its excellent train connections made it a convenient location from which to visit Rita's family in the eastern Campagna hill town of Artena. Florence itself can often be fearsomely congested, of course, between the throngs of tourists on foot and the cabs and delivery trucks trying to negotiate those narrow cobbled streets. So when Rita and I wanted to stretch our legs of an afternoon we would often end up strolling along the Arno. If we hugged the river's northern bank there were only a handful of bridges to break our forward progress, in contrast to the tangle of traffic just a block away. The air was cleaner here, too, and the vistas were more expansive. Following the Arno east, we arrived at a squat medieval tower called the Zecca Vecchia, or Old Mint, which marked the boundary of the city's historical center. We would come to it just as there began to be more space between the buildings and as the nearby roads broadened dramatically. One of these, the Viale Giovanni Amendola, swept across the river toward the auto-strada and Rome.

The Zecca itself was standing here long before Dante was exiled from Florence. On the side of it facing the river a plaque has been affixed with three lines from Canto 14 of the *Purgatorio*.

> *Per mezza Toscana si spazia*
> *Un fiumicel che nasce in Falterona,*
> *E cento miglia di corso nol sazia.*

Charles Singleton offers the following prose translation of Dante's trip-let: "Through mid-Tuscany there winds a little stream that rises in Fal-terona, and a course of a hundred miles does not suffice for it."[7] These lines in effect pose a riddle, the answer to which is "the Arno." Dante the Pilgrim speaks them just after he has encountered two spirits under-going purification on the Terraces of Envy. Startled that someone still liv-ing in his human body should be in that place, they inquire where he comes from and who he is. The Pilgrim answers with this elliptical refer-ence to the river that both bisects and sustains his native Florence, then adds the line "di sovr'esso rech'io questa persona," "and from its banks I bring this body here." Commentators on *The Divine Comedy* note the modesty of this indirect response, and its appropriateness as Dante passes through the region of Purgatory where souls are cured of envy, pride, and anger—his own besetting sins. He is still approaching the place in the poem where his own name can be uttered for the first time. Another suggestion is that he hangs back from a more explicit identi-fication of himself as a Florentine because of shame at what his city has become. Almost immediately after he utters those three lines, and in stark contrast to the courtesy of their preceding inquiry about his ori-gins and identity, one of the two spirits launches into a scornful survey of the communities along the Arno—from the hoggish inhabitants of the mountains to the curs of the plains and the ravening wolves that roam around Florence itself.

Quite unlike Guido del Duca's denunciation of the bestial inhabitants of the Romagna, the lines spoken by Dante the Pilgrim are notable for their focus on the river itself and for their tenderness of tone. The stream from Mount Falterona that marks the headwaters of the Arno is de-scribed with a caressing diminutive, "fiumicel." This effect is reinforced by the word Dante uses to describe the rising of the water: "nasce," "it is born." His way of placing himself in the world thus both avoids naming his city and turns back lovingly to its origins—as if to begin his own new journey back down from the mountains, one that will more clearly map the watershed of his life and will make it possible to begin a more authentic story. Despite Dante's many bitter references to his native place (such as his self-description in one essay as "Florentine by birth but not by character"),[8] his poetry is persistently marked by homesickness—a longing for what *might*, at least, have been. Like the river, he and his city had made such a promising start. His reference to the original mountain spring also suggests another possibility, though; namely, that the story of citizenship can begin anew for those who return to their community's headwaters. In certain cantos of the *Purgatorio*, the penitents climb bent over so that they may read the stories, depicted on the path beneath their feet, of those whose sins resembled theirs. Such scenes reinforce the suggestion that history might be transformed if retraced, and reenacted, with discernment about our former errors.

In the prophetic lineage flowing from Marsh through Aldo Leopold and Rachel Carson, there is a suggestion akin to the lines of verse on the Zecca Vecchia. Marsh, too, believed that unless we can reexamine our recent history, in an effort to recognize where we have gone wrong, we are lost. Connecting the effects of deforestation in his native Vermont with the Mediterranean region's millennial impoverishment was Marsh's own ascent to the historical headwaters. Although the longest serving American ambassador, with his record of twenty-one years in Italy, Marsh felt increasingly estranged from the extravagance and corruption of his native land during the post–Civil War decades. This was, after all, the era for which Mark Twain and his collaborator Charles Dudley Warner coined the term "The Gilded Age." Drawing from Marsh's letters of the late 1860s and 1870s, David Lowenthal writes,

America was now a morass of materialist greed. The reign of robber barons portended "the most pernicious of aristocracies," that of wealth, while the "scandalous failures of Jay Cooke" and others that brought on the panic of 1873 "inflicted an [abiding] stain on our commercial honor." Marsh doubted that Hayes's reforms, however radical, could overcome dollar worship and political patronage. From America came such an "uninterrupted succession of mortifying and discouraging moral and political news" that he wondered if "anybody believes in anybody's honesty these sad days."[9]

In George Perkins Marsh's case, as in Dante's, a caustic intelligence seems to hold despair at bay. Marsh criticized the heedless exploitation of natural resources, in particular, with a harshness and specificity rare in Western literature. My point is obviously not to liken him to Dante as a writer. Who but Shakespeare could stand up to such a comparison? Nonetheless there were affinities that struck me forcefully while rereading *Man and Nature* in the city that was lodged so indissolubly in Dante's heart. Marsh documented his environmental polemic with a scholarly and scientific thoroughness equivalent to the great Florentine exile's Thomist theology. His book also mapped the interconnectedness of natural cycles, including forest succession, climate, and hydrology, with a concentric overview as intricate and up-to-date as the poet's own cosmology. These features of *Man and Nature* give it a bristling and intimidating aspect. Readers in our own suave and cautious culture have sometimes been turned away by the thickets of Marsh's writing. But if we can see his comprehensiveness of style as reflecting a passionate desire to reinscribe the world, so that his readers can see and change, we may become more appreciative of *Man and Nature*'s own unprecedented insight.

There is one more important connection between the American diplomat and conservationist and the genius who galvanized vernacular poetry. Neither stops with bitterness. This is worth emphasizing, since so many college students who study Dante stop after the *Inferno*. But as Dorothy Sayers remarked, this is like judging "a great city after a few days spent underground among the cellars and sewers."[10] While Marsh holds no faith, environmental or otherwise, that can allow him a vision of the heavens, he does at least cultivate a hope for ecological and social restoration on earth. He invites his reader to step onto a path that leads, through the rugged terrain of his prose, from a recognition of our devastating errors to a recovered vision of our true sources of health. To reflect on *Man and Nature* beside the river where Dante walked is to feel with new force the healing astringency of Marsh's vision.[11]

Sometimes the conservation movement in America has seemed to take bitterness as the final word instead of as a starting point in the dialectic of reform. There is an echo of Dante's scathing denunciations of his own society in the language with which certain advocates of wilderness have decried humanity as the scourge of nature. Robinson Jeffers, whose poetry proved so inspiring for organizations like Earth First! sometimes consoles himself by imagining the recovery of nature that will follow upon humanity's well-deserved extinction. Here is how he expresses such anger and exultation in section 5 of "The Coast Road":

> Mourning the broken balance, the hopeless prostration of the earth
> Under men's hands and their minds,
> The beautiful places killed like rabbits to make a city,
> The spreading fungus, the slime-threads
> And spores, my own coast's obscene future: I remember the farther
> Future, and the last man dying. . . .[12]

A similar coldness toward the history of our own species is sometimes expressed today by references in the literature of deep ecology and the wilderness movement to our having gone wrong with the invention of agriculture. Only by dismantling Western culture can the balance of nature be restored. I understand the intellectual assumptions of such a position, and empathize both with its emotions and with those of Jeffers's poem. But neither politically nor spiritually is there much promise in a program of self-loathing. I would describe this as the environmental equivalent of standing on the deck of the *Titanic* and cheering for the icebergs. A more promising image might be that of provisioning an ark against an era akin, in some ways, to a universal deluge. But the community of life in an ark, now as for Noah, must include humanity as well as what David Abram calls "the more-than-human world." And the peak where our ark comes aground will always be a new world of challenges to which we have traveled through the storm, not a reductive and sentimental golden age. Neither forgetfulness nor erasure is the way to navigate through history's heavy weather, though what we suffer and lose on such a voyage will forever change our point of view.

Although Dante had a lot to get off his chest in the *Inferno*, he also continued, through the *Purgatorio* and the *Paradiso*, to pursue a vision of personal, social, and cosmic wholeness. I believe that the environmental conversation, too, must look beyond harshness to a more inclusive and participatory perspective. The dizzying speed with which California's sublime landscape was abused and subjugated made Jeffers's bitterness understandable. As he gazed down at the coast road from the stone fastness of High Tor, such desecration and waste must have seemed like a vision of hell. But the longer-settled "middle landscapes" of Tuscany and Vermont may offer a less apocalyptic possibility for relating humanity and nature. The voice of stewardship may be easier to hear in such modest, yet also beautiful and hopeful, terrain. While not as soaring or decisive as the voice of polemic, it is tenacious in seeking to reconstruct, rather than abandon, our cultural heritage. Paradise is not a sustainable possibility in the human realm—neither for the dazzled and blinking pilgrim who falls back down to earth at the end of Dante's *Commedia* nor for environmentalists in present-day Vermont and Tuscany. But we can at least cultivate a certain tempered and progressive hopefulness as we learn to look more closely at the ground and read the stories of our past and future under foot.[13]

. . .

The third line on that plaque affixed to the Zecca Vecchia relates in yet another specific way to the dialogue of Tuscany and Vermont. At first glance, it might have seemed to contradict Dante's preceding verses. Those two lines emphasized the river's smallness, but this one seems to boast of the *fiumicel*'s insistence on following a long meander ("And a course of a hundred miles is not enough for it"). Almost half of the Arno's total length consists of a U-shaped loop before it arrives at Florence; from that point on it proceeds more or less directly west through Pisa to the sea. But just after it has issued from the Casentino mountains, the river turns abruptly south, and even a little east, at Valico. It drops down through Poppi and Bibbiena before making a broad turn to the west again, through Montevarchi. Then it heads north, through San Giovanni and Rignano, to Pontassieve, where it finds its confluence with the river Sieve and makes its final turn back west through Florence.

Such a broad detour, south and west, then north and west again, transcribes the contours of the Tuscan land. A north–south ridge cuts down through Vallombrosa, between the Casentino mountains and Florence, and thus prevents the river from following a direct route. This looping portion of the Arno mirrors a similar detour followed by the Ottauquechee River on its way through Marsh's boyhood home of Woodstock. The Ottauquechee flows south out of the mountains above Sherburne, turns east through the narrow valley that encloses Bridgewater, angles north on its way through Woodstock, makes a tight loop up through Quechee, then bends back southward to its confluence with the Connecticut River. These two rivers' roundabout courses disclose an affinity between the mountainous terrain of Tuscany and that of the Upper Val-

ley region of southeast Vermont. A watershed's character is registered in
its watercourses' accommodations to obstacles; sometimes, only reversals of course allow the land's vital current to keep flowing.

Those garlanding rivers evoke the land's true topography better than
any contour map. Returning to the Arno's source, then following the
water's deliberate meander back toward home, offers the possibility of a
new beginning for Dante the Pilgrim and his city. Just so, recalling the
story of George Perkins Marsh may renew our perspective on the environmental literature and possibilities of our own day. It may allow for a
dialogue between the landscapes of Tuscany and Vermont in which their
beautifully broken terrain and shadowed histories galvanize a new vision of community and work. Marsh's insights are not definitive within
this conversation. Our cultural perspective and scientific information
have both moved on, in ways that require us to adapt his language and
find our own stories in the land. But *Man and Nature* can be a catalyst for
our quest, a narrative to recall along the route of our own pilgrimage.

At the core of Marsh's environmental vision is a yearning for patriotic
and civic vocation. It wasn't that, as a Vermonter in Italy, he felt any
sense of Dantesque exile—far from it. Florence, in particular, agreed
with him very well indeed. But both his scientific studies and his experience of living abroad seem to have intensified the democratic values he
imbibed in his small-town boyhood. Marsh was writing the first edition
of *Man and Nature* in the years just before Ernst Haeckl coined the term
ecology, in 1866.[14] Nonetheless, he conveyed the essence of that science
in a way that also evoked his egalitarian political vision: "Thus all nature
is linked together by invisible bonds and every organic creature, however
low, however feeble, however dependent is necessary to the well-being of
some other among the myriad forms of life with which the Creator has
peopled the earth."[15] Natural history and politics were never separate for
him.

Marsh's tenure as American ambassador placed him in Italy during
some of the most exciting phases of the Risorgimento—when Dante's
dream of a strong, unified Italy was at long last beginning to be
achieved. Beyond his professional relationships with scientists like
Adolfo di Berenger, he was an admirer of Cavour, the nation's first premier, and a close friend of Ricasoli, who succeeded him. Marsh was also
a crucial ally of Garibaldi, the military hero of unification. In his official
diplomatic capacity, he was able to support Garibaldi's efforts in many

palpable ways, at one point arranging to extricate him from an Italian prison. An interesting historical aside related by David Lowenthal is that Marsh was enlisted as an unwilling party to the negotiations when Garibaldi was offered a generalship in the Union Army during a dark moment of the American Civil War.[16] That plan, which never went anywhere, might have given President Lincoln (in the period before Grant's ascendancy) at least one general on whom he could rely.

Marsh's passionate advocacy of the Risorgimento grew from his admiration for Italian culture and his friendship with political and military leaders. But it also reflected his growing sense that, in order to be effective on a whole-landscape scale, conservation required the authority and control of a unified, democratic nation: "[N]othing but the union of all the Italian states under a single government can render practicable the establishment of such arrangements for the conservation and restoration of the forests and the regulation of the flow of waters as are necessary for the full development of the yet unexhausted resources of that fairest of lands, and even for the permanent maintenance of the present condition of its physical geography."[17] Individual self-interest, and the limited duration of a single human life span, could not adequately encompass the much longer cycles of forest, soil, and ocean. Natural resources needed to be managed for the public good—in contrast both to landscapes monopolized by tyrannical states or the wealthy few and to laissez-faire situations in which individuals could build, mine, or cut wherever they wanted.

Frederick Law Olmsted's official report when Yosemite Valley was first protected as a state park in 1864 resonates tellingly with Marsh's hopes for Italy in the same period. Olmsted drew a distinction between this grand new public park and the private estates of England and Ireland, which no one could enjoy except for the owners and their few invited guests. Everyone, he argued, needed the refreshment and edification of natural beauty, and Yosemite represented a democratic alternative to the great private parks in that it would be "held, guarded and managed for the free use of the whole body of the people forever." The people themselves would also have responsibility for "the care of it, and the hospitality of admitting strangers from all parts of the world to visit and enjoy it freely."[18] Lewis Mumford has written, "That an effort to make reparations to nature and to establish a friendly basis for intercourse should have made any headway at all against the reckless gambling instincts of the post-war period was due to the fact that Olmsted gave to Thoreau's and Marsh's principles the benefit of an active demonstration."[19]

It is not surprising that, living in Italy during the Risorgimento, Marsh should have drawn a connection between conservation and nation building. But in our own time we continue to ponder, as he himself did for the rest of his life, how to balance the need for a state strong enough to safeguard environmental health in general and national parks in particular with the need for an open, democratic system of government. A conversation with Rolf Diamant, superintendent of the new Marsh-Billings-Rockefeller National Historical Park in Woodstock, has proven memorable to me in this regard. He expressed his own vision of national parks not just as protecting places of special beauty, ecological value, and historical significance but also as providing landscapes within which our society of the people, by the people, and for the people—and the parks themselves—can continue to evolve. National parks, he affirmed, are places for democracy itself to mature. This perspective is true to the democratic context within which Marsh described the mutual dependency of "every organic creature." It points to stewardship as essentially a civic undertaking. Such a connection may protect us from the sense of competition between social and environmental values, reinforcing human participation and responsibility within a larger community of life.[20]

Marsh was an early advocate of preserving the Adirondacks, both for the sake of nature lovers hungry for an experience of the continent's primeval forest and for the protection of the streams flowing into the Hudson River and the Erie Canal. This kind of dual argument, one side of which might be described as poetic or spiritual, the other as practical or economic, further complicated Marsh's already dense writing. It has sometimes made it hard for present-day environmentalists to know just where to place him. A similar complexity continues to challenge and enrich the identity of the Adirondack Park, the preserve that may express Marsh's influence and vision more directly than any other. In an article in *Sanctuary* magazine, Paul Bray wrote, "When a 'blue line' was drawn on a map around some millions of acres of land under mixed ownership in the Adirondack region in 1892, a very different idea of a park from the public estate model of Yellowstone was initiated. The challenge was not only how to reconcile nature preservation with the demand for recreational use but also how to meet the economic needs of the park's resident population in an ecologically compatible manner."[21] Bray's language differs in telling ways from Olmsted's vision for Yosemite. In part, this is a token of the differences in settlement patterns and history between east and west. But it also addresses an ongoing attempt, in the American conservation movement, to reconcile ecological and economic needs within a politically acceptable model.

Marsh's broad comparative vision reminds us that conservation must now be pursued within an inclusive, evolutionary perspective. National parks and other protected lands must continue to allow for a higher level of protection than private stewards alone could manage. But they must do so increasingly within a context of global environmental awareness and offer their benefits, as Olmsted wrote, to visitors "from all parts of the world." The official announcements for a conference Rita and I attended at Italy's Abruzzo National Park reproduced a painting called *La Natura, "cuore verde" della Terra, assediata dall' Uomo*, "Nature, 'green heart' of the Earth, besieged by Man." Vivid images of wildness, biodiversity, and natural beauty were hedged round in that picture by gray throngs of humans, with all our machines and buildings, our smoke and our waste. But in their color, vividness, and contrast value, the creatures and landscapes at the center also continued to offer a healing resource that radiated *out*, toward all that surrounded them.

Just as, in part under Marsh's influence, in 1892 a protective blue line was drawn around the "mixed-ownership" Adirondacks, we are now beginning to realize that such a line must actually encircle the whole planet—its struggling human communities and its wildlife alike. Marsh's value to us today comes from his awareness that the beautiful world at which he looked so discerningly had already been damaged in grave ways by human heedlessness. From his own vision of the beleaguered heart of nature grew a hope to promote a more inclusive, respectful, mutually protective, and progressive relationship between human communities and the living earth. Marsh aspired to become himself, and encouraged each of his readers to become, "a co-worker with nature."

. . .

If one follows Dante's suggestion about retracing the Arno to its headwaters, one ascends both to the mountains of Vallombrosa and to a summit in the history of conservation. For over eight centuries, until the unification of Italy in the mid-nineteenth century and the subsequent expropriation of church lands, the forest was tended by monks from the nearby Vallombrosian Abbey. It's important not to idealize or simplify the long history of their stewardship. Researchers have recently documented the distinct phases through which their silviculture passed. The early emphasis on coppicing and the production of chestnuts for food gave way to commercial cultivation of silver fir plantations. Because of this shift, pure stands of fir edged up into the higher-elevation beech forest, and firs increasingly crowded in on the chestnuts of the lower elevations. Prominent, single-age tracts of them still rise around the abbey today. These lofty trees were valued for masts, beams, and other construction materials, and by the end of the eighteenth century they accounted for as much as 35 percent of the monastery's income. The monks' decisions about the forest were always influenced by shifting social and economic contexts. Among other factors, shifts in management correlated with the decline of medieval agriculture practices and settlements in the Apennine region, with urgent calls for timber by the Opera del Duomo in Florence and the Grand Duke of Tuscany, and with changes in forestry regulation during the modern era. But over all those years the monks applied themselves to tending a living resource and to protecting it for the benefit of unborn generations.

Today, Vallombrosa is designated a Riserva Naturale, a status equivalent to wilderness in the United States in all but the continued presence of roads and a few public buildings. The Vallombrosa forest retains botanical diversity and beauty to an extraordinary degree. But Mauro Agnoletti, a leading scholar at the University of Florence, has proposed maintaining "the ancient part of the silver fir forest around the abbey as it is. In this way silvicultural techniques, such as clear cuts and artificial regeneration, could still be performed in order to maintain the pure stand of silver fir existing since medieval times, leaving the rest to natural evolution with little human intervention. This might represent an acceptable compromise between environmental concerns, oriented towards a natural based silviculture, and the evidence of a cultural value that cannot be denied."[22]

When Marsh died at Vallombrosa in 1882, he was visiting his good friend Adolfo di Berenger, the founding and recently retired director of the forestry school there. Marsh found both the long history of careful management and the current health of that forest close to his ideal of stewardship. The stories and practices rooted at Vallombrosa since long before the time of Dante were for him a return to a beautiful headwater, the better to begin again. The region's beautiful name, too, has an enduring meaning for the prophetic tradition Marsh initiated. He and his successors in conservation have advanced our collective understanding by facing up to the darkness of society's destructive practices. Recognizing such problems makes it possible both to look backward, in a more informed historical perspective, and to advance toward a more sustainable way of living together on the earth. Shadows have marked out our path toward a more mature land ethic. But the upshot of Marsh's writing is finally not lamentation. Rather, it is a call for balance and restraint, so that we may pursue a more hopeful and sustainable way of life. The environmental disasters that Marsh described, like those we see in our own day, are invitations to creative grieving. By looking steadfastly into and through loss, we may cross the threshold into a new way of life. Leopold writes in *A Sand County Almanac* that an expanded land ethic has now become "an evolutionary possibility and an ecological necessity."[23] One reason I have chosen to frame this book with Marsh's career is that, over the century and a quarter since his death, we can see clearly how many benefits have already flowed from his critical but constructive appraisal of our practices. His story encourages us to continue advancing along the path of chastened resolution.

Dante's verses posted on that tower beside the Arno had as their context the poet's bitter disappointment with the social and political corruption of his native Florence. The downfall of that once-proud republic was not only a domestic failure for him. It also reflected the rapacity of Rome, Germany, and France—those mighty powers that made the Italian city-states their pawns. Though continuing to serve as American ambassador to Italy until the end of his life, Marsh's sense of political disillusionment, as noted above, grew steadily darker. Letters written home to friends during his last years convey a bleak perspective on current events. Lowenthal comments, "For this grievous state Marsh blamed untrammeled corporate power."[24] Surveying the state of Europe in the late 1870s, Marsh wrote, "In the worst periods of the French Revolution & Bonapartean Wars, men may have seen a sky as lurid as ours of today, but there were then *some* bright spots."[25]

Living in Italy during the fall of 2000, Rita and I found our own reasons for discouragement in following the election season at home. Even the center-left newspaper *La Repubblica* maintained a tone of general astonishment at America's unedifying presidential campaign and unimpressive candidates, sometimes referring to the latter not by their names but simply with two nicknames: the Robot and the Deficient. It's not that the Italians were so much better at producing presidential candidates: they were after all preparing to elect Silvio Berlusconi. But our nation's impact on the whole world, including Italy, is so vast that more is expected of us. The highly polarized months that followed the contested Florida election were further causes of distress. And then came the horrific losses of September 11—followed so soon by a confusion of wars —which have continued to instill a deep uneasiness into our national life.

In such a time, it may be helpful to connect our environmental valley of the shadows with the political turmoil of Marsh's day. As he did, we ultimately face a *civic* challenge. In order to meet it effectively we must cultivate a sense of community that is at once alert to good examples in our history and responsible to coming generations. Thus, we hike up to the headwaters on a quest for collective renewal, motivated by our experience of loss and our sense of danger. This chapter introduced the dialogue between Tuscany and Vermont with several lines from Dante. It might thus appropriately conclude by looking at the ending of "Directive," by Vermont's Robert Frost. The speaker of that poem guides his reader up to the ridge where a farming community was once rooted. The only vestige of the fields those farmers so laboriously cleared is an opening in the woods "no bigger than a harness gall," while a pioneer family's home life is recalled only by a broken drinking cup beside a "belilaced cellar hole." But Frost's speaker also seeks to evoke the vitality of the human bond with a place on earth by locating, near the cellar hole, "the brook that was the water of the house." Dipping the broken cup into that "lofty and original" spring, he invites the reader, too, to renew a connection with the land. Frost's poem began, as did both Dante's *Commedia* and Marsh's life, in a ravaged land and in a moment of social brokenness—expressed in "Directive" as "all this now too much for us." But it ends in a project of recollection and reconciliation at the source. "Here are your waters and your watering place," our guide in "Directive" tells us. "Drink and be whole again beyond confusion."[26]

3
COMPATRIOTS

The first time Rita and I visited the forest of Vallombrosa, we took a blue SETI bus that left from the train station in Florence and swung up into the Casentino mountains by way of Pontassieve. It was October, the summer heat had passed, and the resort towns ringing the abbey were largely abandoned. A single hotel, Le Terrazze, remained open in Saltino. We arrived in the late afternoon and checked into a spacious room for half the high-season rate. The next morning we took our breakfast in the hotel's formal salon in splendid solitude. Then we strapped on our day packs and rambled up the ridge through groves of chestnuts. The air was pungent from drifts of brittle leaves going to powder around our boots. We picnicked beneath a lofty hardwood canopy, where we were both disappointed and relieved not to see any of the *cinghiali*, or wild boar, known to frequent these mountains. What we did see, in the course of the day, were several elderly but hale collectors of *funghi*. Two of them were men, one a woman. They were all working alone, with large coarse baskets slung around their necks on leather straps. One man had a dog with him, and we wondered if he might be after *tartufi*, or truffles, a specialty of the region. His greeting was an especially guarded one.

Given the intricacy with which institutional fiefdoms, too, are often guarded in Italian life, I didn't want to knock on a door at the forestry school without an introduction of some kind. Most of the activities of the school had moved to Florence early in the twentieth century, and I wasn't even sure under whose auspices or on which projects the remaining staff up here in the mountains worked. So our images from this first day at Vallombrosa were solely of the mature hardwood forests, interspersed with massive blocks of silver fir. When we returned six weeks later, we were accompanied by Professor Antonio Gabrielli from the Academy of Forest Sciences in Fiesole. Not only was he kind enough to drive us up this time, saving four hours of round-trip travel and the cost of overnight accommodation, but he also prepared the way by making several calls on our behalf. To the Vallombrosa Forestry School, now under the aegis of the University of Florence; to the Corpo Forestale, or Forest Service, a separate public entity under contract to manage the forest on behalf of that school; and to the regional forestry school in Arezzo, which has jurisdiction over the famous arboretum beside the abbey.

In the company of Professor Gabrielli and our green-uniformed guide from the Corpo Forestale, we set off from the abbey to visit the arboretum. We were following a path that led first through a medieval herbalist's garden. The garden was divided into many little beds, some of them dormant at this season but most closely cultivated with shrubs and a wide range of fragrant and low-growing Mediterranean perennials. Over the course of centuries, the monks at Vallombrosa achieved a remarkable level of expertise in growing and processing plants for treating nervous disorders, coronary maladies, urinary infections, diseases of the skin, and many other ailments. Their approach, as in the adjacent forest, was utilitarian, but it was also closely focused, skilled, and patient. In dealing with herbs and trees alike, they adopted a long-term perspective. Their various value-added products also did much to make the surrounding villages, as well as the woods, flourish. The number of monks at the abbey is of course far smaller today than in the centuries before nationhood. The maintenance of this garden is also now under the aegis of scientists, funded in part by pharmaceutical companies that are duly recognized by placards at particular experimental beds.

After leaving the walled garden, we crossed an ancient logging road, then immediately entered another gate. A path between boxwood hedges led into one of the earliest sections of the arboretum. There were five sections in all, each division associated with a particular era in the collection's development and named for a person who had special significance to the abbey or forest during that time. *Viali*, or avenues, traversed this remarkable collection of trees. Over 700 species were represented among the 5,000 specimens of the sloping enclosure. A high fence ran around the collection's perimeter, in order to protect against the *cinghiali* that would otherwise thoroughly root up the arboretum's floor. Our day's conversations were all in Italian. Thanks to the past months of language lessons, I could generally follow what was being said—with the help of Rita's sotto voce commentary and botanical glosses provided by Professor Gabrielli, with his reading knowledge of scientific English.

The Viale dei Giganti crosses by a group of spectacular Douglas firs, chestnuts, and pitch pines. The firs and pines, planted about 120 years ago, are between 125 and 130 feet high. Our guide from the Corpo Forestale gave us the scale by explaining that this was about half as high as Brunelleschi's dome that rises above the cathedral in Florence. The Viale delle Sequoie branches off from the Viale dei Giganti, ascending a nearby hill in order to allow a view of two redwoods that were planted at about the same time as the Douglas firs. Though significantly smaller than the 1,500-year-old sequoias of Muir Woods, where I so often walked as a boy and teenager in Mill Valley, California, both of these trees already convey the majesty of their species. One, a *Sequoia gigantea*, is now about 145 feet high, over 2 feet in diameter at breast height, and with the characteristic buttresses of its species fanning out at the base. To come upon such a tree, growing strongly half a world away from its native Pacific Coast range, reminded me of Wendell Berry's poem "Manifesto: The Mad Farmer Liberation Front." Berry's farmer nurses a hope much vaster than the prevailing "practicality" of his day, with his crazy resolve summed up in the line: "Invest in the millennium: plant sequoias."[1]

Another notable feature of the arboretum, to which our guide pointed with pride, was a beautiful grove of Japanese cryptomeria. They rose beside a gentle fold in the land, upslope from the Viale dei Giganti. Strolling beside these cryptomeria, with their graceful fans of greenery and redwoodlike bark, Rita and I were transported to Nikko and the mighty groves framing the Tokugawa Shrine. These trees would take three or four centuries to rival the stature of those in Japan, just as the Vallombrosa sequoias won't catch up with Muir Woods for another millennium. But such exotic species now rooted in Italy have already attained their own magnificent character; they offer visitors to this ancient Tuscan woods a global perspective on forests.

The original forests of these mountains were largely beech. As our guide told us, in what turned out to be a daylong series of familial metaphors, that ancient beechwood was the mother of the present forest. Scholars like Mauro Agnoletti and Alberto Bronzi have documented the waves of managed forest succession here, as first chestnuts and then fir were favored in the monks' approach. Antonio Gabrielli has made another point that is of special interest to me because of the parallel with Vermont's environmental history, namely, that the much more extensive woods throughout the Tuscan mountains today than in earlier centuries reflect not just changes in forestry but also the steady abandonment of high-elevation farms: "For centuries just an appendix of agriculture . . . , the forest has in recent times broken free from this situation. This happened precisely when mountain and hill agricultural economy was floundering and farm crops consequently gave way again to forest stands. In other words, the forest is regaining (according to the laws of nature and with the aid of man) the land from which it had been dislodged."[2] Even with all these planned and unplanned changes around Vallombrosa, the monks' concern for the long-term health and productivity of these woods has left an environment diverse enough to be considered a "biogenetic reserve." It is a kind of ark for species from throughout the northern temperate and boreal zones. The varied topography around Vallombrosa offers them diverse niches—dry or wet, northern or southern exposure—so that they can prosper far from the landscapes where they have become, in some cases, endangered.

Growing in the "Tozzi" section of the arboretum, along with the monumental firs and pines but with its crown considerably below that lofty canopy, was another tree even more familiar to Rita and me. We'd been looking for it, in fact, since we entered the gate. In the arboretum's catalogue, which we received from Professor Gabrielli when first visiting him at the Academmia in Fiesole, it was number 2405, *Acer saccharum* Marsh.[3] This particular sugar maple (one of two in that catalogue) was not as big as one might have anticipated from a tree over a century old. Both its modest girth and its trunk leaning out to seek the light could be accounted for by the evergreen canopy blocking so much of the sun. In Vermont sugar bushes like ours in Starksboro, the maples are often thinned out so that each remaining tree can develop its own fully rounded crown. This Tuscan maple would probably never attain the girth or vigor of trees growing in such a spacious setting. Our Vermont soils are also rich in lime, as indicated by such marker species as the blue cohosh, plantain-leaved sedge, and maidenhair ferns growing on the floor of our sugar bush. Even without such advantages, though, this Tuscan maple was well over a foot in diameter at breast height—about the same girth as many of the maples in our sixty-five-year-old sugar bush in Starksboro and large enough to be tapped. Rita and I scuffled through the brown leafage, on this second day of December, looking for maple leaves but finding only indistinguishable scraps and a few tattered beech leaves. This trees' leaves must have slid on down into the stream-bed below after falling a few weeks back. Still, here that maple was and here we were—three visitors drawn to Vallombrosa in the wake of another Vermonter.

Although I have found records of this particular tree's planting neither at Vallombrosa nor at the Arnold Arboretum, its age and that of its neighbors indicates that it would have begun growing here shortly after Marsh's letter to Charles Sprague Sargent in 1882. He particularly asked Sargent to send over seeds of "the *sugar-maple*, the American *ash & elm*, the *black walnut . . .* and the *black birch.*"[4] The sugar maple, ash, and black birch are still among the most common trees in Vermont's mixed northern hardwood forests. Since Marsh's day, though, the elm has nearly disappeared in Vermont because of a blight, while the maple has become so much more prevalent as now to be considered the symbol of Vermont.

The clear-cutting Marsh witnessed as a boy and young man gave way in Vermont first to an era of sheep farming and then to a forest dominated by white pines. These coniferous trees germinate well in grassy pasture as long as they have plenty of light. When the white pines were cut down in their turn at the beginning of the twentieth century, deciduous trees sprouted in that muddy ground where the grass had long ago been shaded out by the evergreen canopy. The hardwood saplings burst up from what foresters call "the buried seed-pool" and kept the pines from reestablishing their dominance. Sugar maples now blanket the middle elevations of the Green Mountains and spread down to embrace the valley farms. The maples' fall colors are so splendid that they dominate the conversation of residents and draw throngs of visitors. The closest phenomenon to it we've experienced elsewhere is *hanami,* or cherry-blossom viewing, in Japan. In both cases, a few days of intense natural beauty call a time-out from people's usual routines. In Vermont, such beauty is the unforeseen result of two ferocious episodes of deforestation.

Marsh's use of the word "compatriots" to describe the New England trees he wanted to see planted at Vallombrosa evokes the civic and communal character of stewardship that can arise from social errors and ecological disaster. In the realm of environmental mindfulness, as in that of forest succession, the progress of our lives often has more to do with grace—unforeseen gifts—than with works. Our human role in nature thus becomes a practice of gratitude and stewardship, one of recognizing what has been lost, what might be restored. No one has played a more important part in our evolving attitudes toward the larger community of life than Marsh. From the founding of the Adirondack Park, to its offshoot the National Park system, and including today's explorations of sustainability in forestry and farming, such an evolution may have less to do with strategic planning than with heightened receptivity and carefulness. These are the democratic values imbibed by a small-town boy whose schooling and family life were complemented by untold hours wandering in the nearby woods.

Marsh's significant exposure to the woods while growing up came in part because he was so studious that as a young boy he apparently damaged his vision by excessive amounts of reading under poor light. Thus, his parents had to forbid him books while his sight partially recovered, and turned him out of doors to read the face of nature instead. Thus, in Marsh's biography as well as in his scientific overview, loss became the context for fuller recognition of patterns in nature. Even before his wanderings through the woods began, though, he had an experience that permanently impressed the trees of his native place on his mind, memory, and imagination. Caroline Crane Marsh's handwritten memoir of Marsh's life in the University of Vermont Library notes that Marsh generally did not like to talk about his own early life.

Occasionally, however, he would state some circumstance or fact relating to his very early years, if it were recalled by the immediate subject of conversation. The following is his own account of a drive over the hills with his father, when the latter was called to attend court in a town several miles distant: "I was four years and a half old at the time, and sat on a little stool between my father's knees in the two wheeled chaise in which he always drove. That 'one horse shay' must have been as strong as the old deacons's, for the roads in those days were shocking. But little I heeded that, for to my mind, the whole earth lay spread out before me. My father pointed out the most striking trees as we passed them and told me how to distinguish their varieties. I do not think I ever afterwards failed to know one forest tree from another. Nor did my father limit his lessons to the individual objects in the

landscape. He called my attention to the general configuration of the surface, pointed out the direction of the different ranges of hills, told me how
the water gathered on them and ran down their sides and where the mountain streams would be likely to be formed. But—what struck me perhaps
most of all—he stopped his horse on the top of a steep hill, bade me notice
how the water there flowed in different directions, and told me that such a
point was called a *watershed*. I never forgot that word, nor any part of my father's talk that day, and even now a vivid picture of that country through
which we passed often flashes upon me when my thoughts are very differently employed."[5]

First comes identification of individual trees, focusing the eye on the
surrounding countryside until it can begin to pay "attention to the general configuration of the surface." Then, as one gradually distinguishes
the ridgelines where rainfall flows down in different directions, the notion of a watershed emerges. As David Lowenthal points out in his biography of Marsh, this concept, informing Marsh's thinking about nature
from such an early stage, naturally leads to an ecological perspective. A
system of valleys and ridges that drains into a given waterway delineates
a naturally defined bioregion, one whose circulation comprehends our
cultural currents as well as being influenced by them. Once we have
arrived at such a whole-landscape perspective, awareness of dynamic
relationships becomes the essence of our natural perceptions. Marsh's
description of how that vision from early childhood returned to him
throughout his life evokes Wordsworth's description of "spots of time,"
those natural experiences that localize memory so that ". . . feeling
comes in aid / Of feeling, and diversity of strength / Attends us, if but
once we have been strong."[6]

As lovers of Vermont whose children, too, feel rooted in this place,
Rita and I have felt increasingly eager to participate in the development
of such a whole-landscape vision. This has meant supporting statewide
initiatives like the Vermont Land Trust and Vermont Family Forests. Our
sugaring in Starksboro, too, has felt like a way to enter both into a sustainable forest economy and into the living rural culture of our place.
Until very recently, just about all Vermont farmers would have produced
maple syrup in the early spring. Preparing their sugarhouse, evaporator,
buckets, and canning supplies would have occupied them throughout a
season in which there was little chance of working in the fields. Even today, maple syrup remains one of the few products in which Vermont

leads the nation. Paying attention to this one "compatriot" of the forest has helped people here identify with the topography and seasons of their place—the trees fringing tilled fields in the lower and middle elevations of the Green Mountains and the protracted transition between winter and spring that completes the circle of the seasons here. The flow of sugar maple sap, when the temperature falls below freezing at night and rises above it during the day, defines Vermonters' watershed of home.

Beginning to know our own sugar bush better has been a process of attunement to the seasons and the woods around our home. It's helped us to watch for signs that the sap will soon start running—like the snow beginning to melt in a ring around each maple's trunk—and to listen for peepers announcing the frog run, our last week of usable sap. Sugaring is also a craft to practice with our children, and one they will have a chance to pass on down the line. This has been an exciting way to feel our family putting down roots in Vermont, not just in the sense of affiliation and loyalty, but also in our physical skills and seasonal rhythms. The fact remains, however, that all love of natural beauty is under a shadow in our time. Even, or especially, in a little pocket of land graced as Vermont has been.

This green and pleasant place lies within an easy day's drive of New York, Boston, and Montreal, so that the pressures of development are hard to stave off and mountain villages like Bristol can soon be destabilized. As the value of rural land increases, it becomes harder and harder for people "whose house is in the village, though," to afford property producing little financial profit beyond a few cords of firewood and a few gallons of maple syrup. Dairy farmers, for whom sugaring has been a sideline, are increasingly hard put to maintain their milk-producing operations in this era of cheap food, long-distance refrigeration trucks, and massive subsidized dairies in places like Texas and California. Beyond these local economic concerns, the maples themselves are increasingly stressed by acid rain from the power plants of the Midwest and by global climate change that has advanced the coming of spring five to six days over the past several decades. A canopy begins to close over these long favored maples, then, equivalent in its way to the one that has stunted and tilted the legacy tree at Vallombrosa.

If there is one lesson we should have learned from the environmental crises of the past half century, it is that the world is one living system. This is sometimes hard to remember in landscapes as fresh and diverse as the mountains of Vermont and Vallombrosa. Much of the land in both regions has been protected by legislation or other covenants, and people in the surrounding communities are committed to preserving both the natural legacy received from previous generations and the locally rooted cultures that protect and sustain such landscapes. But whatever may be going on at ground level, the most staunchly defended forests still lie open to troubled skies.

Camel's Hump in Vermont, our first wilderness preserve thanks to the will of Joseph Battell at the end of the nineteenth century, has also become one of the most studied sites for acid-rain research over the past several decades. The smoke from coal-fired electric generators in the Midwest, streaming eastward across the country in a parody of the beautiful migrating geese that annually traverse our state north to south, undergoes a malign alchemy as it falls on the highest ridges of New England in the form of acid rain. Spruce and fir, holding on in a last sparse band below the tree line, were already stressed, contorted, and dwarfed by exposure to extremes of wind and cold. They had previously shrunk and turned together into the huddled adaptations of krummholz. But when further assaulted by the leaching effects of acid rain, they dropped below the gradient of survival. At the crowning elevations of the Green Mountains' spine, you will now find increasing numbers of bleached, skeletal trees. At Vallombrosa, too, the 1960s and '70s were a time of alarming die-off in the high-mountain fir populations. Our guide from the Corpo Forestale said that he thought the main cause was a lack of sufficient rainfall during that period, rather than the impact of acid rain per se. But he agreed that the margin for survival was a very narrow one, despite the grandeur and extensiveness of the forest. The biggest forest is as exposed to the sky as a single tree, and the higher the mountains, the more precarious may be its purchase on survival.

It is not so hard to conceive of substantially eliminating acid rain. Installing scrubbers on the stacks of coal-fired generators arrests much of the particulate matter before it enters the atmosphere. And forcing the Midwestern producers to begin paying for the damage in New England would soon help them see the advantages of using more expensive but also cleaner-burning varieties of coal. But global climate change is both a much graver challenge and a more intractable one. It is already seriously underway, by the almost universal consensus of the world's leading climate scientists. Even if the United States were now to join with other industrialized nations and ratify the Kyoto Accord, the carbon that has already been pumped into the atmosphere will continue to cycle around the planet and interfere with our weather patterns for many years. If we do not change our ways but in fact continue to aggravate the problem, as with the recent craze for sport-utility vehicles spiking America's use of petroleum, the damage will come that much faster. Such danger does not come from distant, sinister smokestacks. It purrs out of our own tailpipes every time we drive to work or to the store. It also streamed behind the wings of the plane that carried Rita and me to Europe on this pilgrimage. This is not a problem solvable by legislation or attributable to isolated, sociopathic tycoons. It is a reflection of our common way of life, and an incentive to pursue a conservation model that begins with the personal responsibility and community orientation of stewardship.

. . .

Our sugar bush is on a pretty steep slope, so that while we do use buckets for collecting sap right around and downhill from the sugarhouse, we also string pale-blue sap lines up into the woods. These branch lines angle into the thick, gray main line, mimicking the grace of limbs sliding down from the crown to join a maple's trunk; each of them adds its bubbling stream of sap to the gallons collecting in our holding tank. This is a stainless steel bulk tank, originally intended to hold milk and given to us by our friend Bill Scott in Ferrisburgh. Since forty gallons of sap must be boiled down to make a single gallon of syrup, when the sap is flowing sugar makers have to keep their evaporators boiling around the clock. This is a time of festive excess, and often a kind of family reunion in the woods. Parents and children, uncles, aunts, and cousins, stay up all night in the clouds of fragrant steam. Celebrants drink a bottle of beer frosted down in a drift outside the sugarhouse or dip a mug into the boiling sap to make a cup of maple tea.

All the forests surrounding this spring festival, and not just the sugar maples, are threatened now. Our graceful eastern hemlocks, already at the southern extreme of their range, will probably be the first species to vanish in Vermont. With their disappearance, a mysterious northerly note will be lost from the music of our woods, as well as a species of tree whose spiraling, progressively offset branches make it particular good cover for wintering deer. The sugar maples are much more abundant and more robust in Vermont. But their survival may eventually be brought into question, too. And in the meantime, the predictable cycles of sugaring are already being thrown off. In a forest as in a garden, the healthier the plants are, the better they can withstand pests, cold, and other stresses. Our sugar bush in Starksboro is a vigorous one, with its calcium-rich soil, abundance of water, and good drainage. We hope to strengthen the maples growing above Maggie Brook further by trucking bags of leaves and other organic matter up into the woods and by thinning the stand to give the remaining trees space and light to develop full, mature crowns. These efforts are no less urgent and important for being overshadowed by global climate change. But in such an era especially, environmental stewardship must cultivate an appropriate humility. This may finally be an opportunity for stewardship to transcend the lordly confidence of our traditional approach to "natural-resource" decisions. Humility, gratitude, and an earnest desire to collaborate with natural systems damaged by human heedlessness will be the starting points for stewards today. Such a shift of attitude may be one crucial benefit of this shadowed moment.

Vallombrosa, which we first visited because it was the place where George Perkins Marsh died, turned out to be a focal landscape for this meditation in a time of environmental crisis. It has a tradition of active stewardship unmatched in Italy, if not in the world. For almost a thousand years the Vallombrosian monks, and the surrounding villages under their jurisdiction, protected and cultivated their huge forest domain. These forests retain a magnificence, despite the signs that, like our woods in Vermont, they have sometimes been ravaged, enduring several episodes of clear-cutting and other abuse over the past two and a half centuries. The first of these was at the end of the eighteenth century, when Napoleon swept through with his armies of conquest. The next came in the 1860s, when the nation of Italy was finally unified and the church properties (including Vallombrosa) were expropriated. Finally, these woods were both logged with little restraint from the beginning of the Fascist era and severely damaged by Allied bombardments near the end of World War II. Still, within the total expanse of this forest, enough of the deeply rooted diversity survives that, in its new designation as a fully protected Riserva Naturale, these woods make up Italy's richest "biogenetic reserve." The individuals in charge of the remarkable arboretum here are aware of preserving a number of species that have practically become extinct in their native habitat elsewhere in Italy or the world. The forests of Vallombrosa have thus become a sort of ark—a capacious vessel bearing a biological and cultural heritage of importance for the whole world.

The beauty of the word *Vallombrosa* resonated for Rita and me with the forest's amazing setting. It reminded us of certain high valleys in Vermont that feel like havens held up under the sky. The name of this forest also has a special resonance for lovers of poetry. Milton refers to it in one of his most famous epic similes, in Book I of *Paradise Lost*, where Satan gradually recovers his self-possession, rising from "the burning marle" of Hell where he has been cast by God and turning to gather his fallen forces.

> [He] call'd
> His Legions, angel forms, who lay intranced
> Thick as autumnal leaves that strow the brooks
> In Vallombrosa, where the Etruscan shades,
> High over-arch'd, imbower. . . .[7]

Book I is the easiest place in the poem to accept Blake's assertion that "Milton was of the Devil's party without knowing it." Subsequently, the poet strategically whittles Satan down to size, but especially in the epic similes of his beginning, Milton's descriptions of the fallen angels in Hell are magnificent. This particular reference emphasizes the fallenness and lack of consciousness of those "angel forms" by comparing them to autumnal leaves. But it also conveys what a mighty force they still are. The redundancy of the name Vallombrosa and the word "imbower" serves to bring out the darkened glamour of the scene.

Milton's tone and strategy are clarified by another epic simile occurring just fifteen lines earlier. Some scholars argue that Milton actually reached Vallombrosa, others that he just lifted that glamorous reference from a description of the landscape in Ariosto.[8] But there is no disputing that he visited Galileo during his journey to Florence as a young man, or that he looked through the scientist's telescope on that occasion. In the earlier simile, Milton shows Satan moving toward his fallen troops, with his "ponderous shield" slung over his back like a Homeric hero's.

> [T]he broad circumference
> Hung on his shoulders like the moon, whose orb
> Through optic glass the Tuscan artist views

At evening from the top of Fesole,
Or in Valdarno, to descry new lands,
Rivers, or mountains, in her spotty globe.[9]

Satan's stature is amplified here by both the perpetual mystery of the full moon and the heroic achievement of Galileo, "the Tuscan artist." But one who inspects this grandeur through a sharp enough lens, as Milton will increasingly be doing in *Paradise Lost*, can see clearly enough that, for all his magnificence, Satan's is an extremely "spotty globe." Such poetic chiaroscuro is the context through which the name of Vallombrosa entered English literature. It introduces a world of drama and struggle, sudden reversals and determined counterattacks, carried out under a full moon and under the "over-arch'd" boughs of a forest at once ancient, embattled, and rustling with human stories.

. . .

Almost every day of our sojourn in Florence, I would walk past a shop specializing in antique prints and finely bound books located just across Borgo San Jacopo from our apartment. In the morning, the elderly proprietor hung out a number of prints on the wall beside his door, taking them in again each night. I noticed with surprise that the largest of these were usually several pictures from Audubon's Elephant Folio of *The Birds of North America*. Ever since I was a first grader at Audubon School in New Orleans, where we wore T-shirts adorned with Audubon's showy oriole, I have been in love with this set of pictures. They evoke the origins of nature writing and conservation in America, combining a high degree of visual focus and a large amount of scientific information with a palpable sense of wonder. Such amazing creatures Audubon's birds are —often life-size or even larger. What has always struck me about them, though, even when I was a boy, was their sadness. They feel like elegiac celebrations, stop-action portraits so vivid they make a viewer think of the individual, long-since-deceased, birds. This has always been part of the experience of human observers who gaze deeply into nature, as captured in Virgil's phrase "the tears of things, mortal affairs that touch the mind." We look and look, in the knowledge that what we see is passing away before our eyes.

While three of the birds so beautifully portrayed on that stucco Florentine wall (the red phalarope, black-billed cuckoo, and the Louisiana [now Harris] hawk) still have stable populations, the fourth, the passenger pigeon, is extinct.[10] Ours is a day when the affecting transience of nature, so bound up with our own mortality, has been overtaken by a new kind of death. The natural systems with which we identify, and from whose continuity we draw consolation, are themselves increasingly susceptible to decline and death—not in the natural course of things, but because their methods of self-perpetuation have become obsolete. Whole forests are cut down, and the species that coevolved with them also disappear. Passenger pigeons may have been the most numerous species of bird ever to inhabit our planet before their extinction by a combination of mindless slaughter and the destruction of the American hardwood forests on which they relied. Audubon himself described standing in such a woods in western Pennsylvania as a flock of them passed overhead, so thick that they darkened the sky and so extensive that their continuous passage lasted for four days. There were millions of birds in this living shadow. Forty-five years later not a single passenger pigeon survived.

Vallombrosa.

4
SAINT BEECH

On a mild December afternoon, several weeks after our visit to the Vallombrosa arboretum, Rita and I stood beside an ancient beech in the forest above the abbey. Its solid gray bark had the characteristic scoured texture we recognized from Vermont. But much more massive branches than we were used to seeing on a beech undulated out and up in their centuries-long dance with the filtered light. A stone wall shored up the embankment where the beech was rooted, while a small chapel stood nearby. Inside the chapel hung a portrait of San Giovanni Gualberto. The altar before his picture was covered by petitions of the faithful, written on scraps of paper and held down by pebbles, fragments of wood, chestnut burrs. One close to the front asked for the gifts of "salute e serenità"—health and serenity.

The journey that brought Giovanni Gualberto to Vallombrosa began on a Good Friday almost a thousand years ago. He was riding his horse up the hill from Florence to attend Mass at the Church of San Miniato when he came upon the man who had killed his brother. The murderer begged for mercy with his arms outstretched in imitation of the Crucified One. And the young aristocrat forgave him, violating every expectation of his class and era. As he continued into the basilica for worship, he passed a fresco where Christ bowed his head in approval of his actions. Within several months, Giovanni had overcome the opposition of his father to become a member of the Benedictine community there at San

Miniato. But just a few years later he was lucky to escape with his life, fleeing the wrath of Florence's bishop, whom he had denounced for electing a corrupt man as the monastery's new abbot. The Vallombrosian order of Benedictines, which was subsequently founded by this refugee to the mountains, would be devoted both to contemplation and to reforming monastic life and the church itself. And the new community's spiritual energy would soon be widely recognized and supported. In 1039 Giovanni Gualberto received the surrounding forests as a gift to the monastery, and a beautiful stone church was completed and consecrated at Vallombrosa in 1058.

When the young Florentine first arrived in this rugged terrain, though, he did not have patrons, a clear sense of mission, or even the necessities of food and shelter. Another significant event in the story thus relates to his finding protection from the elements below a beech that interlaced its branches over his head to keep him dry and warm. For centuries, a chapel has commemorated this act of compassion by the Faggio Santo, or Holy Beech. In the English translation included in a guidebook we purchased at the abbey, the honored tree was referred to simply as Saint Beech. The ancient specimen rooted here now is considered by the monks to be the third successor in a direct line from the original protector of San Giovanni Gualberto. Leonardo, the uniformed Vallombrosa forester who brought us to see this current incarnation of the Faggio Santo, remarked in a matter-of-fact way, "It's the same every year. This beech always gets its new spring leaves earlier than any other beech in the forest."[1]

Further donations followed the original bequest of land. By the end of the thirteenth century the abbey's property stretched from the confluence of the Vicana and Arno rivers all the way up to the summit of Monte Secchieta—several thousand acres in all. By that point, the monks had already established a tradition of careful forestry. They coordinated their efforts with local farmers and furniture makers, developing a value-added economy that kept villages in their region considerably more prosperous than most communities in Tuscany. The Vallombrosian monks were twice expelled from their abbey and forest—first for a few years under Napoleon and then again for over a century after the 1861 unification of Italy. They were finally allowed to move back into their abbey in the 1960s, though the forest itself has remained both a publicly managed Riserva Naturale and a field station for Italy's only state forestry school. The forest as a whole has remained one of the most beautiful, diverse, and culturally prestigious in Italy. Its designation today as a Riserva Naturale perpetuates a tradition of reciprocal protection between trees and human beings that was inaugurated by the Faggio Santo almost a thousand years ago. And Giovanni Gualberto continues to be recognized in Italy today as the patron saint of forests.

. . .

The story of San Giovanni Gualberto and the Holy Beech is colored by a medieval piety that feels remote from our own world, yet it may have much to teach us about conservation. In fact, being able to listen respectfully to such stories may help those of us who consider ourselves environmentalists to find a more comprehensive and adequate land ethic. The American conservation movement has focused on wilderness from the time of John Muir through the career of David Brower. In my mind, the wilderness ethic represents a breakthrough in our thinking—an affirmation of nature's value, and its sacredness, transcending the narrow calculus of "natural resources" and human utility. It represents one of America's greatest contributions to world culture. But the initial strategy of separation—drawing boundaries beyond which roads, mechanized transport, and permanent dwellings are not allowed—needs now to be integrated more fully into our other practices on the land. It is not that such a strategy has been wrong in itself. The Wilderness Act of 1964, the Alaskan Wilderness Bill, and the Eastern Wild Areas Act have all been triumphs for American conservation, and the exclusions described above have been necessary for the preservation of such extraordinary lands. But we are called upon to take a further step and to uphold higher standards in the lands outside the boundaries of wilderness, where we live and work. While continuing to focus on the forests, we need to cultivate a spirit of gratitude toward individual trees.

Rita and I have raised our family in the village of Bristol, Vermont, sheltered under the heavily wooded ridge of the Green Mountains that runs from Mount Abraham to Camel's Hump. We celebrate the resurgence of these Vermont forests over the past two centuries, as well as the increasing diversity of animal life that makes our state so much wilder in important ways than at any time since the Civil War. But such an ecological recovery has another side. In the mid-nineteenth century almost all the food and fiber consumed in Vermont came from within the state's borders. Our houses and furniture came from the trees of our own wood-

lots, just as the energy to heat those houses did, and our clothes were often woven from the wool of our own flocks. But today, when these mountains are so much less ravaged, we also import an overwhelming proportion of our energy—in the form of oil, natural gas, and hydropower from
Quebec. Much of our food is grown in places like California, New Jersey,
Ohio, and Florida. Even our houses and their furnishings include quite a
bit of wood from elsewhere. I do not intend to argue for a new isolation-
ism. But the fact remains that the rewilding of our forests is part of a
larger pattern. The increasing greenness of a beautiful place like Vermont reflects the degree to which we have become implicated in the industrial agriculture practiced far from our borders, in the clear-cutting
of the Pacific Northwest, the Amazon rain forest, and Indonesia, and in
the manufacturing carried out at low wages throughout the developing
world.[2] It's important for us to bear this whole picture in mind, but hard
to do. We need daily, visible reminders of the true environmental costs of
our lifestyles, as well as local sources of inspiration for a more mindful
and modest way of life. Both in the preservation of wilderness and the
conservation of sustainably managed forests, we need to remember the
holiness of individual trees.

As we hiked through the woods of Vallombrosa with Leonardo, we
talked about the relationship between the Vallombrosian ethic of stewardship, in which more or less the whole forest was managed, and the
Franciscan ethic, in which major tracts were set aside beyond all human
use. Leonardo said that, although employed at Vallombrosa, he had long
held the Franciscan model to be the loftier one. In recent years, however,
he'd become concerned that environmentalists in wealthier countries
like Italy and the United States might be protecting our own wilderness
by, in effect, sacrificing the rain forests of Brazil. This had led him to feel
that a spiritually grounded model of stewardship was an essential complement to any wilderness ethic. If we become governed by a more
restrained and strategic use of our own resources—as opposed to our
present consumption of distant forests, hidden from us behind a veil of
distance and money—we may also begin using, and wasting, less. This is
not an alternative to wilderness protection. It is a fulfillment of it, inspired by the millennial dialogue of wilderness and stewardship, and by
the example of a single tree.[3]

We were following Leonardo along the Circuito delle Cappelle, the
path connecting ten chapels that commemorated important sites in the

life of San Giovanni Gualberto and the monastic community. This itinerary was developed during the sixteenth through the eighteenth centuries, in the aftermath of the Counter-Reformation. Like similar paths
throughout Italy, it was conceived of as a "calvario," a circuit on which
one could enact a walking meditation on the life of Christ and the path of
sainthood. It marked the whole landscape as a "sacro monte"—a topography at once physical and spiritual, where the walkers' devotions could
be concretely reinforced.[4] Another stopping point on the Circuito was
the Cappella del Masso di San Giovanni Gualberto. This is the place
where the saint was tempted by the devil to cast himself down from a
cliff. But the surface of the rock, or "masso," behind him softened like
wax and Giovanni stuck to it, unable to fall even if he'd wanted to. Just
weeks before, Rita and I had visited La Verna, an important site in the life
of Saint Francis which we'd read about in Gary Nabhan's *Songbirds,
Truffles, and Wolves*. So we had in mind a very similar story from the life of
Francis, about two centuries later.[5] The devil tempted him to jump from a
cliff, too. But the rock once again saved the saint, hollowing out behind
him and extending around each side in an embrace, the traces of which
can still be seen today.

At the core of these stories is a sense that the lives of both saints were
imitations of the life of Christ. The Gospel according to Matthew describes how Jesus was tempted by the devil to cast himself down off the
Temple and thus to prove, by the divine intervention that would keep
him from hitting the ground, that he really was the Son of God. Believers
in the eleventh and thirteenth centuries could feel that in the saints' stories they were in effect rereading Christ's career in updated Italian trans-
lations. The sense of Francis's life as reiterating the Savior's was developed more elaborately than in the case of Giovanni Gualberto. Not only
was La Verna the site of his temptations, but it was also the place where
Francis received the stigmata. But the substitution of a Tuscan cliff for
the Temple in Jerusalem makes another point more fundamental than
the details of such parallels: that spiritual experience flourishes when
rooted in a local landscape, where it can be seen and touched and walked
on as well as spoken or prayed about. To seek such grounding in the
mountains, as both saints did, rather than in the streets of Florence or
Assisi, was an attempt to renew spiritual images and topography that
had been exploited by the ruling hierarchies of church and state. It was a
way to reenter what Baudelaire calls the "forest of symbols," where mys-

teries could once more become personal, immediate, yet still ineffable. Such forays can also sometimes be fatal. One of the other sites at Vallombrosa is La Cappella del Masso del Diavolo. On this high rock a young monk, who had despaired of his vocation and was forsaking the monastery, was tempted by the devil and in fact cast himself off the cliff to his death.

One way I can understand these three stories of mountain-top temptation is in relation to the challenge any wilderness presents to our human capacity for self-control. The streets of a city channel our energies, while its buildings are containers for our social roles, our relationships, and even, in a grandly liturgical city like Florence, our theology. But the human drive for power and self-assertion is a molten core beneath these sliding social plates. In the eruptions of war or revolution the structures that have defined our lives may crack and fall. We tend to view such catastrophes as extraordinary accidents caused by forces from without. Going into the mountains, however, we encounter the primal reality of our unmediated human will. A wild forest, unaligned with social expectations or theology, challenges us to enter a larger order that transcends our human conceptions and self-assertion, and to be incorporated into something inconceivably complex.

In graduate school I had the good fortune to study Spenser with Bart Giamatti, who found in the Renaissance epic a profound anxiety about the failure of language and the loss of control. With reference to the vocabulary of Ariosto, whose *Orlando Furioso* so influenced the English poet, Giamatti proposed that *The Fairie Queene* could be interpreted in relation to two Italian words—*frenare* and *sfrenare*. The first means literally to rein in or control—whether with relation to a steed, an impulse, or a situation that could easily gallop away from us. Such control calls for strength, skill, and discipline, as well as for good fortune. *Sfrenare*, in contrast, means to break the reins, to run wild like an out-of-control horse or a mob. Such a runaway state is all too likely to prove fatal. For the two saints, the world of prayer and fasting in the wilderness, and of turning away from the shopworn but familiar structures of their day, could well have been a kind of free fall. They might have cast themselves to their deaths, as they testified they were both tempted to do—tempted to fly, in fact, in a supreme though short-lived expression of the unrestrained and triumphant will. Their ability to withstand such temptation came, at least in part, from the grounding, and the active collaboration, of the landscape itself. Our own survival today depends, as theirs did, on more than the sublime experiences of spirit and wilderness. Every day, we also need the concrete, local realities of that tree, this rock to keep our lives in balance.

. . .

I had never heard of the Circuito delle Cappelle before our first visit to Vallombrosa. Nor do I have a Catholic background or any comparable theological structure into which to fit these shrines. My most vivid experiences of the sacred have been in the mountains and in literature. Yet visiting and thinking about these chapels, nestled amid an ancient forest on a path by a thousand-year-old abbey, has completed a kind of circuit for me, too. It has connected Native American spirituality, so deeply rooted in North America but often feeling so inaccessible to mainstream Western culture, with the piety of medieval Italian monastics. While I can't claim membership in either circle of faith, the dialogue between them clarifies some principles that bear on the possibility for an integrated environmental vision—one that includes both wilderness and stewardship and that finds its wholeness in the intimate physicality of a familiar landscape.

Fifteen years ago, Rita and I had the opportunity, with all three of our children still in tow, to take another sabbatical abroad. That time it was in Japan, where in our walks in the mountains we sometimes came upon notable boulders or lovely old cryptomeria trees that had been recognized as having special spiritual power. In the indigenous Shinto tradition of that country, *kami*, or spirits, are present throughout nature. In reverent acknowledgment of the particular natural phenomena housing such kami, priests will girdle them with a knotted rope, from which long strips of white paper hang in a zigzag pattern reminiscent of lightning bolts. Coming upon such a venerable presence, whether in a Kyoto shrine or on a pilgrimage route in Shikoku, we were always arrested by its beauty and stateliness. It was as if the encircling rope framed the power that was already in rock or tree and let us see what we might otherwise have missed. Standing quietly there, we could also take in the energy of other, nearby, trees, their upper boughs lifting and falling mysteriously though we could feel no breeze. We could see the glint of gray from distant boulders, also socketed into the fragrant slope by the first gardener of the forest.

On our way home from Japan we were fortunate to be invited to a conference on religion and the natural environment being held in Chiang Mai, Thailand. The enormously valuable teak forests of that region had been ravaged over the past several decades. But shortly before our arrival a nearby community of forest monks found a way to protect a magnificent stand of teak scheduled to go under the saw. When the loggers arrived they found that the trees facing them had been ordained as Buddhist monks, with orange robes bound around them. Thailand is the most Buddhist country on earth, and when those men saw the robes they refused to take their saws to the tree-monks. The sacredness of the forest became visible when wrapped in a more familiar human story of holiness.

Perhaps all deeply rooted peoples have evolved stories that allow them to live sustainably within the specific limitations and possibilities of their place on earth. Leslie Marmon Silko generalizes this process with relation to her own people's traditions: "The oral narrative, or 'story,' became the medium in which the complex of Pueblo knowledge and belief was maintained. Whatever the event or the subject, the ancient people perceived the world and themselves within that world as part of an ancient continuous story composed of innumerable bundles of other stories."[6] To live successfully, and beautifully, in the same place over centuries requires stories fitted to that landscape. These stories are a necessary medium both between human beings and the land and between generations, who need to have a context of restraining and inspiring wisdom passed down from their ancestors.

I have come to believe that without the stories that integrate the face of nature with the drama of our human lives society will not have the power to restrain our appetite and respect the larger balance of nature. *Sfrenare* is the verb that describes the wild gallop of extraction, expansion, and "development" in the era since World War II. But there are reins dangling near the runaway steed's neck which we might be able to pick up now. These are called stories.

Specifically, what we need now are more stories that help us imagine the life, and the individuality, of trees. The central argument of Marsh's book is that deforestation has always been the most far-reaching, and oddly invisible, form of environmental degradation. It has generally happened as the cumulative effect, over generations, of unrestrained cutting, not through an active policy of eradicating forests. On the contrary, heedless logging proceeded from the assumption that the woods could never be depleted, from blindness to the fact that communities can cut the woods at a rate faster than new trees can grow. The alternative to such destructive oblivion is a mindfulness informed by both ecological insight and reverence. In a sentence that anticipates both John Muir and Aldo Leopold, Marsh writes that "we can never know how wide a circle of disturbance we produce in the harmonies of nature when we throw the smallest pebble into the ocean of organic life."[7]

Such an awareness of interconnectedness continues to grow today. Tom Wessels has directed me to a recent study in *Nature* indicating that the roots of different species of trees may be so thoroughly intergrafted at the mycorrhizal level as to make the whole forest community one almost-continuous circuit of nutrients. Even stumps may continue to add annual rings as they benefit from the photosynthesis of nearby trees to which they are connected at the root level.[8] Such interdependence, invisible until severed by the shovels of our analysis, accords with the piety of the Circuito delle Cappelle as well as with a reverential voice that continually emerges within Marsh's heavily documented argument: "Thus all nature is linked together by invisible bonds, and every organic creature, however low, however feeble, however dependent is necessary to the well-being of some other among the myriad forms of life with which the Creator has peopled the earth."[9]

Long before San Giovanni Gualberto's encounter with the Holy Beech, restraint in our approach to forests has been schooled by religious awe. In his book *Pan's Travail*, J. Donald Hughes remarks that sacred groves were essential to the biodiversity of the Mediterranean world, even as deforestation took its toll in much of that region. There were hundreds of such groves throughout the region, making their impact significant. "The reservation of sacred groves was probably the greatest single means of conservation in the ancient world; as Greek and Roman writers note, plants and animals survived within them when they had disappeared from surrounding areas."[10] Hughes quotes Seneca in arguing that the ancients didn't simply preserve groves because they had been designated as sacred. It worked the other way around. Such a designation came from the intuitively perceived quality of these woods: their holiness was recognized before any more specific divinity or ritual meaning had been attached to them. "If you come upon a grove of old trees that have lifted up their crowns above the common height and shut out the light of the sky by the darkness of their interlacing boughs, you feel that there is a spirit in the place, so lofty is the wood, so lone the spot, so wondrous the thick, unbroken shade."[11] The special power of these groves was first experienced directly and intuitively and only then expressed through the tales of gods who resided in such noble beauty, or of maidens, shepherds, and other human beings who had been transformed into trees and whose personal stories or qualities thus lived on in those trees.

One of the most beautiful tales of human beings metamorphosed into trees is Ovid's account of Baucis and Philemon, whose hospitality to Jupiter and Mercury allowed them to be transformed into two beautiful trees at the end of their long life of mutual devotion. The two gods were traveling in disguise through a rural district where they had found no hospitality. "They tried a thousand houses, / Looking for rest. They found a thousand houses / Shut in their face." But then they came to the "humble cottage, thatched with straw and reeds" where Baucis and Philemon welcomed them to their table and offered them of their best—rest on a sedge and grass mattress, a few black and green olives, a cabbage from the garden. In a delightful narrative detail, the elderly couple became aware of their guests' divinity because the level of wine in the earthenware jar never grew lower during the repast. Then the two trembling old people were taken up onto a hill where they could see that the surrounding countryside, and all their less hospitable neighbors, had been covered by a flood. Their own dwelling of sticks and branches was transformed before their eyes into a grand temple to the gods. When invited by Jupiter to ask for a favor, they requested to live together as priests in the temple and to die in the same hour.

> And the prayer was granted.
> As long as life was given, they watched the temple,
> And one day, as they stood before the portals,
> Both very old, talking the old days over,
> Each saw the other put forth leaves, Philemon
> Watched Baucis changing, Baucis watched Philemon,
> And as the foliage spread, they still had time
> To say "Farewell, my dear!" and the bark closed over
> Sealing their mouths. And even to this day

The peasants in that district show the stranger
The two trees close together, and the union
Of oak and linden into one.[12]

The power of this story comes not only from the way it suggests human nobility *reflected* in the graceful maturity of trees, but also in the ways it shows marriage and hospitality as human virtues that can be *enacted* by trees. Giovanni Gualberto met with such hospitality from Saint Beech, whose overhanging, interlaced branches offered him comfort, security, and protection from the grasp of Florence and its corrupt hierarchies. The flood of retribution visited on the countryside by the two gods also becomes a motif in environmental narratives from the Romantic era to the present—a cataclysmic erasure and, at the same time, an opportunity to reaffirm deeper values of fidelity, empathy, and hospitality. A story like that of Baucis and Philemon grows from the perception of something sacred in the mysterious, shadowed beauty of an ancient forest. But it also amplifies that beauty, inviting readers to pause respectfully amid a forest of stories, and to identify our own personal dramas with the stories of the trees.

A writer like Ovid arose out of a society in which such myths still had living religious force, in which Jupiter and Mercury were both figures in a story and deities worshipped in their own grand temples across the empire. But in other ways the situation of Ovid and his readers was not so far from ours today. He was a cosmopolitan poet, writing for an audience that extended beyond Italy into modern-day France and Spain. And his tale of Baucis and Philemon was set in Phrygia, far from any of those lands. Neither he nor most of his readers could stand and look at the actual trees in question, and few of them would have ever been to that landscape. Still, a seed was planted in *The Metamorphoses* that germinated, grew, and has been transplanted in poetry from his time until ours. It was the sense of imaginative, emotional kinship between human beings and the lives of other plants and animals with which we share this planet. We have reached a moment in our cultural history when we need to reconnect such sympathy, and its finely honed imagery, with the trees of our home.

Our culture today, however, is much more cosmopolitan even than Ovid's. Not only do we have access to a range of stories extending around the world and going back to the beginning of written culture, but those of us living in Europe, on the Pacific Rim, in North America, and in other affluent parts of the world have also become highly mobile. Both of these factors pose challenges to the task of finding rooted stories that help us, too, live lives more rooted in the world. But even our travels, and relocations, can be part of such a process, insofar as we keep our eyes open for stories of reciprocity and respect, like that of Saint Beech, that have become authentically rooted in their particular landscapes. A grounded culture is not necessarily a parochial culture. As Gary Snyder once reminded my class when visiting Middlebury College, various bioregions' stories have the capacity to reinforce each other. They can be both delightful and clarifying, keeping everybody loose. Today, we may be less like grounded people who need occasionally to travel than like perpetual travelers needing to settle down. We also may not always be clear which stories are ours and which belong to someone else. But, even in the mobility that continues to be many Americans' lot, we can become more attuned to the different places we live. Befriending our local trees is a good way to start.

The tradition of American nature writing has encouraged such personal, attentive relationship with our local environments. John Muir, whose book *The Mountains of California* appeared in 1894, thirty years after George Perkins Marsh's *Man and Nature*, wrote as vividly and knowledgeably about trees as anyone in American literature. His section "The Forests" is a masterpiece of scientific description, not only evoking precisely and comprehensively the structure, life cycles, and succession of all the major Sierra trees, but also bringing out their individual character, as conveyed by texture of bark and needles, shape of crown, and abundance of cones. Muir comes to trees with an exhilarated naturalist's gaze. But my favorite passage about trees in this book comes from another chapter, called "A Wind-Storm in the Forests." In the midst of "one of the most beautiful and exhilarating storms [he] ever enjoyed in the Sierra," Muir climbs a hundred-foot-high Douglas spruce. He rides out the winds on that day when "[i]n its wildest sweeps my tree-top described an arc of from twenty to thirty degrees." From such an experience of thrilling participation in the tree's wild motion, Muir comes away with a deeper identification with both the life history and the spirituality of such forest giants. "When the storm began to abate, I dismounted and sauntered down through the calming woods. The storm-tones died away, and, turning toward the east, I beheld the countless hosts of the forests hushed and tranquil, towering above one another on the slopes of the hills like a devout audience. The setting sun filled them with amber light, and seemed to say, while they listened, 'My peace I give unto you.'"[13]

The danger and excitement of the storm, as well as its beauty, opened Muir up to the life of trees, and to his own life, in a new way. They took him on a trip beyond his usual categories and conceptions. Travel, in some sense or other of that term, can help open our eyes to the world again and renew our sense of belonging and kinship. Just as that has been true for Muir astride the Douglas spruce, and for the indigenous people whom Snyder described traveling to trade, among other goods, their stories, so too it may be required for those of us living in America today. It may be true that on one level travel is what we need *less* of—with our hypermobile, ungrounded way of life. But by the same token, what we do need is a path to travel back *home*—passage to identification with a particular place on earth as well as with the trees and animals belonging to that landscape and to which in turn that place belongs. And stories are an essential part of such sympathetic regrounding. They can be the doors through we walk back into the life of the places we are calling home.

Gary Nabhan discusses the term "ecosystem people," coined by the ecologist Ray Dasmann to describe groups "who have lived for centuries or longer in the same places, without major sources of supply from the outside," developing a "working relationship with the species surrounding them." Finally, though, Nabhan prefers to speak of "cultures of habitat": "In contrast, the term habitat is etymologically related to *habit, inhabit,* and *habitable;* it suggests a place worth dwelling in, one that has *abiding* qualities. I could not make a machinelike *ecosystem* my abode for long, but I could comfortably nestle down in a *habitat.*"[14] Whatever the language with which we approach them, deeply rooted stories of home have a special value for people seeking to reground ourselves. This is a tricky one. Native peoples, who have so often been dispossessed of their lands, among other oppressions by the majority culture, are understandably reluctant to see outsiders appropriate their stories—taking them out of context and sometimes even reworking them. So in these cases, even more so than with the careful documentation of scholarly writing, it is crucial to attribute any local story or myth to the particular Native storyteller from whom one received it, whether orally or in writing, and to respect its original language and form. There is thus a better chance for a story's traditional *context* to be transmitted when being introduced to newer settlers in a bioregion.

A particularly reverberant story for me as an inhabitant of Vermont is Joseph Bruchac's retelling of his Abenaki people's story of the origin of human beings among our eastern woodlands. Here is the way he relates it in one of his collections called *The Faithful Hunter:*

> . . . Gluskabe made the first people out of stone. Because they were made of stone they were very strong. They did not need to eat and they never grew tired or slept. Their hearts, too, were made of stone. They began to do cruel things. They killed animals for amusement and pulled trees up by their roots. When Gluskabe saw this he knew he had made a mistake. So he changed them all back into stone. To this day there are certain mountains and hills which look like a sleeping person. Some old people say those are the first ones Gluskabe made, whom he changed back into stone.
>
> Then, instead of making more stone people, Gluskabe looked around for something else to make human beings. He saw the ash trees. They were tall and slender and they danced gracefully in the wind. Then Gluskabe made the shapes of men and women in the trunks of the ash trees. He took out his long bow and arrows and shot the arrows into the ashes. Where each arrow went in a person stepped forth, straight and tall. Those people had hearts which were growing and green. They were the first Abenakis. To this day those who remember this story call the ash trees their relatives.[15]

My family too lives in these woods. Amid the dominance of sugar maples, the straight gray ashes still stand out in their dignity. And Bruchac's story also helps us picture our own vertical forms as arising in and enlivened by the forests of western Vermont. It is a reminder to be very careful in all our actions, proceeding with a grateful heart and a slowness to destroy and fall back into the ways of stoniness. This would be a good story for every Vermont schoolchild to know, in order to remember our Abenaki predecessors and neighbors in the land as well as our kinship with the trees. Perhaps bearing it in mind might help us begin a thousand years of mindfulness in the Green Mountains, just as the story of the Faggio Santo inspired, and inspires, stewardship in the forested mountains around Vallombrosa. Joan Chittister, like Giovanni Gualberto a Benedictine, has entitled her recent volume of ecofeminist theology *Heart of Flesh: A Feminist Spirituality for Women and Men.* She takes as her epigraph Ezekiel 36:26, a verse that reinforces the possibility for dialogue between what might have seemed disparate traditions and landscapes. "I will give you a new heart and put a new spirit in you; I will remove from you your heart of stone and give you a heart of flesh." A heart of flesh requires a departure from stony error, a pilgrimage to venerable stories of relationship, and a celebration of our kinship with the woods.

· · ·

I picked up a brittle beech leaf from beside the Cappella. It was different from ours in Vermont—smaller, rounder, browner, and stiffer than the beech leaves I was used to. And it was already on the ground when ours at home would still be bleaching and rattling on their twigs. Vermont's beeches hold many of their leaves throughout the winter, when the surrounding deciduous trees, except for a scattering of red oaks, have all lost their foliage. Still, this was recognizably a beech leaf, with its fish shape and its little spines at the end of every vein. It was a reminder, from one forest to another, of the holy bond that sanctifies trees in our minds and ordains us all as inheritors of the forest.

5

AFTER OLIVE
PICKING

And the dove came to him in the evening; and, lo, in her mouth
was an olive leaf pluckt off; so Noah knew that the waters were
abated from the earth. —Genesis 8:11

The olive trees of Impruneta live in two eras at once. Their lower trunks
are often centuries old, as twisted and muscled as the bases of our cedars
in northern Vermont. But smooth new trunks emerge from these rugged
vestiges, with branches curving up from them in turn like wands. On a
cold morning in December, the trees spangle as cold gusts flip over the
powdery gray surfaces usually hidden beneath the leaves' glossy tops.
They pulse at a slower frequency, too, as the slender branches bend back
and forth within that scintillation of leaves. One of the stories these cen-
taur-olives tell on their rushes through the wind is of the 1985 cold snap
that coated Tuscan groves with ice, shattering over 90 percent of the
trees and interrupting centuries of continuous cultivation in this region.[1]

Tuscany marks the northern edge of Italy's major olive oil production
and is the region where the world's most distinctive oil has long been
made. The cooking here emphasizes excellent local ingredients—beans,
fennel, sage, pork—rather than the subtle blends and sauces characterizing some other Italian cuisines. But all of these elements are unified
and enhanced by a drizzle of extra-virgin oil when a dish is cooking, an-

other few drops when it is brought to the table. The Christmas season is made more festive by the arrival of the new oil. This green, slightly murky oil has a special pungency and freshness. Restaurants put signs out by their front doors to announce when it has arrived; their patrons build their meals around it—as in *pinzimonio*, where a platter of raw, sliced vegetables is served for dipping in oil, with a basket of unsalted bread on the side. True Tuscan oil is an *artigianale* product, and much more expensive to make than the *industriale* olive oils produced in such quantities around the Mediterranean region. It had already become difficult for growers here to stay in business before the freeze of 1985 came. And then the supply of this traditional oil was abruptly cut off. With one winter's storm, the taste and the look, the rhythm and the feel of Tuscan life was changed.

Fortunately, the sturdy old roots survived, and after a couple of years were thrusting up new shoots and setting fruit again. By the late 1990s, the level of olive production had just about returned to its former level, although the trees themselves were so much slighter, with few branches robust enough for pickers to brace their ladders confidently against. Rita and I participated in gathering this fragile bounty during the olive *raccolta* of 2000, when we picked for our Impruneta friends Janet Shapiro and Stefano Magazzini. Janet and Stefano tend and pick 3,000 trees, some on their own land and others on property they lease, producing a premier oil sold under the Sagittario label in Italy and the Della Robbia label when exported to the United States and elsewhere. These names come from a series of glazed ceramic friezes produced in the mid-fifteenth century by Luca della Robbia to depict the signs of the zodiac. His design for Sagittarius, the period from late November to late December, shows a man sitting in an olive tree and picking into a traditional Tuscan basket. Only in Janet and Stefano's (and Della Robbia's) Tuscany does olive picking take place this early in the season—when many of the olives are still green. Elsewhere around the Mediterranean, the fruit are allowed to ripen and fall. The earlier picking, which is so much more labor intensive, both avoids the bruising and mold possible with the later harvest and imparts a mixture of flavors that includes the lively, almost hot, taste of the green olives. It makes the new oil markedly green in color as well.

The distinctiveness of Tuscan oil also comes from the four specific varieties of olives predominant in the region. The Leccino, Moraiolo, and

Pendolino olives all ripen on the earlier side, with the Leccino and Moraiolo being hardy strains well suited to Tuscany, the chilliest of the major olive-producing regions. With olives—as with vineyards—marginal slopes, soils, and climates sometimes produce the most memorable flavors. Then there are the Frantoio olives, which have small tolerance for cold and are also rather late in maturing. These constitute a significant proportion of the green olives in a given year's harvest, and are essential to the new oil's burstingly fresh flavor. Within a couple of months after pressing, Tuscan oil clarifies as the fine suspended particles settle out, and the color gradually becomes more golden than green. It remains a subtle, extra-virgin olive oil, and the basis for Tuscan cuisine throughout the year, but unlike wine, it will not continue to improve. In this regard, it is more like Vermont's maple syrup: a pure, unstabilized product, the fragrant blossoming of one particular year, and best consumed before the next year's production.

Such links with Vermont became increasingly important parts of our experience living in Florence and traveling around Tuscany. In following Marsh's footsteps to Europe, we had hoped to strengthen our global perspective on conservation and stewardship and to return to Vermont with a clearer sense of our state's place and mission in the world. While his life and thought remained important to us, the day-to-day experience of living in Italy also opened us up to more immediate and sensuous affinities between Tuscany and our home in the Green Mountains. Making friends, sharing meals with them, and experiencing the regional traditions that are so essential to Italians' quality of life, we gained a richer perspective on the culture and environment of our own rural state—a perspective that achieved its sharpest focus in the experience of picking olives.

Rita and I learned various techniques for picking, depending on the trees' location and size. With smaller, isolated trees, we stood beside them wearing traditional baskets around our necks on leather straps. Each basket was shaped like a quarter of an apple, with the open top as one of the flat cuts and the other noncurved side resting against our bodies. These baskets were made of olive twigs woven around a pine frame. Most of our work was up in ladders, though, leaning against the bouncy branches and with no way to use a basket. Sometimes we stretched out to rake off clusters we could barely reach, holding little plastic claws that imitated the traditional ones made from olive wood. Sometimes we stripped thickly fruited twigs with a gizmo made of two hinged pieces of aluminum with rubber bumpers between them; we would squeeze these together around a twig and pull toward us. Or we would just pick by hand, grabbing and dropping handfuls of mixed green and brown olives onto the sturdy nets or army surplus parachutes fanned out on the ground around each tree or each closely growing pair of trees. When those trees were totally picked clean, a couple of people would begin lifting and folding the net or parachute beneath, tilting the olives into a growing pile that could finally be poured into one of the twenty-kilo crates in which the harvest was transported to a beautiful old stone barn Stefano and Janet used for storage and bottling.

The pickers worked in two teams. One team included Janet and Stefano with friends who could join them, as we did, for the occasional weekend, and who were rewarded with the comradely pleasure of participating in the harvest and with a few bottles of oil after the next pressing took place. Then there were the professionals, whose crates were carefully kept separate for the tally at day's end. "Professionals" may be misleading, since these people were still only paid in oil. But their team worked every day during the season and received half of the product from their day's picking. These gallons were used to meet the needs of their extended families in the coming year or occasionally sold in their neighborhood stores. Janet and Stefano reported that it was getting harder and harder to find pickers with the time, skill, and motivation for this job. Many of them have traditionally been retired people, and as the current group begins to die off it's not certain there will be a new crop of pickers to replace them. This question of continuity becomes even more urgent for the proper pruning of the trees, which starts early in the New Year. Janet and Stefano are both skilled pruners, but their most knowledgeable helpers tend to be in their seventies, as hardy as Moraiolo trees but in need of assistance by new pruners whom they could also be helping to train.

For Stefano and Janet, the production of premier Tuscan olive oil is as much a process of cultural conservation as a form of agriculture. It is an expression of love for their place on earth and hope for its future prosperity, not only economically but also as a distinct topography and lineage of the human experience. Janet, who was born in San Francisco in 1949, came to Italy during her college years and decided to spend the rest of her life here. While she eventually returned to America to complete her undergraduate degree, that was a brief interruption of her chosen life in Tuscany. Stefano, who had grown up in San Casciano, about ten miles south of Florence, met Janet in 1976. He had heard about "this young American woman who knew how to prune olive trees and lived in a small country house in Impruneta" and was eager to meet her. Janet and Stefano ended up getting married, buying the olive grove near her house—where they still live and have brought up their girls, Tina and Livia—and devoting themselves to producing the very finest traditional Tuscan oil. In a special issue of the Italian magazine of food and wine *Gambero Rosso* dedicated to the subject of olive oil, their Sagittario oil was identified as one of the region's top twenty and described as having "an elegant and intensive fragrance with fruity and herbaceous aromas; the green fruit taste is soft and substantial and has hints of artichoke."[2] A connoisseur's terms for olive oil, like a wine list's evocation of the nose and finish of various vintages, can seem whimsical to those of us who are not initiates. I'm not sure I can vouch confidently for the hints of artichoke, but "fruity" and "green" I can guarantee.

For Janet, this excellent olive oil distills the region and culture she fell in love with. Many people in our day discover rather than inherit their place on earth—a deep affinity that, once they recognize it, they must find a way to integrate into their other choices and practices. For Rita and me, similarly, the flavor of maple syrup has increasingly symbolized our attachment to Vermont, to which we have come as adults but to which we have also made our own lifelong commitment. In building a sugarhouse and learning to make syrup ourselves, we have tried to enter into the living tradition of our adopted rural community. For Stefano, in contrast, meeting Janet provided the inspiration to leave his job as a technical draftsman in a Florentine factory and return to the agrarian traditions of his Tuscan family. Rather than adopting a rural lifeway new to him, he was reclaiming a legacy and shouldering responsibility for perpetuating it.

On our last night in Italy, before our spring return to Vermont and the new sugaring season, Rita and I had supper with Janet and Stefano in their stone cottage in Impruneta. Their kitchen is dominated by a wood-burning cookstove similar to the old Glenwoods one still finds in so many Vermont farmhouses. As we sat at their table sipping good Tuscan wine, Stefano browned some chewy, unsalted bread on the stove and rubbed a clove of garlic on top while the toast was still hot. Then we dripped some of the last new oil over it to make the simplest, most delectable *bruschetta* imaginable. As Stefano continued to prepare and serve this memorable meal, the dishes were graced again and again with a little of the new oil. We added it to the *ribollita*, a hearty vegetable soup served over another piece of toast, as well as to the slices of potato and whole leaves of sage crisped in a lightly oiled pan. Oil was even applied to our dessert of *scacciata a l'uva* as it came out of the oven—a flat, dimpled bread into whose dough red grapes had been individually pressed and crushed. Grape juice and the savor of green olives permeated the moist, dense pastry, complementing Janet and Stefano's *vin santo*, the Tuscan dessert wine made from shriveled grapes, which they had barreled seven years ago. They were offering us not just their hospitality but the essence of their landscape and culture. We carried Tuscany with us, as we returned to Vermont, in the lingering taste of this meal with deeply rooted friends.

Janet and Stefano's stewardship of their olive groves is a matter of cultivating both a landscape and a cuisine; a direct, personal commitment to their place on earth and the community it supported. Before beginning our stay in Italy, while still walking across southwestern France, we glimpsed a political movement expressing values akin to theirs. This was a protest against the spread of American fast-food franchises. Such establishments felt like a foreign irritant to many French people, like the English words elbowing into their language with the vigor of starlings flocking around North American airports and cane toads foraging across Australia. They seemed to violate the regionally based French cuisine and to undermine the tradition of long midday meals *en famille*.

On July 13 we had arrived at the ancient pilgrimage city of Saintes and found an article in the local paper whose headline read "On a kidnappé Ronie." The statute of Ronald had been stolen from the McDonald's in town by a group calling itself FROC, Front de résistance à l'oppression capitaliste. The newspaper had been sent a photograph showing "Ronie," blindfolded but still grinning, with a man in camo and a stocking mask standing behind him. The main difference between this photo and one that might have come from a Corsican terrorist was that this masked man cradled a baguette in his arms rather than an Uzi. The accompanying letter, which began "Le FROC a frappé," went on to make a number of demands, including Camembert in the McFlurrys and traditional costumes of the Charente region for the counter staff. This was political theater, playful but also serious in its identification of American fast food,

globalization, and mass marketing as dangers to a traditional rural culture. Rita and I might not have understood the point of this protest if we
hadn't spent the previous weeks experiencing how the landscape, agriculture, food, and wine of France shifted in a continuous, coordinated,
and festive way. It's not hard to see how a fast-food establishment whose
products remain uniform in every season and around the world, and
whose conveyor-belt cheapness, giveaway plastic toys, and movie-linked
advertising make them such a draw for young families, might feel threat-
ening to a community that prized its distinctiveness not only from other
countries but also from other parts of France.

Similar anxieties led to the founding of the Slow Food movement in
Italy. In fact, the immediate inspiration of its founder, the food writer
Carlo Petrini, was the 1985 opening of a McDonald's in Rome's Piazza di
Spagna—which was for him the most beautiful public square in the
world. Though in its own way as political as the French reaction, Slow
Food has gone beyond that reactive, partisan phase to take a more creative and playful approach. (Such a tendency might be innate to Italian
food culture. As Rita has noticed, the endless variations on the shape of
their staple, pasta—strings, tubes, pillows, butterflies, bow ties, seashells
—reflect centuries of Italians playing with their food.) The Slow Food
emphasis is thus less on protests against international franchises than
on making sure that the widest array of traditional alternatives survive.
Its culturally oriented approach to food reverberated for us with Janet
and Stefano's more personal and land-based commitments. By 1989 the
movement had spread to over two dozen countries, and a manifesto was
approved five of whose central principles follow below. The mock seri-
ousness of its language makes me think of Joyce's coinage "jocoserious"
in *Ulysses:* diction that at once makes fun of itself and suggests great
significance in aspects of life we usually take for granted.

*A firm defense of quiet material pleasure is the only way to oppose the universal
folly of Fast Life.*

*May suitable doses of guaranteed sensual pleasure and slow, long-lasting enjoy-
ment preserve us from the contagion of the multitude who mistake frenzy for
efficiency.*

*Our defense should begin at the table with Slow Food. Let us rediscover the flavors
and savors of regional cooking and banish the degrading effects of Fast Food.*

In the name of productivity, Fast Life has changed our way of being and threatens our environment and our landscapes. So Slow Food is now the only truly progressive answer.

This is what real culture is all about: developing taste rather than demeaning it. And what better way to set about this than an international exchange of experiences, knowledge, projects?[3]

I had the opportunity in Florence to meet with Nanni Ricci, one of Slow Food's vice presidents who lives in the nearby town of Greve-in-Chianti. Over some Chianti Classico Riserva of the celebrated 1995 vintage, we chatted about the movement's history, mission, and evolution. His own emphasis, like that of the manifesto, was less a polemic against globalization per se than a call for establishment of a new food culture. When I asked about his sense of Slow Food's core mission, he immediately responded, "the defense and promotion of the right to pleasure." Such language is reinforced by the terminology describing individual chapters of the organization: *convivia*. One of the most promising aspects of Slow Food is its festive nature. Too often, we American environmentalists fall into a heavy litany of "Thou shalt nots" as we focus on the very real problems of pesticides, SUVs, suburban sprawl, and the like. But it's crucial, if we don't want to come across simply as grim, forbidding voices in the modern conversation, to remember how to play and party too. We need to convey the image of a life more inviting than the prevailing model of consumerism. Indeed, as with so many things Italian, the Slow Food movement seems especially attractive to many Americans now. Nanni Ricci said that, within the last couple of years alone, thousands of members had joined from the United States, with *convivia* in most states. (We had originally heard about Slow Food from our friend Jeff Roberts, one of the leaders of the Vermont *convivium* and an activist trying to connect our state's farms more directly and creatively with our best restaurants.) Nanni stated that good taste—meaning sensual enjoyment, not conformity to others' preferences—was the foundation of the movement, with diversity as its result. By way of expressing his conviction that this is an international movement compatible with pluralistic, local values, he said that good food enjoyed in the context of its own distinctive culture and traditions was always "the best meal in the world."

Slow Food's emphasis on diversity is another way in which it seems a timely addition to the environmental discourse of our day. One of the hardest questions facing those who propose a locally grounded, "bioregional" sense of place is how to avoid a separatist or intolerant sense of community. Indeed, as writers like Simon Schama and Jonathan Bate have both discussed, the Nazis were in certain regards the greenest of modern regimes.[4] That uncomfortable fact should help us remember to pursue an inclusive, pluralistic environmentalism based on celebration of many local landscapes and cultures and resolutely avoiding the lexicon of purity, separation, and exclusiveness. Perhaps the best metaphors to sum up Slow Food and the bioregional approach to environmentalism would be such open-ended ones as a menu, a cookbook, and a festival. Of course these images, too, become problematic in a world where many starve and many more are malnourished. I was interested in reading the Slow Food publications to note that one of their programs, called Fraternal Tables, is in fact dedicated to food relief, medical assistance, agricultural support, and other attempts to promote social justice and equality. Celebration must be complemented by compassion.

Another Slow Food program Ricci and I discussed was the Ark of Taste, an initiative to identify excellent foods that are closely tied to, and even symbolic of, a particular locale but that are also in danger of becoming extinct—"lost in a world of standardized food." Maintaining the maximum diversity is thus one of the fundamental principles of this movement, just as it is of America's Wildlands Project. Further, Slow Food focuses on those foods which, with economic support and consumer education, might still have a commercial future. Because of our country's prominence in biogenetic engineering, not to mention in the fast-food industry, America might seem far from such a localizing, conservative approach. In fact, though, the Spring 1999 issue of *Slow* magazine contained an article, "The American Ark," describing some of the foods indigenous to particular regions of the United States whose quality and distinctiveness give them promise for survival if celebrated and promoted. In California, these include the Sun Crest peach, "one of the last truly juicy peaches," a handmade cheese called Dry Monterey Jack, and Chipotle peppers. In the South there are, among others, the Limbertwig, an heirloom apple; such favorite strains of field peas as Red Ripper, Babyface, Whippoorwill, and Hercules; and the pungent wild onions known as ramps. It's fine with Ricci if people want to grab a bite to eat in a fast-food restaurant. The important thing is not to lose all the other options. His fear is that globalization might sweep over the world like, in his words, "a universal flood."

. . .

Beyond its associations with the stories of Noah and of Baucis and Philemon, the image of a deluge has special force in Florence, where plaques throughout the city's center commemorate the devastating flood of 1966. In the Santa Croce Piazza, a sign is posted nearly eighteen feet up one wall reading, "Il 4 Novembre 1966 L'Acqua D'Arno Arrivo A Quest' Altezza." The perennial danger to Florence of such inundation is indicated by the sign posted about three feet below that one: "A Di 13. Settembre 1557, Arrivo L'Acqua D'Arno A Quest' Altezza." This remarkably compressed city, whose historic core can be walked across, east to west or north to south, in less than an hour and whose Renaissance treasures are unequaled in the world, is so easily overrun by flood waters—soaked and torn and caked with mud. In the museum beside the Church of Santa Croce hangs Cimabue's famous painted crucifix from the thirteenth century, largely effaced when the last flood swirled around it. Even more vivid emblems of such destruction, for me, are Paolo Uccello's frescoes in the Green Cloisters of Santa Maria Novella, across town. Paolo, one of the most mystical artists of the early Renaissance, received the name Uccello for his fascination with painting weirdly angelic birds. In the cloisters named for his frescoes' strange greenish tint, he depicted his unearthly vision of the Universal Flood. But those dreamlike scenes of animals winding onto the Ark amid the rising tides are rendered even more powerful by the fact that they were themselves partially washed away in 1966. Splotches of intact fresco are interspersed among watermarked stretches of stripped, tan plaster, like memories glimpsed through the clouds of sleep or age.

There could scarcely be a better place than Florence to think about the fragility of beauty, and of the arts that sanctify our daily lives and the life of our community. In the decades since the last great flood, curators, architects, and clergy have been deliberating about how to protect the treasures entrusted to their care when the next deluge arrives. Slow Food's Ark of Taste is a sister strategy of stewardship and faith.

The Ark has long been an image holding special power for conservationists. The devastations of our post–World War II era can feel like an onslaught of such magnitude as to threaten the very existence of our beautiful natural world. Protected areas, too, like federally designated wildernesses and biosphere reserves, can feel like arks. They are places to preserve at least a modicum of biodiversity, sheltering the wild stocks from which, in a postdiluvian time, the world may be replenished. There is an implied historical perspective behind such efforts—one with which I agree—namely, that our current way of life in much of North America, Europe, and the Pacific Rim is simply unsustainable. This has in effect been a post–World War II binge by the wealthiest nations. Entering E. O. Wilson's "century of the environment," we will need to come back into balance, whether through wisdom and restraint or in the wounded aftermath of a crash. The most recent demographic studies sponsored by the United Nations show a complex and challenging picture. On the one hand, human population growth is already declining significantly in western Europe and East Asia; the total population of the world is in fact expected to begin falling by the end of the present century. On the other hand, for the poorest nations—including much of Africa as well as such south central Asian countries as India, Pakistan, Bangladesh, and Afghanistan—this will be a century of devastating population increases, given their current difficulties in feeding their people.[5] At such a moment of crisis, only a global perspective will see us through. Those of us in affluent nations must learn to see our suffering neighbors as part of one human community and to restrain our own use of natural resources. Just so, humanity as whole must commit to holding on, for the next troubled century or two, to species that millions of years would not suffice to reevolve. We are challenged to see ourselves as stewards on behalf of a larger ecological community as well as of the entire human family.

It's important, at such a moment, to emphasize that attempts to launch an ark can never be more than temporary expedients. Even with its divine commission, Noah's Ark was only provisioned for a voyage of 150 days. After that, it struck ground on a summit that biblical scholars now identify as Mount Ararat. It was definitely time, then, to open the windows and send out some birds as scouts. A wilderness area, too, is finally a stopgap rather than a solution. Even if the grizzlies and bison of Yellowstone don't wander over the borders of that magnificent park and get shot by irate ranchers, their protected populations within those boundaries are not big enough to allow for adequate genetic vitality through cross-breeding. And even if adequate corridors are established, allowing their populations to mix it up by traveling among the currently protected but separate refuges of the American and Canadian Rockies, these animals will still be dependent on a healthy ecosystem, spiraling through a stable climatic pattern and watered by a sufficiency of non-toxic rainfall. The Ark can only succeed in its conservationist mission when there is, at the receding of the flood, solid ground for it to settle on; when there is a green branch somewhere out there in the world, even if out of sight, where a dove can find the leaf of hope.

An imaginary Ark of Taste stocked with apples, peppers, cheeses, and ramps might seem sadly inadequate in the face of the universal flood already lapping across our thresholds. Such perishable, easily bruised cargo. Finally, though, the fragility of this Ark may eloquently express two truths about our human community's relationship to the Universal Deluge of our time. The first of these is that the earth itself is only a transitory phenomenon. As "For Nothing," a poem from Gary Snyder's volume *Turtle Island*, has it, earth is "a flower . . . on the steep slopes / of light."[6] Snyder invites us to see our planet as a merely a moment of color, as brief as the blossoming of an alpine phlox at the edge of Sierra snowmelt. The ideal of sustainability only makes sense within this context—not as a value of permanence or even security but rather as a pause of appreciative mindfulness along the path. Earth itself is the closest thing we know to a complete and self-contained watershed, and our most fully provisioned ark as well. It is a circuit of energy sustaining our equivalent of Noah's 150 days. Remembering the temporary nature of our world, and of our lives within it, we may be less inclined to squander the time we have been given together. Coming to the table as to a celebration, or to communion, is a way to bear the world in mind, and to be borne along with it in the voyage of diversity and gratitude.

. . .

On a bright winter's morning in Florence, Rita and I got on a train bound for Mantua. We were going to visit Giuseppe Moretti, a farmer in the Po River valley who is also a founder of Italy's bioregional network, the editor of its newsletter *Lato Selvatico*, and the Gary Snyder's Italian translator. He lives in one of the flattest, most fertile, and longest-settled parts of Italy. But as our train traveled into the foggy north, we also felt how much more developed than Tuscany this stretch of Lombardy was. Even away from the cities and stations, the tracks were paralleled by frontage roads, lined with postwar cinder block warehouses and sheet-metal sheds. Intensively cultivated fields of vegetables were ditched around by murky water and criss-crossed by power lines. The golden hills rolling around Florence, their fields framed by olive trees, cypresses, and umbrella pines, punctuated by ancient villas and churches, were far behind us. This was a good place to test conclusions reached in the groves of Impruneta.

We were met by Giuseppe at the Mantua station. A slightly built man of fifty-two, with his sandy-colored hair in a ponytail, his feed cap, flannel shirt, jeans, and work boots, he could easily have been an organic farmer from northern Vermont. We had arranged to visit him several weeks earlier. Then, when we realized that his farm had just been flooded out and he was living with his wife and their two grown children in a temporary apartment in the town of San Benedetto Po, we wrote back suggesting that it might be better to put the trip off to an easier time. But Giuseppe insisted we come ahead, and with his quiet eye and serene manner he reassured us again at the station that it was very good to have us there.

He drove us first, in his old Fiat, to the apartment provided to his family as victims of the flood that had devastated the entire Po valley several weeks earlier. It was a sparsely furnished flat with a makeshift stove and propane tank set up in the kitchen, drying lines strung over the bathtub. But Giuseppe's wife and son joined us there for the midday meal, and for the celebration of food and family that clears a space in every Italian day; a time to be reminded why one works, and to remember as well that the earth is bountiful. His wife, Gabriella, was employed as a seamstress in a nearby clothing factory, while their son was a mechanic in a local garage. Their daughter was unable to make it home for lunch, since she worked in an office in Mantua. We had ravioli filled with *zucca*, the yellow squash Italians use in so many buttery concoctions. Giuseppe commented that this was the traditional Christmas Eve dish when he was growing up, and he always adored it. Once he was grown and cooking for himself, he realized he could have it on any occasion he liked. Like now, after a flood!

The one room in this apartment that was jammed absolutely full was Giuseppe's study. He had managed to save his books from the rising water, and they covered the walls on their jury-rigged shelves. Almost all of them were American paperbacks, from the poetry of the Beats up through an excellent selection of contemporary environmental writers like Richard Nelson, Wendell Berry, and, above all, Gary Snyder. Giuseppe had grown up on the nineteen-acre farm in nearby Portiolo which he now cultivates himself. He dropped out of school early to help his parents, and described himself to us several times as a "peasant." But in the 1970s he discovered Snyder's writing and found that it spoke to the questions facing his rural community in Lombardy as well as Italy as a whole. His region's emphasis on traditional cuisine as a focus for family and community struck him as akin to the views expressed by bioregional writers like Snyder. At the same time, he could see even his own local culture changing under the pressures of fast food, television marketing, and other aspects of the globalized society. Many of his neighbors shared his anxiety that the young people would lose their sense of connection with their place and its food, that they would fall into the wasteful, irresponsible practices of those without roots. But people had trouble imagining constructive alternatives, so strong did the tide of what Nanni Ricci called Fast Life seem to be running. That's why, over the past two decades and more, Giuseppe Moretti has devoted his evenings to studying English and reading widely in environmental literature. It's why he helped to found Italy's bioregional *rete*, or network, and has now finished translating an excellent collection of Snyder's poetry and essays entitled *Reabitare nel grande flusso, Reinhabiting the Main Flow*. He wanted to present a useful resource to his community, and his nation, so that they would be able to construct a response to the present flood of placeless commerce. The fact that such helpful literature came from the same country that was so powerfully behind globalization seemed, finally, unsurprising.

After lunch, Giuseppe's wife and son went back to their jobs, while he, Rita, and I climbed back into the Fiat and drove out to inspect the farm and feed the animals—a drive Giuseppe took twice a day. The road ran along the top of an ancient earthen dike enclosing a wide expanse of farms and fields known as the Golena. The farms on the river side of the dike were of course all boarded up and abandoned, amid the standing water, twisted fences, uprooted vineyards, and downed power lines. The fields around them had begun to dry out but were coated with an oily, gray residue. Farther along, the dike had been breached at several spots, inundating previously protected farms like Giuseppe's. As we drove toward his home over a final network of gravel roads, we saw a few other farmers rattling along in their trucks or surveying their littered fields with hands on their hips. They too had come back to care for their livestock and begin the laborious cleanup—though it might be weeks or even months before their homes were reinhabitable. When we reached the Moretti farm, we found a scene of devastation, with vines collapsed over their trellises, some of the fruit trees broken, and that same oily residue on top of fields that had so long been carefully tended for producing organic vegetables and grain. Some of this soil will simply need to be removed and replaced. Giuseppe's mother had been living in the original farmhouse, a traditional structure of stone and plaster, until forced out by the flood waters. At eighty-nine, she was now in a nursing home in San Benedetto Po, unlikely ever to return to her old home. Giuseppe and his family had lived in a log cabin he had built nearby, one of the few wooden dwellings we saw in Italy. Every room in his house had been affected, and he had just finished shoveling mud off the downstairs floors, between interior walls green with mold.

Giuseppe didn't know when the cabin would be ready to move back into, though he was working on it every day. Nor was it clear when the promised governmental relief funds would appear for cleaning up the land itself. He had already missed the fall planting and couldn't anticipate when the next planting would be possible. But at least he could feed the animals. We climbed ladders with pails for the rabbits in their hutches on the upper story of the barn, then descended to scoop out grain for the chickens ranging in and out of the ground floor. A band of cats was waiting patiently in the farmyard. They had sought refuge on this rise of land when the flood waters receded from it as from a little Ararat. Perhaps some of the cats had even arrived on the crates, chairs, and lumber that floated to ground here like so many arks. Wherever they had come from, or how, Giuseppe calmly accepted them as his responsibility and brought over a big pan of kitchen scraps for them in the trunk of his car.

When the animals had all been fed, we went for a walk along the section of the dike that had collapsed and opened this Golena to the flood. Several men were standing by their cars when we reached the dike. An unoccupied folding chair marked where one older gentleman had been sitting when his friends arrived for a chat. Apparently, he came over every morning to watch the flood-swollen river sweep by, remaining until sunset. Flood watching had become his job, just as Thoreau had appointed himself Concord's unofficial Inspector of Snowstorms. Rita's Italian is excellent, and I can usually understand what is being said, though my command of the spoken language is considerably less than fluent. Still, when Giuseppe stopped to converse with that little group of men, we heard with amazement the local Lombard dialect for the first time. I'm not sure whether, in another context, we would have recognized it as Italian at all; with our utmost concentration, we could only make out the odd word. Giuseppe remarked to us afterward that it was unlikely any Italian from more than about thirty miles away would have understood that conversation. The continuing prevalence of dialects in Italy was for him an important aspect of bioregional culture in Italy. Like food, it was a mode of membership in the local story.

The adjacent section of the dike had no road along its top, though a muddy path marked where walkers and bikers had been using it. This massive earthworks had been built in the last century, an astonishing effort achieved exclusively by human muscle power. In retrospect, Giuseppe said, the dike had probably allowed for more cultivation and construction than was really sustainable in the floodplain of a major river. But the limits of human control had been revealed more quickly than they might have been because of heedless construction, road building, and logging in the skirts of the nearby mountains. Here, too, in the lowlands, almost all the trees had been cut; there is no equivalent in this part of Italy of Tuscany's ancient beech, chestnut, and oak forests. On the river side of the dike we did see occasional forested blocks where hybrid poplars had been planted in precise rows. These trees grow quickly, then are harvested after twelve years in order to produce pulp. When we arrived at the place where the massive dike had finally collapsed and then dissolved before the river's pressure, the steep walls of that gap looked as if they had been cut by a large, sharp shovel. This was a perfect illustration of George Perkins Marsh's insight into the relation between deforestation and flooding, which he formulated in Italy at just about the same time the dikes were being shoveled up in the first place: "The face of the earth is no longer a sponge, but a dust heap, and the floods which the waters of the sky pour over it hurry swiftly along its slopes, carrying in suspension vast quantities of particles which increase the abrading power and mechanical force of the current."[7]

What we saw, standing at the edge of that ruptured dike, was both a confirmation of Marsh's prophecy and an affirmation of Gary Snyder's

concept of the Main Flow, from which Giuseppe's new volume of trans-
lations takes its title. In a way, the flood was a comforting reminder that
nonsustainable human practices will be brought back into balance with
the earth, one way or another. To put this another way, insofar as our
practices align themselves with the larger balance of creation, they
are already in line with the Main Flow. We talked with Giuseppe about
Snyder's essay "Entering the Fiftieth Millennium," which discusses the
painted caves of the Dordogne that Rita and I had recently visited on our
walk across France. An astonishingly rich culture flourished in that region during the period between 35,000 and 10,000 years ago. Recognizing the prevalence of such hunter-gatherer societies over 25,000 years of
what Snyder has termed our 40,000-year-long "Homo sapiens calendar"
also underlines the importance of caves and other sacred sites, and of
the animal-based spirituality they often celebrated, in our human story.
Further, the fact that the Chauvet cave (discovered only in 1994) dis-
closes an artistic magnificence from 32,000 years ago that was fully
equivalent to the art of Lascaux 15,000 years later confirmed Snyder's
nonprogressive perspective on art and culture.

Rather than seeing human society on a steady curve of improvement
or, on the other hand, falling into nostalgia for an idyllic world before in-
dustrialism, Snyder sees excellence and harmony as recurrent qualities
in human culture. They perpetually reemerge, as the seasonal harvest of
humanity's dialogue with the living earth. Rather than forging forward
or fleeing backward, we thus need constantly to come back to the vibrant possibilities for groundedness in the present. This is the world in
which people seem to have lived for most of our history. In projecting human culture a further 10,000 years into the future, Snyder writes, "We
might wonder through what images *our* voices, our practices, will carry
to the people of 10,000 years hence. Through the swirls of still-standing
freeway off-ramps and on-ramps? Through the ruins of dams?"[8] These
images evoke the aftermath of a universal flood, like the ebb tide through
which the Italian farmer Giuseppe Moretti is now navigating. But the implied timeline is also much vaster than the postwar half century from
which we usually draw our norms. It allows a student of bioregional literature like Giuseppe to affirm calmly that, as he said to Rita and me,
"The first lesson is not to move." Stay put in the place where you were
born, where your parents were born. Improve the soil a little every day.
And through literature and networking, improve the cultural soil as

well. As Giuseppe was driving us back to the train, he said, "I don't expect conditions to improve much here in my lifetime. Even in a century or two, things might still be going downhill. But I'm hopeful that in 500 years we might have remembered where we live and who we are." In the meantime, he'll continue growing high-quality produce for his neighbors and grain for the nearby producers of organic livestock.

· · ·

The story of the flood in Genesis is one of hope as well as disaster, crowned by a new covenant between God and the descendants of Noah. In my conversation with Nanni Ricci, he had spoken of the setbacks to Tuscany's wine tradition in the 1970s as a providential disaster. Although it has always been a wonderful zone for grape production, for some of the same reasons that make it yield extraordinary olive oil, the Chianti area until recently had a very mixed record for wine. Fine vintages were certainly produced, though overshadowed by crudely concocted reds in their trademark straw-covered flasks. There were also few quality-control regulations of the sort governing France's regional appellations. This lack of oversight allowed a situation where, in the 1970s, certain unscrupulous producers added methyl alcohol to their blends, with the result that a number of people died from drinking Chianti. At that point, Tuscany's wine growers had a choice of either losing their industry or committing to a new level of integrity and quality. They rose to the challenge, policing themselves with a new regulatory system and embarking on an ambitious program of education for their agricultural community. Today the region is producing wines that are increasingly admired around the world, and little towns like Greve and Radda have become prouder and more prosperous than ever. As Ricci looked at the current European crisis related to *mucca pazza*, or mad-cow disease, he saw a similar opportunity to find a new beginning in disaster. This may be a chance, he believes, to do much more than rethink the grotesque use of ground-up offal as cattle feed. It's an occasion to think about Europe's diet, and ecology, as a whole; to confront the dangers implicit in genetically modified organisms; and to reaffirm the traditional, and culturally important, pleasures of the European table.

· · ·

Our final night in Tuscany, as we ate with Janet and Stefano in Impruneta, we discussed the way in which the ice storm of 1985 had offered a similar opportunity to recognize and protect the place of olive production in their region. Even before that ice storm, the premium oils produced in the hills around Florence were finding it harder and harder to compete with mass-produced oils. In a story familiar from Vermont, where so many of our dairy farmers live close to the line of bankruptcy, owners of groves near Florence were selling out to wealthy purchasers from other parts of Italy and abroad. Even if the newcomers didn't actively develop the land, they generally knew nothing about tending and cultivating the olives and thus let the groves die out without even knowing they were doing so. But when the trees broken off by the storm were burned, leaving barren hills around Florence, many people suddenly realized with a shock the extent to which the meticulous, traditional production of oil had also protected the Florentine landscape so beloved of their painters and architects—had in effect created that landscape, in a way that made it and the traditional agriculture inseparable.

Janet and Stefano hunted up a clipping from L'Unità, in the winter of 1985, headlined "Firenze senza olivi e sempre Firenze?" "Is Florence without olives still Florence?" The article began by recalling the flood of almost twenty years earlier, when the overflowing Arno had endangered so much of the city's artistic heritage. It continued, "Today a new flood is destroying the hills that make a crown around Brunelleschi's dome, the heights of Fiesole, Impruneta, Bellosguardo that have always formed a unique architectonic complex with the city. Is it possible to think of Florence without her hills?"9 In sweeping away the trees that framed and defined the city, the ice had posed a question that might otherwise have been difficult to articulate. What made this more than simply a lamentation was the fact that the millions of trees whose above-ground portions had been broken off and subsequently burned were soon sending up new shoots from those groves of stumps. Olives have always produced fruit exclusively from the new growth; hence the importance of a thorough annual pruning. Within six years after the disaster, though the trees had no sturdy branches to support pickers as in the Della Robbia plaque, they were once again producing at their prestorm rate. Growers like Janet and Stefano have been better able to make a case for their product's higher cost, as the restaurants and food lovers of Tuscany have celebrated the return of their traditional new oil with the joy of recovering something they feared they'd lost forever. And the olive growers have organized to promote legislation, education, and marketing efforts on behalf of their distinctive and superb product.

It's no use preparing for a flood that has already come and gone; Noah's blueprint, with all those measures in cubits, is not what will see us through this time around. Sometimes the threat is of inundation, sometimes of destruction by mud or ice. Other floods may be harder to get a fix on at first, like the permeation of traditional rural cultures by television and mass marketing or the carbon that whispers ceaselessly, though largely unseen, from our automobiles. The only thing that stays the same with all these deluges is our perpetual need to settle back down on the solid earth. A new beginning may start with something as simple as an olive leaf, reminding us of a familiar, nourishing world close to home. A meal with friends and family around a table may be a daily invitation to renewed community with the earth, as olive oil from the trees outside the window is drizzled lightly over the soup and bread in a benediction over whatever comes next.

PART II
LANDMARKS AND COVENANTS

6
HUNTER IN
THE SKY

Harvesting olives for the production of traditional Tuscan oil turned out to be the climax of our Italian pilgrimage. By deepening our awareness of what it meant to produce maple syrup, this experience also represented the first step in our return to Vermont. Perhaps it is often true that once one has traveled far enough into a new landscape, it becomes possible to see within it the familiar lineaments of home. A. R. Ammons writes in *Sphere: The Form of a Motion*, his book-length poem on relativity, "things go away to return, brightened for the passage."[1] For me, our curve of departure and return inscribed a trajectory through *Man and Nature* as well as across southern France and Italy. Just as getting to know about Janet and Stefano's work in Impruneta enhanced my sense of the cultural meaning of sugaring, so too connecting George Perkins Marsh's prophetic vision of conservation with the historical landscapes of southern France and Italy enriched my sense of conservation and literature alike. It prepared me to resume my teaching in Vermont, as well as our family's work in the woods, with a stronger appreciation of our culture's wholeness.

Marsh offers a view of history more complex than the assumptions that have sometimes characterized environmental discourse. I believe that it is also finally a more hopeful one. From the "dominion" language of the book of Genesis through the impact of science and technology on natural systems, the Western tradition itself strikes many environmentalists today as the cause of our global problems. But pinning one's hopes for preserving biodiversity on an international collapse of cultural, political, and economic systems is not a very hopeful approach. A more promising, and increasingly prevalent, metaphor is that of an Ark built to preserve not just biodiversity but also human values and community. Such an image reinforces the idea that technology (in the vessel's efficacy and speedy construction) and religious faith (in the divinely ordained blueprint) can each contribute to the success of the entire project. In this sense, the Ark can offer an emblem of a chastened yet ambitious new form of stewardship. If we want an environmental philosophy that goes beyond the fatal glamour of a shipwreck or the resolution of an extinguished conversation, we need to build a strategy for survival that works with the resources of our culture.

While Marsh called attention to the destructiveness of deforestation in Vermont and to the millennial impoverishment of the Mediterranean world, he also drew on examples of sustainability like that at Vallombrosa. His hundreds of references to current scholarship in forestry, agronomy, and hydrology make it clear that science, too, can be part of the solution as well as of the problem. Marsh found in Western culture countervoices to the ignorance and carelessness he decried, and both his critique and his constructive suggestions are informed in important ways by the vision of his Romantic predecessors. For Marsh, our culture's ecological errors become landmarks by which reformers might orient themselves. They can thus be essential parts of a tragic pattern of enlightenment. Within such a perspective, Marsh asserted that "the pioneer settler" in an abused and abandoned landscape could "become a co-worker with nature in the reconstruction of the damaged fabric which the negligence or the wantonness of former lodgers has rendered untenable. He must aid her in reclothing the mountain slopes with forests and vegetable mould, thereby restoring the fountains which she provided to water them."[2]

As Rita and I walked across parts of England and France on our way to Marsh's Italian haunts, his story helped us to be more alert to a resonance between the conservation movement and the foundations of European culture. In the pilgrimage country of the Dordogne, we encountered ancient sites where the spiritual testimony of our ancestors illuminates the present global crisis of the environment. Two of these sites frame the present chapter's meditations, while the next chapter will relate such physical relics to a specific literary lineage. Not just in southern France but also during our first days of hiking in Wordsworth's Lake District, we came upon stone reminders, from monoliths to cathedrals, of previous pilgrims' journeys. Witness stones were frequently of special interest to the English Romantics, since they both drew from the Western tradition of spirituality and cultivated a religion of nature that has been essential to the wilderness movement in particular and the conservation movement in general. Wordsworth's vision, because it is so emphatically localized, also reverberates with that of Bashō in Japan of the previous century, and of the Pueblo writer Leslie Marmon Silko in our own. Thus, while it is possible to trace the direct influence on Marsh of a succession of Western writers including Wordsworth, Emerson, and Thoreau, it is also possible to relate him to insights and values developed outside this tradition. This ratifies Marsh's own international and comparative perspective—the alternating rhythm of references to his Vermont home and the larger world.

Marsh was, along with his niece Susan's husband, Senator George Edmunds, one of the most prominent Vermonters of his day. But he grew increasingly disgusted by the corporate profiteering of the post–Civil War years. He never returned to America during the final years of his life, even as he continued his service as ambassador to Italy. While following his path through Tuscany, though, Rita and I always planned to return to Vermont, and to take the next steps in our family's effort of stewardship. The third chapter of this second section, "Landmarks and Covenants," focuses on a particular poem of Robert Frost's that both extends the Wordsworthian tradition into the landscape and environmental history of Vermont and addresses the ways in which physical labor on the land can reinforce our awareness of its mystery and foster attitudes of mindfulness and stewardship. Frost's "Mowing" amplifies the challenge, posed by the tympanum at Conques, for wholehearted and discriminating action in the world and encourages us to place our own stone marker along the way.

. . .

A rainbow of carven stone fans out above the western portal of the pilgrimage church in Conques. This tympanum of the Last Judgment dates from the early twelfth century when the church was erected and dedicated to Ste. Foy. She was the twelve-year-old daughter of a fourth-century Franco-Roman family. Following her conversion to Christianity, she was martyred for refusing to sacrifice to other gods. After 819, when her remains were transferred to Conques from her native Agen, this church became one of the most splendid and revered on the pilgrimage route to Compostela—the Chemin de St. Jacques. All of the pilgrims streaming into the church would have paused, as Rita and I do now, below this majestic Romanesque frieze. It is truly a "Bible de pierre," or Bible in stone.

After we've stood in the small plaza for a few minutes gazing at the tympanum, Rita enters the church. Her family background and personal practice are Catholic, and the centuries of religious art in the West illuminate and reinforce her faith. Over the thirty years of our marriage, I've often accompanied her to Mass. As she takes communion, I sit in the pew silently reciting the Lord's Prayer and Twenty-Third Psalm from my Southern Baptist boyhood, as well as the Kanzeon chant I've learned at the Vermont Zen Center. These are my litanies of goodness and mercy, following me all the days of my life. But as often as I've encountered Last Judgments on earlier visits to Catholic churches—above other medieval portals, in paintings and frescoes, or covering the interior dome of Renaissance cathedrals—this is the first one that's seized me so powerfully. In fact, I don't know when I've last felt so physically arrested by any work of art, literally halted in my tracks.

This was especially unexpected, since from my earliest recollection, hellfire and judgment were the aspects of Christianity I most resisted. My parents' Baptist faith, like Rita's Catholic experience, was a beautiful one—tolerant, generous, and literate. But on a couple of occasions during my growing up, as we were visiting family in northern Louisiana, we attended old-fashioned revival services in tents set up beside the local church. I remember the pounding of the preacher's fist on pulpit and Bible, reinforcing the imagery of sinners consigned to fiery punishment. I remember excruciatingly prolonged altar calls, when tearful men and women stumbled forward to rededicate their lives to Christ. Some children went up too. One sweltering night I began to wonder whether the service might be allowed to end if I got up and walked to the front myself. My mother's cool hand held mine with a little extra firmness on this occasion, though, both offering comfort in the storm and implying that it might be just as well if I stayed right there beside her. I never discussed these confusing experiences with either of my parents but did think about them quite a bit. I decided that while I believed in God and Heaven, and I loved Jesus, I just couldn't square those feelings with Hell. I guessed most people acted badly by mistake or habit; it shouldn't take an eternity of flame to punish such sinners or to scare the living onto the straight and narrow.

Over the intervening years, I've come to realize how much of this resistance to judgment was temperamental rather than theological. Not only were my parents unusually nonjudgmental people, but they were also extremely forbearing to my older brother, Lyn, and me. From the first thick pencil and wide-lined workbook in first grade, I relished school and applied myself happily to assignments. This brought approval from teachers that complemented what I received at home. Because I've been so blessed in my marriage with Rita, and so fortunate in my teaching situation at Middlebury College, it has been easy enough to maintain a contented outlook with no particular leaning toward judgmentalism. Still, issues of judgment have impinged on my life in ways that have felt more disconcerting every year. I've always disliked the institutional necessity of giving letter grades to students and, in becoming a senior member of the faculty, have faced the more excruciating task of making professional recommendations about faculty colleagues. As I've written and published more, I've faced the inevitability of comment, some of it critical, by readers who don't know me and to whom I have no chance to explain myself in person! Though hellfire is invoked in none of these occasions of judgment, they remain anguishing for me. The extent to which I brood over them suggests a fundamental issue needing to be confronted. If judgment is not, in fact, either an avoidable error or an extraneous force disrupting the inherent harmony of my life, how can it be integrated into a more comprehensive and balanced viewpoint?

. . .

At the center of the Conques tympanum is Christ in Majesty, right hand up for the righteous, left down for the damned. He is gazing straight ahead, absolutely centered in his own composure, a look not especially comforting for the boy who always shrank from the mandate "Let the dead bury the dead." Christ is haloed, wreathed in stars, borne up by flammifers—candle-bearing angels. Right beneath his feet the Archangel Michael and a tenured devil weigh the departeds' souls in a balance scale to determine their destinations. Like a bad sleight-of-hand magician, the devil tries to distract Michael with a gesture of his right hand while pushing down on the hellward pan of the scale with his left. Nonetheless, the pan on the angel's side keeps dipping lower still, toward mercy. This is the side I've always wanted to cling to.

Abraham and the Patriarchs, representing the history of earthly righteousness that prepares for and mirrors heaven, are seated in panoply in a segment of the tympanum beneath Christ's right hand. On that same side, a procession of the redeemed advances toward the Savior's throne. Mary leads the way, taking precedence over the various popes and patrons. The entire frieze would once have been vividly painted—almost hallucinatory in its power. Now only a tinge of blue remains on Mary's cloak, like a distant odor of sanctity. Charlemagne himself, one of the early benefactors of this pilgrimage church, takes part in the procession. But he has the good grace, unusual in such allegorical scenes, to look sheepish as an abbot leads him along by the arm. Perhaps he's aware of some incongruity between the acts of blood that consolidated his power and the deeds of religious beneficence that expressed it. As Bodhidharma replied when the emperor of China asked how much spiritual merit he would win for building Buddhist temples across the realm, "No merit."

Two details in these panels to Christ's right are especially delightful. At the end of a procession whose participants' stature has been steadily diminishing along with their spiritual celebrity, there is one very small figure who seems to have recently been heading in an entirely different direction. But his head has swiveled back toward the tympanum's center and his torso is beginning to turn there too, even though his feet are still pointing away. This seems to be the image of one who, to his own astonishment, has been converted at the last minute. On our way to Conques, we passed through the city of Angoulême, with its museum dedicated to the art of *la bande dessinée*, or comic books. There's an antic character to this frieze that echoes the comic-book exuberance we found in Angoulême, while at the same time enhancing the Last Judgment's dramatic impact. In addition to the little man's consternation at his unanticipated conversion, there's also the matter of those popping coffin lids. A segment wedged just above the gathering of the Patriarchs and below the Procession of the Righteous contains a little line of coffins. The coffin farthest to the left is still closed, but one by one the lids rise a little higher and the bewildered inmates first peer out and then sit up.

Presumably, the last trump has just sounded. So the coffins' sequence offers a kind of time-lapse photograph of the dead rising to the occasion like so many hermit crabs frisking out of their shells. This unfolding of a temporal sequence within the spatial divisions of the frieze makes for a wonderful distribution of energy across the arc of stone. In another little wedge beside the one with the coffin lids is a portrait of Ste. Foy herself, hands clasped in prayer and in devout prostration. She is being welcomed into heaven by a giant outstretched hand suggestive of God himself. Such a portrait of the saint has a sweet simplicity amid the crowded spectacle of righteousness on Christ's right and the explosion of violent retribution to his left. It reminds me of the story of Ruth—always such a cool drink of water in that noisy and dangerous neighborhood of the Bible.

If the side of redemption shows history as an avenue to grace, and righteousness as the earthly model of heavenly blessedness, the other side focuses on depravity and its harvest of hellish torment. At the bottom, a devil looks longingly across the divider between two panels. He is staring at souls—being welcomed into heaven by an archangel—that he would have liked to snare himself. Even as he gazes, though, his club is raised to knock another of his own constituents into the mouth of the ravening monster that is Hellsgate. Immediately above that scene on the devilish side of the tympanum is an allegory of damnable sins (or as Dante will insist, misplaced loves). Infatuations with wealth, power, pride, sex, and heretical beliefs are all portrayed and punished here. One example is the depiction of a knight, arrogantly armored and lifted up, at the moment when he is also being hurled headlong over his horse's neck. A warning to all viewers is carved between these pictured tiers: O PECCATORES TRANSMUTETIS NISIS MORES IUDICIUM DURUM VOBIS SCITOTE FUTURUM, "O sinners, if you do not mend your ways, know that you will suffer a dreadful fate."[3]

It's notable how great a role clerics play in the section of the tympanum to Christ's left. Perhaps such an antihierarchical tilt helps to explain how the whole composition was able to pierce my Protestant, academic resistance so sharply on this July morning in the year of our Lord 2000. Monks lead the pageant of damnability off, including one abbot/ bishop being crushed down over his own crozier by a demon. In the panel just below him stand a king and a pope having their crown and miter wrenched and bitten off, respectively. In an era when the power of secular and ecclesiastical hierarchies was so overwhelming, corruption and self-aggrandizement seem to have been correspondingly pervasive. But they were evidently no less infuriating for all that, as indicated by Chaucer's devastating portrait of the Pardoner and Dante's headfirst consignment of Pope Boniface VIII to a particularly unpleasant hole in Hell. The punishments of these ravening shepherds at Conques anticipate such literary treatments.

If part of my captivity by the tympanum at Conques came from its antiauthoritarian flavor, part from its Escher-like and antic intricacy, it was also true that we had arrived at Conques in a way that prepared us for a powerful revelation. We had been struck by the richness of early human sites in the Dordogne, but in studying our maps we realized that these were scattered so widely as to preclude visiting them on a single route of march. So despite having been self-propelled for almost five weeks, we decided to take a week off and rent a car. We worried that this might feel like an interruption or a defeat, but in fact it was great. Not only did it let us get to Les Eyzies, Pech-Merle, and Lascaux within the week, it also made it possible to visit Conques in the nearby valley of the Lot. Huguette Knox, a colleague in French at Middlebury College, had mentioned that this was for her France's quintessential medieval town, and one of the several most remarkable sights in the entire country.

Thus it happened that, on a late July morning of gorgeous sunshine, we were racing up mountain roads in our rented, aphid-green Renault Clio. Even before we arrived at the town or encountered the tympanum, this landscape felt like something in a dream. The speed of travel by car amazed us—trees flashing past, rivers splashing up beside the road then rippling away. It was like being Mr. Toad in his shiny touring car. Or like a blissed-out dog with its head thrust through a car window. No wonder we forgive our cars so much! Beyond the sheer velocity, there's the drama of topography—the rising of the map around you. As we climbed above the Lot we also moved from the fat pastureland that had been all of France we knew by foot to forested highlands that reminded us of our Vermont home on the slopes of Mount Abraham.

Conques, like Vallombrosa, is set in that most magical of landscapes—a valley high in the mountains. Its name comes from the Latin *concha*, "shell," and indeed the village seems to hang in a little scoop or swirl of space. Slated turrets face a steep slope of mature conifers amid which the *sangliers* (France's answer to Italy's *cinghiali*) wander, grubbing up roots and fungi. Despite our delight in the giddy speed with which we entered

Conques, we did feel a twinge of regret when we climbed out of the car and spotted the familiar red and white *balisage* leading into town. In the square before the church, we also met a number of pilgrims who were on foot. They were carrying their own *conques* in the form of scallop shells symbolizing the Chemin de St. Jacques—either hanging on their staffs or around their necks. Despite the wistfulness with which we observed them, however, there was something surprisingly valuable to us in the way we arrived. It felt as though we were leaning forward and staggering, as if from a rush through space. We were sucked into the rapids of that tympanum before we had a chance to orient ourselves or find a stable footing on that stone shore.

As I gazed at the tympanum, turned away to read about it, came back with guidebook in hand to study the sculpture's components and design, then gazed some more, I felt transported. I was moved to tears, my heart pounding, in the weightless, breathless hush of the deepest dream. It was an encounter with the needs and potential of my own soul, and of the dangers of placing too much weight on feeding and defending our own individuality. The fact that this work of art is finally focused less on those vivid scenes of condemnation and suffering, vindication and glory than it is on the viewer's own moral education is reinforced by the direct statements carved into the pediment. One inscription, dividing the segment of the Patriarchs from those featuring Ste. Foy and the resurrected, reads, CASTI PACIFICI MITES PIETATIS AMICI SIC STANT GAUDENTES SECURI NIL METUENTES, "The chaste, the peace-loving, the gentle, the pious, are filled with joy and, secure, have nothing to fear."

The tympanum at Conques is above all a strategic work, intended to promote an immediate, visceral, and motivating encounter with one's own spiritual condition. As is also true about the self-damned sufferers of Dante's *Inferno*, written two centuries later, external adjudication is far less to the point than existential self-definition. *The Tibetan Book of the Dead*, and the grinding, crushing horror of those Buddhist tankas with their monstrous blue bodhisattvas, offer similarly purposeful images for contemplation. Jonathan Edwards, with his sinner-spider dangling over the flames, pursues a kindred strategy in his own Locke-influenced Puritanism. Such staggering religious imagery is finally about conversion, through terror at the implications of believers' usual, day-to-day choices. Such an intent can also be seen in Marsh's evocations "of impoverished production, of shattered surface, of climatic excess . . . [that]

threaten the depravation, barbarism, and perhaps even extinction of the species."[4]

Indeed, up through the hellfire imagery of David Brower's speeches about environmental destruction that he collectively referred to as "the sermon," the prophetic tradition of conservation, like its religious forerunners, has been meant to galvanize the soul. Increasingly, environmentalists' emphasis is not only on government policies but also on the all-devouring power of consumerism. Religious traditions have always pointed out the danger of unrestrained appetites. They can mislead us so that we forfeit the Kingdom of Heaven that is within; they can condemn us to the deep suffering that comes from worshipping false gods (Lord Stomach, Lord Crown). They finally cost us no less than our soul: our capacity, through love, for ecstatic union with the All that is finally all there is. And as Wendell Berry has written, the blandishments of consumer culture finally lead only to "the hysterical self-dissatisfaction of consumers that is indigenous to an exploitive economy."[5]

Such a connection, reinforced by the antic complexity of the design, eventually helped me get past my rationalist, middle-class revulsion in order to inspect more closely the scenes of torment on one side of the design. It allowed me to register the tympanum's generous offer of insight into the origins of my own anxiety, narcissism, and constant need for affirmation by others. As I gazed, I began to make a connection whose pertinence had not been effaced by the passage of almost eight centuries. I may not gorge myself as the carven image of Gluttony seems to have done. But what of my American consumption of the world's goods, even as forests are eradicated and children starve? How far am I from the condemnation of "false usury" as I track my TIAA-CREF fortunes in a stock market I neither toil for nor understand? It was a shock to find myself in this picture I was used to turning away from.

As I've said, my lifelong resistance both to judging and to being judged is at the core of my difficulty with any Last Judgment. My desire was to be loved by all those closest to me, and to be considered above reproach by everybody else! This is as ludicrous an emotional agenda as one could adopt, and fifty-nine years of living have done much to modify it. Just as I've struggled to gain composure in my professional life, so too have I found myself challenged as a parent—never knowing where to draw lines. Rita's greater clarity, and decisiveness, about such matters has helped us as parents and allowed my own temperament to offer its own contribution. Still, parenthood, especially in the period while we had three teenagers in the house, has proven both my greatest challenge and my best opportunity to cultivate love without the cover of constant mutual approval. It has been a doorway out of the enclosure of my neediness. The joy of this chapter in the life of our family has been coming to see our children as comrades and teachers as well as charges I have been given to parent.

I think about them now in looking at the "phylactery," a carven ribbon of stone on the outside strip of a massive arch that frames the tympanum. A small angel's head and wings rest atop the phylactery. But on either side of it, spaced evenly down to the columns that support the whole tympanum, are humorous little faces—exposed just from the nose up by their little hands that bend down the ribbon on either side of their heads. They make me think of the little "Kilroy was here" doodles my father learned to draw during the war. These faces are part of the larger design, though running along the outside of it and in a plane closer to the viewer. They're peering slyly *out* at all of us who've been gazing so earnestly in. Rachel, Matthew, and Caleb, you're the comical observers peeping out from behind the phylactery that encircles *my* tympanum. (One tympanum per customer?) Actually, I can just about make out all your faces among the little individualized watchers—which makes me wonder who those *others* are. Are you finding some element of your own tympanum in me? The humor and pathos of sharing a world so intimately with our parents and children is that we always remain generationally out of phase with them. What wouldn't I give to talk with Dad and Mom now, with all of us in our late fifties—Rita's and my age now and theirs when we were married. Or to talk with each of our children when they've arrived at this stage of life but we're also somehow still here ourselves! There's a fantasy for you, and probably, like other fantasies, just as well left alone. I have just one partner with whom to pass through life hand in hand. And she's exploring the church's interior as I hover by the tympanum. Time to go inside myself.

. . .

I find Rita at a side altar dedicated to Ste. Foy, the twelve-year-old whose faith, commemorated in her name (*foi* is French for "faith"), and courage inspired the community of this church through centuries of pillaging and desecration by foreign raiders, rival parishes, Huguenots, and revolutionaries alike. Such faith, and devotion to a local patron saint, seem distant from most of us these days. Still, Rita and I light a three-day candle before the saint's altar and repeat this suggested prayer: "Sainte Foy, puissante and gracieuse patronne, priez-vous pour nous, notre famille, notre pays, and pour le monde entier" (Ste. Foy, powerful and gracious patronness, pray for us, our family, our country, and the whole world). This amazing site was rediscovered in 1837 by Prosper Mérimée, who was France's *inspecteur général des monuments historiques.* Since that time, the town and church have been carefully restored and are now considered to be cultural monuments of world significance.

It wasn't until the twentieth century that the windows were restored, not with medieval stained glass, but with a strikingly austere modern design. As in a number of other restored cathedrals around France, these are composed of leaded panes in the ancient manner but remain plain rather than representational. The basic color is a pale gray, though with subtle shadings of mauve and blue. The leading generally divides the windows with curving diagonals, though sometimes the segments of glass are more nearly horizontal. The thickened, grainy quality of the glass itself suggests its medieval lineage and further complicates the quiet richness of the effect. No rich crimsons or Chartres blues flood the pilgrimage church at Conques on a sunny July day. Rather, it is suffused with a soft glow, pale gray like the floral decorations of the carvings and the fretwork of the lofty ceiling. Confident faith does not come as easily for most of us today as it may have for our ancestors. But perhaps a sacred structure like Conques can help us mend and reconceive the tall windows in the sacred edifices that we inherit.

Rita and I walk back into the plaza facing the church's western entrance and stand once more before the tympanum. I increasingly sympathize with that last little figure in the procession, his feet pointing in one direction but his head jerked back in the other. There's so much in this tympanum that just won't hold still. It reverses a viewer's expectations—especially when that viewer is an emotionally vulnerable pilgrim, very much still en route. Inseparable from the tympanum's shockingly dynamic quality is all the violence that it contains in the panels of punishment. This part of the design has a bearing on my own tendency toward anxiety, which may in turn reflect the fact that my life has been almost devoid of violence. My society is also one in which, at least for many middle-class Americans, physical violence is rarely part of day-today life. This is not normal from a larger evolutionary perspective. My nerves and heart, as well as my adrenal system and the fast-twitch muscle fibers of my legs, may be getting jumpy while waiting for the next shoe to drop. The previous shoe, for our own family, came on D day.

Despite our abundance of food and clothing, freedom to make our own choices (religious and otherwise), access to education, and even travel beyond what our grandparents' generation would ever have dreamed of, there's a jumpy, apprehensive quality in American society. In our compulsiveness about wealth and consumption, we sometimes act as if we were barely surviving, while by all outward measures we're living in Fat City. This seems equally true in Britain, Germany, Italy. And I don't think it's only because of a disorienting vacuum of violence in our day-to-day lives. Even more, it may express our uneasy denial of the violence against the planet and the unenfranchised millions of the world caused by our very way of life. Though an American president has taken office who denies the gravity of global climate change, people all around the country and the world can still feel the patterns of the year changing. Vermonters wearing T-shirts out of doors in December may enjoy the milder days, but it's a nervous pleasure, made edgier when spring arrives a week earlier than expected. We don't have to stretch our imagination or compassion as far as drought and famine in the Horn of Africa. In the midst of our Green Mountains' pastoral beauty, we can see the shifting calendar of our maple sugaring and can begin to wonder just how elastic the maples that clothe our mountains will prove to be after the hemlocks of Vermont have already come to extinction because of the warming year.

Since the coining of the phrase by William James, proponents of idealistic social programs and causes have spoken of the need to view them as "the moral equivalent of war." Brutal aggression in both eastern and western hemispheres pulled World War II–era America together into as concerted and creative a community of effort as our country has ever experienced. Citizens were able to visualize all too clearly the dire results of a victory by Hitler and his allies. But we have not yet been able to form a similarly focused response to the dangers posed to the health of our atmosphere, our forests, our oceans, and the wildlife of the world. And one obvious reason is that for those of us leading comfortable middle-class lives there is no enemy external to our own heedless consumption, to our society's destructive transportation systems, and to the grotesquely unequal distribution of the world's resources. The enemy is within. The violence of the world expresses our disorientation.

Hell, for Dante as for the sculptors of Conques, can be understood as the landscape of misdirected loves; purgatory as the painful climb toward true love and a consciousness concentric and harmonious with the universe. Reflecting both our mistakes and our potentially more luminous choices, the tympanum at Conques offers an emblem of what, in our own terms, society must somehow now achieve. We need a way to *see* both error and redemption, hanging in the sky above us as we circulate around the public square. The story must be concrete, recognizable, and compelling. Without our own equivalent of the tympanum at Conques, we will never change our ways. With it, we might recover a spiritual grounding and faith that let us look more closely at our own lives. We might move, as in the prayer to Ste. Foy, from concern for our own family and place to a tender and sincere regard for the entire world. As David Lowenthal has pointed out, Marsh's ecological insights germinated before he ever left America, on the basis of his observations while growing up around Woodstock and of his wide reading. But the tympanum of Europe, with its errors and sufferings as well as its conversions and repentance, matured his vision. The many centuries of land-use history around the Mediterranean allowed him to achieve a tempered and constructive global perspective.

. . .

If our walk toward Italy was a pilgrimage in marriage for Rita and me, it was also, as mentioned, a quest for each of us in our individual ways. Rita's father, like my parents, was of Scottish extraction. But he died when she was less than six months old. She was raised by her mother and her grandmother, who lived with them, spoke mainly Italian, and managed to have her granddaughter named for her own patron saint, Rita of Cascia. For the first five years of her life, Rita often heard Italian. She attended Catholic schools and attained a steady faith that has been a special gift to our family, given my own less fixed religious identity. But growing up with no nearby Italian community and then spending her entire married life in Vermont, where Yankees and French Canadians are the dominant ethnic groups, she had few chances to explore her Italian heritage outside the immediate family.

As Rita and I stepped together toward Italy, the spiritual heritage of the Mediterranean world became an essential part of this pilgrimage in the footsteps of Marsh for me as well. The stories of saints, with their roots reaching down into the pre-Christian era, and the tympanum's elaborate structure of repentance and confession are all foreign to my own Protestant background. But I began to see them, like the notion of pilgrimage itself, as a potential resource for the environmental movement today as well as for me in this moment of my life. The path through all those towns we had never visited before and would be unlikely ever to see again was charged with mysterious significance for both of us. And visiting the painted caves of Pech-Merle in the same week we saw Conques helped me see both Marsh's contributions and our own life in Vermont within a more expansive and challenging context.

Because of Rita's claustrophobia, the descent into the caverns of Pech-Merle was one I made without her. Being separated after five weeks in which we'd been together for just about every minute of the day was disorienting. It helped me identify with the artists, questers, and priests who left their normal lives to descend here during the period when it was decorated and frequented, between 25,000 and 10,000 BCE. Scholars of this Magdalenian era agree that human beings would never have actually lived in caves like those at Pech-Merle and Lascaux. The subterranean world was too damp for such a purpose. It seems much more likely that bands of hunter-gatherers would have sheltered under lean-tos, or under the dramatic overhangs so prevalent in this region of limestone cliffs and outcrops. Most members of these groups may never have gone down into the depths of Pech-Merle, and the identity of those who did remains only speculative. What is clear, though, is that these caverns were visited regularly during bands' annual migratory circuit, along with the associated cave site of Conguac. It was a holy place for pilgrimage or initiation. As individuals cautiously made their way down from the surface to the depths of their world, they would have carried little stone dishes of fat, lit to give off a modest, flickering light. The irregular surfaces of the cave's interior, and the paintings created in certain chambers, would have swum up into sight as the hand holding the light got close enough to a wall.

Even with the electric lights that were switched on as our small tour group arrived at each new chamber, the turning path and side chambers made this a shadowy procession. The initial caverns through which one passes at Pech-Merle are relatively close to the surface and have several uncannily organic features. An ancient oak on the surface has somehow penetrated the roof of the cave with a long flexible root, which sways from the ceiling of the first chamber in way that suggests a vein, a nerve, or an umbilical cord. It quivered in the wind of our group's passage. The impression of having entered a living body was heightened by the effect of centuries of seepage down the limestone walls. The smooth, bubbling transparency of these ropy traces made them gleam as if wet. Sometimes delicate pink fans of calcium deposits hung on the walls, like corals or mysterious organs. The hunters of Pech-Merle, whose bands depended almost entirely on the herds of reindeer they followed, must have felt a connection, at once dreamlike and familiar, with the ritual skinning and dismemberment of their prey and the shining evisceration of those bodies so like our own. This was a sacramental journey within.

One of the most striking of the painted areas at Pech-Merle seems to express this sense of organic exfoliation and profusion. In the Black Frieze a design almost twenty feet across depicts horses, bison, long-horned cattle, and mammoths. Often, the animals closest to the center are superimposed on one another, in a gesture that seems to convey an ecology of the spirit. It offers a meditation on the flowering and flowing of distinct but overlapping forms within the mysterious house of life. I've never encountered a more eloquent exploration of what is, for me, the meaning of evolution—the arising of bodies from bodies, like mandalas emerging and disappearing in a kaleidoscope. Forest succession, inheritance and mutation, and predator-prey adaptation all figure in the revolutions of the Great Dance. An early interpretation of the Magdalenian cave paintings took them to be a kind of ritualized hunters' magic. But as evidence accumulated about how overwhelmingly reindeer dominated in these people's diet and hunt, the question arose why these other species should have been so much more prominent in the paintings. Perhaps it was their remarkableness, and the profusion of their different forms.[6] There's comfort in a world offering such diverse companionship.

Coming out of a fundamentalist background (like John Muir, David Brower, Dave Forman, and an interestingly large number of other environmentalists), I have had to cultivate the taste for complex religious imagery. One of the main differences between us Baptists and the Catholics, in the minds of my Sunday School teachers in denominationally polarized Louisiana, was that *they*, despite the Bible's clear warnings against idolatry, allowed *statues* in their churches. Fortunately, I'd gotten over that one long before this year's journey to Florence—a city that seems to have more statues than trees. But my instinctive preference in a space for meditation or worship has remained for plain wooden floors and unadorned white walls. Over thirty-six years of attending Mass with Rita, I've been mulling this over, trying to reconcile my respect for her religious experience with my own entrenched aesthetic.

An important opening to the value of a more highly elaborated religious setting came when we were on a previous sabbatical in Kyoto. While Zen centers in America were often remarkably similar to Quaker meeting houses, the great Zen temples in Japan generally had more in common with Italian basilicas. Paintings, sculptures, carvings, candelabra, and clustered chains of gold and silver did much to confuse my personal association between traditional Zen and radical Protestantism. But one site in Japan pulled together these apparently disparate traditions and left me with a much more wholehearted appreciation for Catholicism's enormously rich artistic tradition.

In the venerable temple of Sanjūsangendō, built in the century following the construction of the cathedral at Conques, there is a vast, dim hall containing one thousand bodhisattvas. These life-size wooden statues, each with individualized features, were once brightly gilded. But like the tympanum at Conques, they have faded over the centuries to a mellow brown. Each bodhisattva has many arms, meant to represent a thousand arms each. As the statues recede from a viewer, separated from them by a railing, they align into ranks like the tree trunks of an ancient forest, their arms thickening the sacred grove like branches. These statues represent Kanzeon, the Bodhisattva of Compassion, and their many arms and hands are meant to suggest the bodhisattva's availability to every human being, no matter what the nature of his or her suffering. As the nonidiomatic but memorable English translation of the plaque by the door of the temple puts it, these thousand thousand-armed bodhisattvas were created to symbolize "the numerousness of compassion."

The "numerousness" of bodhisattvas in their grove at Sanjūsangendō mirrors the profusion and diversity that make forests and wildlife such important spiritual, as well as physical, resources. The deeper meanings of our lives do not need to be sought away from nature. They are bodied forth by the earth and available to be encountered by us on every level of perception. Attentiveness to nature brings an experience of saving grace. Within the caverns of Pech-Merle, not only do the bodies of magnificent wild creatures emerge in the profusion of the Black Frieze, but it also seems in some cases as if their form, posture, and placement were actually created by the living irregularities of the rock. No less than the tympanum of Conques, the Black Frieze is a rainbow, a circuit of permutations and combinations that express the cosmic principle of plenitude. Two of the most beautiful creatures in the frieze are horses, in the big-bellied, small-headed, slender-legged, and elegantly shaded and mottled "Chinese" style of Lascaux. They face away from each other, but their hindquarters are partially superimposed, and the head of one is outlined by a crooked fissure in the cave wall so that it seems to be shoving out of the stone surface at that point.

This dynamic effect—at once physical and imaginative in impact—is felt even more powerfully in the figure of a mammoth separated from the main group of animals. At that point there are five vertical folds in the rock, evenly spaced and with a slight rounding of each stretch of stone beneath two seams. Recognizing a mammoth in this simple gestalt, the artist completed the picture in the most economical way, drawing a curved line to evoke the massive animal's back, suggesting a tusk, and then adding a group of vertical lines toward the beast's front to suggest its shaggy coat and beard. The paleobotanist Steve Young speaks of the "antic" quality of evolution, all those elaborate, ever-changing costumes pouring out of the clown car of nature. The interpenetrating movement of life is erotic as well as comic. (Perhaps those two categories are always one.) Our little group's guide in Pech-Merle pointed out the faint red outline of a pikelike fish riding along the neck and spine of that rock-faced horse on the right—another overlapping within the profusion. But for me it also suggested the mesmerizing countermotion of a mane—the brightness of a fish that swims and spangles behind the arched neck of a running horse.

No one can know exactly how these caves at Pech-Merle were used, or precisely what the animals depicted here meant to the artists and to those who descended with their smoldering grease lamps to look at them. But the carefulness and amplitude of these paintings feel like prayer, and their beauty like celebration. Modern visitors notice how few human figures are in evidence, and how small and relatively crude those pictures are. The "buffalo woman," "wounded men," and "hunters in distress" that do occur feel scribbly—marginal, ambiguous, precarious. But, in a way, that is consistent with the loving, knowledgeable eyes so evident in this art of a hunting people. In the Museum of Early Man at Les Eyzies there are a number of stone knives and scrapers. Each is chipped into a keen, shallowly beveled blade on both sides and referred to in the exhibition materials as a "biface." Such doubleness expresses the natural but profound ambivalence of the successful hunter—the gratitude that the people would now eat, and the passionate identification when skinning and evisceration disclosed kindred flesh, glowing like a vision in the light of flames. I believe that the paintings at Pech-Merle are both what the people did with these overpowering feelings and where they returned to recover and refine the language of their hearts.

Such needs are with us still. Early on in my teaching career at Middlebury College, almost thirty years ago, Erika Goldstein, a student who had gone on to medical school after her graduation a couple of years earlier, dropped by my office to chat and to tell me about her experiences at the University of Rochester. She had enjoyed her studies there and had done very well. But one event at the end of her second semester had had a profound impact on her. All year long her four-student class on physiology had been disassembling a human cadaver as they exhaustively studied each system of the body. They sliced and analyzed the eyeballs, disclosed the ligaments that moved the fingers and the limbs, gazed into the forests of the lungs and traced the articulation of the skeleton. It was an intense educational experience, and one that did much to make their class into a community of physicians in training.

But at the semester's conclusion Erika and her fellow students told their instructor that they all felt a need to commemorate the woman whose body they had so thoroughly dismantled and from whom they had learned so much. As respectful as the atmosphere in their dissection room had been, to look at an extracted eye with one's own similar eye, to separate the sinews of the human hand with one's own dexterous hand, had been emotionally confusing, even unsettling, for them. The instructor, to his credit, was able to meet their concern. Together they decided to hold a chapel service honoring this person whose body had been their companion and teacher throughout the year. Not only the class but many other members of the medical-school community had attended. Several of the students had risen to speak of their gratitude to the cadaver whose personhood they had gathered to affirm. And many of those who were present, student and faculty alike, wept. I've recalled this story ever since Erika told it to me as a model of education that integrated heart and body with the mind. I think about it now, having experienced Conques and Pech-Merle, and about our need for ceremonially designated spaces in which to encounter the wholeness of our lives, and in which to heal the wounds of our dividedness.

. . .

When I was a boy, silently registering my mental reservations about hellfire, and also when I was looking askance at earlier visions of the Last Judgment that were presented to me, I assumed that the "sins" on which such—to me disproportional—punishments were being visited were to be understood as infractions. It felt like a medieval code of justice in which someone might have a hand chopped off for stealing a loaf of bread. But from my father I learned that beneath the Latin word for "sin," *peccatus*, was the Greek *hamartia*—a metaphor from archery meaning "to miss the mark." From this angle, sin was a problem of separation, a failure to connect. The medical students at Rochester felt their separation from the full humanity of that body with which they'd been so intimately involved. They needed to integrate this aspect of their lives before they could find wholeness. I feel certain that, over the intervening decades, they have been more compassionate listeners and physicians because of having had such an experience. For the faith that erected the church at Conques, that remarkable tympanum was like the top half of a concentric target, with Christ at the center and the human spectacle filling the plaza around the church's western portal completing the circle's lower half. And what of those of us living today in a world so expressive of our own inattentiveness and dividedness? Where will we find the circling mind of ceremony that allows us to recognize ourselves in kinship with the world?

. . .

Of all the stirring images harbored deep below the pleasant French countryside in the caverns of Pech-Merle, the most moving was a remote side passage containing a dozen or more ancient footprints. Researchers identify them as having been made by a twelve- or thirteen-year-old on some solitary trek away from the main, painted chambers. Who knows what vision, errand, or initiation was involved? One print, gleaming under our electric light and showing the individual impress of toes and heel, looks as if it could have been left yesterday by a barefoot teenager following a muddy path. No one can say exactly when these prints were made, except that it would have been over 10,000 years ago. That is when the glaciers' aftermath of heavy gravels and debris sealed off the cave and put an end to its use as a shrine by this band of hunter-gatherers.

That one footprint reminded me of our three children, who have so recently passed through their teenage years and who were, as Rita and I pursued our European pilgrimage, taking important steps in their education and their independent, adult lives. And of course footprints have a strong association with our own slow journey, encountering the world foot first as we forge toward our common and disparate goals. We've left our waffly boot prints in many a muddy patch—from the Yorkshire bog above Nine Standards disingenuously characterized by our guidebook as a "moist bit," to a similarly disastrous stretch called "humide" by a villager pointing us toward our path in the Charente. The evidence of our passing lingered long after we had crossed the further horizon, just as the muck and sphagnum clung to our boots and traveled in our socks for days.

In "The Tuft of Flowers," Robert Frost's speaker goes out to mow a field only to find a broken swath where a previous mower has scythed around and spared a spray of flowers growing tangled in the grass. This "message from the dawn," indirect as it is, speaks to the second mower's heart of a kindred sympathy with the earth. It leaves him, paradoxically, able to affirm the possibility of human community, "whether we work together or apart."[7] I felt personally connected with the teenager treading Pech-Merle's muddy path. Sympathy, community, even the wholeness of our lives, are easier to believe in when we can stand beneath the tympanum, laugh when the mammoth steps out of the wall toward us, and gaze down at the footprint in its prehistoric mud. Such visions are both corrective and affirmative, reminding us, in both regards, that we are not alone.

Often, the visions that most galvanize our imaginative and sympathetic powers are those that take dramatic force from being at once remote, in time or space, from our usual lives and, in another sense, immediate and personally recognizable—even intimate. Freud spoke of the essentially uncanny (*unheimlich*) quality of dreams. Figures and circumstances present themselves as familiar but unsettlingly changed, often by the admixture of another person's hair or features or voice, or by significant details wrenched away from an entirely different situation. Such incongruities give dreams their puzzling quality and cause us to puzzle over them. The scriptures of the world, Freud's *Interpretation of Dreams*, Jung's *Memories, Dreams, and Reflections*, and the testimony of indigenous initiation traditions still practiced in North and South America, Australia, and elsewhere all agree about the integrating power of dreams in the landscapes of our lives. But one must be ready in order to see, recall, and reenter a dream of this transformative power. Such special alertness often comes at an intersection, or a crisis, in the dreamer's life, lending openness to mind and spirit, and urgency to the dreamwork of insight and maturity.

In walking toward George Perkins Marsh's life in Italy, where he consolidated the experience of damaged landscapes in the Vermont of his boyhood and wrote his prophetic book, I was focusing on a related question. We live in a day when the world's scientists have reached a broad consensus about the realities of global climate change. The corollaries of even a modest rise in mean average temperatures are also widely agreed on. One of the first results, as Bill McKibben has described, is that in many areas the trees will die, since their longer reproductive cycle and rooted life prevent them from shifting habitats as animals can. But the animals, too, are imperiled in a world where highways bisect the land and deforestation diminishes alternative habitat. Meanwhile, the birds are often threatened by pesticide use in one part or another of their migratory range; although the United States banned domestic use of DDT after Rachel Carson's witness, we still sell it to Latin American countries, so that the same songbirds can be poisoned by a toxic food chain there instead of here. And our overfishing of the ocean, most recently with immensely long dragnets that scrape the bottom bare at many places, has gone far toward devastating one of the richest habitats on earth, one on which human beings have long depended. None of these catastrophes is news to anyone who reads the papers or watches television. Yet somehow we can't focus on the reality of our own society's destructiveness, even as we approach the point where our survival may be imperiled.

Marsh's book documents the extent to which the deforestation by ancient civilizations around the Mediterranean changed the climate, eroded the soils, lowered the water table, and destroyed much of the wildlife. Donald Hughes refers to Marsh's argument in *Pan's Travail*, citing the famous passage in the *Critias* where Plato says that the mountains of Attica were heavily forested shortly before his lifetime but have now been rendered arid and unusable by unrestrained cutting and grazing. In this connection, Hughes recalls a particularly impressive myth that resonates with what Marsh called "man's ignorant disregard of the laws of nature": "An awareness of the possibility that wildlife might be totally extirpated is found in a Greek myth. According to it, the mighty hunter Orion offended Artemis, goddess of the wild, or as some versions have it, Gaia (Ge, Mother Earth) by boasting that he would kill every wild beast in the world. In retaliation, the goddess sent a giant scorpion to sting him. Before this could happen, Zeus set both the hunter and his arachnid enemy in the sky as constellations opposite each other."[8]

An implication of the myth may be that humanity shares with Orion the Hunter a rapacious appetite, one that can only be curbed by a threat of death. Such a crisis requires that a larger intelligence impose itself in order to prevent a disaster. The fact that this story has at least as much to do with human beings as with the gods is reflected in the facing positions of the two constellations. Paired in this way, they remind observers here below of the perpetual need for restraint. We can still go out under the night sky and look from Orion to Scorpio. Seeing them, we may recall an old story whose pertinence is undiminished. Granted, these guiding stars will only be visible once we have made our way back into the darkness. This may mean moving well away from the illuminated house, or taking a long walk into the country. Even if neither of those choices is currently available to us, though, we still retain the power to read the myth, close our eyes, and give ourselves over to remembering the world. When day returns, we can decide upon our next steps.

7

GIFTS OF PROPHECY

In order to enter the animal dreaming of our ancestors at Pech-Merle, we must first climb down into the darkness of the earth. To remember the balanced constellations of Orion and the Scorpion, we have to leave our houses, walk past the last street lamp, and feel ourselves falling out into the sky. Beyond all its ecological insights and political stratagems, conservation requires a relinquishment of our floodlit confidence in human prerogatives. This is a recurrent need. Stepping away from our masterful routines, we recover membership in the larger circle of life. At the heart of the prophetic tradition associated with George Perkins Marsh is a restorative rhythm of darkness, interrupting our technological and social momentum so that dawn can come again in mindfulness and hope. As writers in Marsh's lineage point to the destructive consequences of environmental carelessness, they cut us off from certain roads where we have gotten in the habit of traveling pretty fast. But they also reconnect us to the forgotten sources of our real vitality. Acknowledging the errors of our ways is an opening into darkness that amplifies echoes of the love, health, work, community, and mystery giving life wholeness. It opens the door to an inner ecology of excursion and return.

In commenting on the fairy tales of the Brothers Grimm, Padraic Collum has suggested that the old stories attained their full richness only when darkness fell. "A rhythm that was compulsive, fitted to daily tasks, waned, and a rhythm that was acquiescent, fitted to wishes, took its place." But he also notes how, both in the Grimms' German homeland and in his native Ireland, this shift in consciousness was eliminated by people's ability to live under artificial lights right up until the moment they went to bed. First kerosene lamps and then electricity meant that "in towns and in modern houses the change of rhythm that came with the passing of day into night ceased to be marked. . . . The prolongation of light meant the cessation of traditional stories in European cottages."[1] Without the blurring and release that come to our minds in the dark, it is harder to be fully receptive to the magical transformations or talking animals that convey so much of humanity's accumulated wisdom. We're held in thrall to our own rationality and assertiveness, compulsively re-enacting our dailiness, no matter how unnourishing it may have become. Freud's attention to dreams reflects his insight that such stories and images, coming toward us in the darkness, might mark a path back to the wholeness of our lives.

We seem to have forgotten, as a society, how to turn out the lights of our striving and acquisitiveness. Our projects keep the generators thrumming all night long and dry up the rivers. This is what it means to say that the environmental crisis is ultimately a crisis of culture. It's time to give ourselves again to the wisdom of old stories; to reawaken, in the retrospective dark, to the relationships that make our lives whole. Earlier stages of the conservation movement assumed that damage to the natural environment could be prevented or repaired by legislation; advances of scientific knowledge would stimulate and reinforce our progressive policies. Such floodlit confidence will not guide us to the roots of the problem, though. Thus, when we speak of "the stories of home," we are referring to more than ecologically sophisticated narratives. We are also invoking an era before our glittering cities dimmed the night sky. Until we can find our way back to what Collum calls the "acquiescent" darkness, we will languish in a kind of collective Alzheimer's, unable to make out the constellations or remember the pattern that connects.

. . .

George Perkins Marsh inaugurated a prophetic tradition in environmental literature and thought. He did so by facing the darkness of our environmental catastrophes and by suggesting a more restrained and respectful approach to forests and other natural systems. In *Man and Nature,* Marsh addressed the relation between our individual choices and social practices and humanity's growing discord with the natural world. He sharpened his analysis by placing the problems of his contemporary society in a much broader historical context than people were used to thinking about. As important as both of those achievements were, however, neither was his most original contribution. In the decade before Marsh's book appeared, Thoreau's *Walden* challenged the era's economic, social, and spiritual imbalance in an even more trenchant way, while Darwin, in his *Origin of Species*, was framing human history in the much vaster panorama of natural selection. But *Man and Nature*, while registering similar insights in its own way, also undertook an entirely new task. It documented the cultural and economic costs of rampant deforestation in particular and related its damage in his own time and place to the gradual impoverishment of the Mediterranean region. By combining the language and insights of science with a thoroughgoing social critique, and by continually bringing his analysis back to the level of policy, Marsh introduced a prophetic rhythm. He looked steadfastly at the worst effects of our actions in order to encourage more constructive measures. Within the sometimes daunting meticulousness of his research and documentation, he tracked a circuit of healing from catastrophe to insight.

While Thoreau likens himself to the Preacher in Ecclesiastes, Marsh is closer to the Bible's prophetic tradition. And in contrast to Darwin's grand vision of continuity between human beings and the process of natural selection, by which "endless forms most beautiful and most wonderful have been, and are being evolved,"[2] Marsh focuses more specifically on human history as a long gathering toward the present moment of crisis. It is illuminating to compare some of the language of *Man and Nature*'s final paragraph with Darwin's, quoted above from the concluding paragraph in *On the Origin of Species*. Near the start of his paragraph, Marsh writes that "in the vocabulary of nature, little and great are terms of comparison only; she knows no trifles, and her laws are as inflexible in dealing with an atom as with a continent or a planet." But he ends with this sentence: "The collection of phenomena must precede the analysis of them, and every new fact, illustrative of the action and reaction between humanity and the material world around it, is another step toward the determination of the great question, whether man is of nature or above her."[3] Despite the ecological insight evident throughout *Man and Nature*, Marsh reverts several times to this confusing assertion of man's special status. It does not represent Christian orthodoxy, since, despite his appreciation of the writings of Horace Bushnell, Marsh was a skeptic in religious matters and for much of his adult life did not regularly attend church services. Rather, his sense of "man" as "above" was an attempt to get at the possibility for rising out of ignorant and repetitive behavior. In this way, though the language is so different, he anticipates Aldo Leopold's "land ethic," and the creative tension between being "a plain member and citizen of the land community" and holding ourselves to a new and higher standard of mindfulness.[4] Marsh and Leopold are akin not just in the observation of ecological patterns and the chronicling of human disruptions in living systems. Both writers take those as data yielding, in Leopold's term, an "upshot" of new perspectives and actions.

To connect *Man and Nature* with biblical prophecy does not imply that Marsh's book is merely an ecological diatribe. Even the book of Jeremiah, though it lacks the messianic hymns of an Isaiah, still looks toward restoration for Israel and Judah once the folly of the people and their leaders has been corrected. But because that scourging is such a big job, and because the people need to encounter the suffering already beginning to be visited upon them in a much more immediate and creative way, the prophet focuses primarily on their errors.

Neither Jeremiah nor the lineage of environmental prophecy founded by George Perkins Marsh looks ahead to a simple or self-evident future. Prophets are essentially time jugglers, intent on helping people understand the chains of causality linking present sufferings to past abuses, and looking ahead to even worse outcomes that might be predicted if such practices continue. The product of such prophecy is not a set of rules or instructions. Rather, it is an enhanced vision of alternative futures which comes from tracing the consequences, many of them unintentional, of our present actions. The most important link between Marsh and his successors like Leopold and Carson is that they, too, begin by looking at ecological disasters and then project alternative futures that would follow from either continuing our present errors or taking a more informed and responsible approach. Scientific information about our errors cannot by itself offer a solution to environmental problems. But it can invite a more imaginative and historically expansive perspective in our civic choices. Hope, for the writers in this prophetic tradition, is not an unwavering beacon at the end of a dark panorama; it is an intermittent gleam, a spark that may or may not be blown aflame. This outcome cannot be guaranteed by any book but will instead be determined by readers' own practices, both personal and collective.

The tangled sequence of Jeremiah, chapters 23–25, is characteristic of prophecy in this key, and specifically of much environmental writing since Marsh's day. In chapter 23, verses 5–6, comes a great promise of restoration for the people: "Behold, the days come, saith the Lord, that I will raise unto David a righteous Branch, and a King shall reign and prosper, and shall execute judgment and justice in the earth. In his days Judah shall be saved, and Israel shall dwell safely: and this is his name whereby he shall be called, THE LORD OUR RIGHTEOUSNESS." But just four verses after that promise, Jeremiah returns to the present moment, with its abundance of false prophets deluding the people with their comforting lies, their fantasies, and their "lightness." As verse 10 expresses, the cycles of nature itself are disrupted when the community becomes so misled and debased: "For the land is full of adulterers; for because of [swearing] the land mourneth, the pleasant places of the wilderness are dried up, and their [course] is evil, and their force is not right." The easy "dreams" of bogus prophets are part of this collapse, not any solution to it; an era of violence is the people's inheritance, but also finally their path toward release. Jeremiah foresees both the subjugation of the people of Judah by Nebuchadnezzar and the Babylonians and, "when seventy years are accomplished," the overthrow and destruction of those conquerors. Jeremiah couches this historical sequence in the language of both a threat and a terrifying promise, in verse 15, chapter 25: "For thus saith the LORD GOD of Israel unto me; Take the wine cup of this fury at my hand, and cause all nations, to whom I send thee, to drink it." There is no promise here that suffering and oppression can be avoided if the people only mend their ways. It is too late in the day for such an escape. The hope Jeremiah holds out is that suffering may be seen as a path of recollection and restoration, a harrowing invitation to righteousness and faith.

The voices of Jeremiah and George Perkins Marsh are good ones to listen to now. Though stringent, they are a healthful alternative to the consumer fantasies of television advertising—life perfected by a new car or a long-distance calling card. And they also provide a firm foundation for contemporary critiques of ecological carelessness. In *The Future of Life*,

E. O. Wilson couches his authoritative biological overview in language as apocalyptic as that used by either of those earlier figures, surveying "the erasure of entire ecosystems and the extinction of thousands of million-year-old species."[5] The twentieth century was a time of exponential scientific and technical advance. But as the human community and our home the earth begin a new century, populations are projected to explode among the poorest nations of the earth, climates to become less temperate and predictable, soils and oceans to be impoverished, and the purity of our food and water to be harder and harder to guarantee. If we can see such a cataclysm, not as a random disaster, but as the direct outcome of all our previous and present choices—and the transition to a more chastened and mindful sense of community—then we can see within stark prophecy a true vision of hope.

In the century following its publication, Marsh's *Man and Nature* had two great successors in the lineage of American environmental prophecy. Aldo Leopold's *A Sand County Almanac* (1949) and Rachel Carson's *Silent Spring* (1962) are the volumes whose influence on twentieth-century environmentalism has been the greatest. Just as Marsh's book led to the passage of landmark forestry regulations, to the founding of the Adirondack Park, and, more indirectly, to the National Park System, Leopold's is often held to be the chief influence behind the 1964 Wilderness Act and Carson's is seen behind the founding of the Environmental Protection Agency. If one were to continue filling in the list of influential books in the field of conservation and environmentalism, John Muir's 1894 volume *The Mountains of California* would also certainly come to mind. This collection of essays, originally published in the *Century* magazine, was decisive in convincing Congress to protect the Yosemite Valley. Along with his later work through the Sierra Club, it earned Muir the title of Father of the National Parks. Muir's writing is often vivid, particularly in his adventures like the ascent of Mount Hoffman, his experiences of climbing mighty trees during "a wind-storm in the High Sierra," and his loving portraits of individual species of trees. But even though Muir decries destruction of beautiful places, his vision is different from those of Marsh, Leopold, and Carson in a fundamental way. He celebrates the glories of the Sierra in order to call for their protection as a "Range of Light" transcending and apart from human industry in the lowlands. The other three writers are prophets to Muir's priestly celebrant in that they more fully integrate human history into their ecological perspective and call for far-reaching changes in the attitudes and practices of society as a whole.

Leopold's and Carson's books remain central references in our discourse today about nature and culture, much more so than Marsh's, in fact. Their greater accessibility has to do with the fact that, though solidly grounded in science, the two more recent figures write in a much more conversational voice and subordinate documentation to strong narrative lines. But by connecting Leopold and Carson with their great predecessor it may be possible to see the contours and implications of both writers' work with a new clarity. Like Marsh, each of them begins with a tale of violation and loss. Like him, they step back to offer a more inclusive historical perspective, on the basis of which they formulate a more sustainable ethical and ecological framework. Leopold is particularly close to Marsh in that he too begins with an account of heedless clearing and exploitation. Deforestation, drainage, burning, and plowing of slopes had combined to impoverish large areas of Wisconsin within living memory. The resultant "Sand County" was just one more chapter, transferred about a century later and 800 miles further west, of the same story of greed and carelessness George Perkins Marsh was born into in southeastern Vermont.

One divergence in Leopold's telling of the story, though—and a link between him and Rachel Carson—was the special emphasis he placed on loss of wildlife within this general despoliation. When he read backward through Wisconsin's century, in sawing through the rings of an ancient bur oak, he saw changes in the land that also led to the death of the last elk, the disappearance of the Wisconsin wolf, and the extinction of the passenger pigeon. Marsh understood that deforestation had led inevitably to the siltation that filled harbors and the desertification that destroyed agriculture, and eventually as well to the demise of proud and ancient civilizations around the Mediterranean. Leopold honed this insight by showing how loss of habitat destroyed wildlife, and how the killing of certain predators accelerated the general process of ecological impoverishment.

In personal correspondence, the scholar and essayist Eric Freyfogle has expressed to me his sense of how pervasive the awareness of loss is in Aldo Leopold. In Freyfogle's view, there were several key periods in Leopold's life that strengthened his sense of environmental loss. First, there were his "early professional years in the Southwest, when he saw dramatically the ill effects of overgrazing, waterway alteration, and wildlife mismanagement." Equally momentous was his 1935 trip to Germany, "where he saw glaring evidence of how long-term, artificial forestry ruined soil and degraded wildlife communities." Then there were his 1936 and 1937 trips to the Rio Gavilan and Sierra Madre region of Mexico. Here he saw land "that was more pristine and lush than any he'd ever seen; in their vitality they contrasted markedly with lands in the U.S. Southwest that, while once similar, had been degraded through human use." Finally, there was his sense of ecological decline associated with "the unwise reduction of predators and the consequent destruction of ranges brought on by excessive herbivore populations."[6]

Leopold's sensitivity to the ecological importance of predators is a defining characteristic of his writing, and the heart of *A Sand County Almanac* is his account of killing a wolf in "Thinking Like a Mountain." It brings Marsh's millennial history of carelessness into the compass of a single man's action and insight, at once a grievous violation and loss and a conversion giving rise to new understanding. Though Leopold's book as a whole belongs in the prophetic tradition inaugurated by Marsh, its personal frame of reference and narrative force also relate it to the nature-writing tradition running from Thoreau through writers like Mary Austin, Edward Abbey, and Terry Tempest Williams. In this combination of elements, it brings new literary power to Marsh's vision, profound and constructive as that was but also sometimes muffled by its density of documentation or muted by its abstraction. Such a confluence offers hope to an arid and eroded culture.

Leopold's account of shooting a wolf, and of the new insight that came from his realization of his mistake, resonates both with Marsh's perspective and with the biblical tradition lying behind it:

> Only the ineducable tyro can fail to sense the presence or absence of wolves, or the fact that the mountains have a secret opinion about them.
>
> My own conviction on this score dates from the day I saw a wolf die. We were eating lunch on a high rimrock at the foot of which a turbulent river elbowed its way. We saw what we thought was a doe fording the torrent, her breast awash in white water. When she climbed the bank toward us and shook out her tail, we realized our error: it was a wolf. A half-dozen others, evidently grown pups, sprang from the willows and all joined in a welcoming melee of wagging tails and playful maulings. What was literally a pile of

wolves writhed and tumbled in the center of an open flat at the foot of our rimrock.

In those days we had never heard of passing up a chance to kill a wolf. In a second we were pumping lead into the pack, but with more excitement than accuracy: how to aim a steep downhill shot is always confusing. When our rifles were empty, the old wolf was down, and a pup was dragging a leg into impassable slide-rocks,

We reached the old wolf in time to watch a fierce green fire dying in her eyes. I realized then, and have known ever since, that there was something new to me in those eyes—something known only to her and to the mountain. I was young then, and full of trigger-itch; I thought that because fewer wolves meant more deer, that no wolves would mean hunters' paradise. But after seeing the green fire die, I sensed that neither the wolf nor the mountain agreed with such a view.[7]

This narrative has a significance in *A Sand County Almanac* equivalent to Rachel Carson's "A Fable for Tomorrow" in *Silent Spring.* The following passage, with which Carson chooses to open her book, resembles Leopold's account in offering a story to frame her complex visions of ecology and social responsibility:

There was once a town in the heart of America where all life seemed to live in harmony with its surroundings. The town lay in the midst of a checkerboard of prosperous farms, with fields of grain and hillsides of or-chards where, in the spring, white clouds of bloom drifted above the green fields. In autumn, oak and maple and birch set up a blaze of color that flamed and flickered across a backdrop of pines. Then foxes barked in the hills and deer silently crossed the fields, half hidden in the mists of the fall mornings.[8]

Leopold and Carson both offer a vision of natural wholeness against which to frame their critique of social practices. Both try to make ecological principles available to a broad audience by offering dramatically crafted parables. But each is quite distinctive in accomplishing these goals. In his account of shooting the wolf, and the relationship he draws between that action and the ecological devastation of the western mountains, Leopold also shows himself in error and records the process by which he came to a new understanding. He is an educator as well as a chronicler, with deathly mistakes as the telling examples that bring his points alive. Indeed, following his glimpse of the green fire in the dying wolf's eyes, and his observation over subsequent years of how the wolf-free mountains were denuded by numerous, if starving, deer herds, Leopold became an early and effective advocate of the importance of predators to a healthy ecosystem. Today, we take that insight for granted, just as the crucial role of wetlands, another of Leopold's arguments, has also been established beyond question by scientists and protected by legislation. The insight began, though, not in dispassionate research but rather in reliving a process of violation, repentance, and conversion.

Leopold's dramatic reversal of values with regard to wolves recalls the story of Saul, persecutor of the early Christians, struck down by a blinding light as he followed the road to Damascus. When he arose he was a new man—Paul, the follower of Christ and Apostle to the Gentiles. Interestingly, John Muir, the most important conservation figure in the period between Marsh and Leopold, had a parallel experience of blindness and recovery. A gifted mechanic and inventor, Muir was working late in an Indianapolis factory when the tip of a file slipped through his hands and pierced his eyeball. The last thing he remembered seeing as he stood by a window was the aqueous humor from his eye dripping into his cupped hand. The injury in one eye was soon compounded by sympathetic blindness in the other eye, so that Muir had to spend weeks in bed in a totally darkened room. When his sight finally returned, he left behind his promising career in industry and set out on foot to immerse himself in the beauty of the natural creation. He never turned back from this celebration of the earth, or from his tireless advocacy of its wild places.

In neither Muir's nor Leopold's case did personal revelation or a sense of emotional connection with nature trump or displace science. Quite to the contrary, their mystical insights were ratified by scientific research and have become essential to the analysis of ecologists, conservation biologists, and park managers in our own day. To put this another way, Leopold's experience of gazing into the eyes of the dying wolf enabled him to respond with discernment to Marsh's own arguments. With reference to the 1874 revision of *Man and Nature*, retitled *The Earth as Modified by Human Action*, Leopold wrote,

> George P. Marsh . . . was one of the first to sense that soil, water, plants, and animals are organized in such a way as to present the possibility of disorganization. His case histories describe many degrees of biotic sickness in many geographic regions. They are probably the ultimate source of the biotic ideas now known as conservation.

One might offer an ironic definition of conservation as follows: Conservation is a series of ecological predictions made by beginners because ecologists have failed to offer any.[9]

This tribute to Marsh comes from a remarkable essay which Leopold wrote in 1946, but which was published for the first time in Eric Freyfogle and J. Baird Callicott's 1999 collection *For the Health of the Land*. Though not referring specifically to Marsh, this passage from slightly later in the same essay offers a concise summary of *Man and Nature*'s central insight: "Paleontology teaches us that most land was stable, at least in terms of time scales applicable to human affairs, up to the point at which fauna, flora, soil, or waters were radically modified for human use. Disorganization seldom preceded the wholesale conversion of land with modern tools. It is necessary to suppose, therefore, that a high degree of interdependence exists between the capacity for self-renewal and the integrity of the native communities."[10] This insight carries through both Leopold's writing and Carson's. They, like Marsh, are scientifically educated teachers, and the essence of their teaching is that the earth is fragile; human beings can disrupt natural systems and thus have a responsibility, as Marsh expressed it, to undertake "the restoration of natural harmonies." An important element introduced into the tradition by Leopold and carried on by Carson is the appeal, not just to their readers' minds, but also to their hearts.

In his essay "The Land Ethic," from *A Sand County Almanac*, Leopold stated that no significant change in people's policies and practices toward the land was ever accomplished without love. He thus extended the prophetic tradition in conservation in a way reminiscent of the Apostle Paul's statement in the second verse of 1 Corinthians, chapter 13: "And though I have the gift of prophecy, and understand all mysteries, and all knowledge; and though I have all faith, so that I could remove mountains, and have not charity, I am nothing." There is, in effect, an ecology of prophecy, which includes faith and love as well as knowledge and power. This necessarily involves an inversion of hierarchies, and thus may only be reachable along a path of confusion and shaken confidence. Certainly, Leopold's narrative of shooting the wolves conveys the charged emotions and blurred boundaries of a dream. A doe emerges beside a stream in the New Mexico mountains. Then it is transformed into a wolf, then into a "melee" of wolves. As the young men fire wildly downhill, the pack disperses, until we are left with only one young man, gazing into the dying light of a single wolf's eyes. When that light is extinguished, a single idea takes its place: that the mountain may have a different opinion of the place of predators in a healthy landscape than the human hunters ever imagined. And with that insight, the young man too is transformed.

If we are returning to the writings of George Perkins Marsh with renewed appreciation today, that may be in part because of the ways in which Aldo Leopold both perpetuated and transformed Marsh's prophetic vision. Part of this, as discussed above, was bringing more narrative and literary power to a book whose astonishing insights were often couched in the highly documented, scrupulously qualified, and impersonal voice of a scientific journal. Leopold was a professor at the University of Wisconsin when he wrote both *A Sand County Almanac* and the essays now collected into *For the Health of the Land;* like Marsh he was both thoroughly versed in the science of his day and cognizant of contemporary developments in Europe (especially in Germany and Austria). But many of the essays in the recent collection, in which the seeds of the *Almanac* are frequently visible, were published between 1938 and 1946 in a journal called the *Wisconsin Agriculturist and Farmer.* Among Leopold's first readers were quite a few property owners making daily decisions with an impact on the ecological balance of their regions. Accordingly, his focus is frequently on highly local issues, his emphasis on the education and persuasion of individuals rather than on broad policy analysis or legislative initiatives.

It was not that Aldo Leopold did not also have an interest in public lands and public policy. As Freyfogle and Callicott point out in their introduction to *For the Health of the Land,* in 1925 alone he published five articles advocating wilderness preservation, and in 1935 he became one of the founders of the Wilderness Society. But he turned down the society's presidency in order to cultivate his small, worn-out farm in Wisconsin and write personal essays about the cycles of nature in that landscape. "He was at work seeking a lasting, pleasing middle ground between the poles of urban civilization and pristine wilderness."[11] Nora Mitchell and Rolf Diamant have written of the way in which "the middle landscape can promote a respect for and understanding of place, nurture a land ethic, and enhance democratic values and civil society."[12] Stewardship grows in such a middle ground, which may also be understood as an ecotone—the edge between two ecosystems which ecologists describe as having both a higher number of species and greater biotic density than either constituent system. Such stewardship is characterized by an inclusive perspective and expressed by a high level of practical skill.

Leopold follows up directly on Marsh in his argument that both restraint and skill are needed if past environmental abuses are to be avoided. Marsh began by calling for a moratorium on further logging in every state of the United States (with the possible exception of Oregon), but at the end of his life he traveled to Vallombrosa, where the skilled practices at Italy's first national school of forestry won his admiration on both aesthetic and economic grounds. As David Lowenthal discusses, Marsh became quite disillusioned about the civic culture and direction of the United States in his later years. The growing power of corporate interests, and the selfishness of private landowners, whose own interests could not accommodate the longer cycles of forest succession and health, left him feeling that only governmental conservation programs could succeed. Marsh's increasing distrust of private ownership was reinforced by his warm support for the project of Italian unification. Environmental protection, for Marsh, was one of many values dependent upon a strong, centralized state: "[N]othing but the union of all the Italian states under a single government can render practicable the establishment of such arrangements for the conservation and restoration of the forests and the regulation of the flow of waters as are necessary for the full development of the yet unexhausted resources of that fairest of lands, and even for the permanent maintenance of the present condition of its physical geography."[13] But Leopold focused on the large portion of the country that was already in private hands and on which, as he knew as a hunter, much of the wildlife depended. Perhaps one difference between the two writers was that, living abroad for most of his last two decades, Marsh's perspective on his native country became broader, while Leopold's, after he purchased a small farm in the last third of his life, grew more practical and immediate. At any rate, Leopold sought to educate farmers about the principles of ecological health, to show them how preserving biodiversity could actually increase their income, to cultivate in them a love for wild beauty that would both inspire them to foster it on their own lands and, accordingly, enrich the quality of their daily life.[14]

A crucial element of love for one's home landscape, from Leopold's perspective, is skilled care for it. This is more than love of the beauty all around one's farm; it takes responsibility for its continuation or, in the case of the abused piece of land that surrounded Leopold's "shack," it sets about restoring it. In an essay called "The Farmer as Conservationist," Leopold makes this point through a distinction between the two necessary qualities of "restraint" and "skill."

> Certainly, conservation means restraint, but there is something else that needs to be said. It seems to me that many land resources, when they are used, get out of order and disappear or deteriorate before anyone has a chance to exhaust them. . . . Conservation, then, is keeping the resources in working order, as well as preventing overuse. Resources may get out of order before they are exhausted, sometimes while they are still abundant. Conservation, therefore, is a positive exercise of skill and insight, not merely a negative exercise of abstinence or caution.[15]

This aspect of Leopold's environmental philosophy would not have meant as much to me before my family and I became involved in tending the sugar bush in Starksboro. The history of this particular piece of land is typical of the lower elevations in the Green Mountains. Hill farms were established at the beginning of the nineteenth century, but almost all were abandoned between the Civil War and World War II. Thin, flinty soil and a challenging climate wore those families out. They often logged off the land in a final effort to keep their farms. But there was no further recourse then, and they had to go. Our land, 142 acres of sloping ground, is typical in having been pretty much clear-cut about seventy years ago. Skidders can go straight uphill more safely and easily than they can traverse slopes, so that dozens of eroding roads climb through our woods, where loggers abandoned one skidder track after another in bringing out the last trees. When such a piece of Vermont is thoroughly mined and abandoned, the forest does come back. In the case of our sugar bush, it is a woods dominated by sugar maples but also with a fair sampling of paper birch, yellow birch, ash, poplar, red oak, hardhack, butternut, basswood, white pine, red spruce, and hemlock. But having all started more or less at the same time, rather than with the diversity of age that would have come with natural forest succession, the trees of such a recovering forest reach a point of gridlock. Neither nutrients nor water nor, most crucial of all, light is sufficient to allow them to grow much further. The woods fall into a kind of suspended animation.

Here's where skill can come in. Single-stem selection can gradually thin the forest out, allowing some trees to expand their crowns and establish a canopy higher and fuller than would otherwise have occurred for centuries. This can't be done all at once, or the remaining trees would be too vulnerable to winds and pests. Another principle of forest health that a skilled steward attends to is diversity. Although we do favor maples right around the sugarhouse and sap lines, we also look for ways to foster other trees, like butternut and basswood, that, though rarer, are important parts of the forest community. We close off the higher logging roads, allowing those woods dominated by oaks and pines, which were never as thoroughly cut, to be an unfragmented habitat for deer, moose, and bears. Similarly, we map out and then stay away from wetlands and other special habitats. We regrade the few main roads we do continue to use, installing water bars to prevent further erosion. In the field remaining open at the lowest part of the property, we cut around apple trees now surrounded by encroaching forests, "releasing" them as an important source of food for bears, deer, turkeys, and partridge. In late summer, when the ground-nesting birds have raised their new broods, we brush hog the meadows so that they will continue to be a habitat for these species.

These are fledgling efforts by Rita and me—two teachers, and not of forestry—and our children. We are guided in working with the old meadows and orchard by Vermont Coverts, which seeks to make landowners more alert to their property as habitat. We are slowly being educated about tending a forest by Vermont Family Forests, a local network of small landowners. Such organizations serve us in the way Leopold informed and inspired his Wisconsin farmer neighbors. They don't undermine our commitment to expanding the wilderness areas in Vermont. Indeed, Vermont Family Forests begins with the premise that such preservation is essential, just as Leopold saw wilderness as a necessary complement to the work of skilled farmers and other land stewards. "Completely wild lands have one function which is important, but as yet ill-understood. Every region should retain representative samples of its original or wilderness condition, to serve science as a sample of normality. Just as doctors must study healthy people to understand disease, so must the land sciences study the wilderness to understand disorders of the land-mechanism."[16] A continuing dialogue in this prophetic tradition relates to the question whether public or private stewardship is more effective in the long run. Leopold suggests that the government is best at preserving vast blocks of wilderness—which are less likely to grant a profit to any individual landowner or even to any one generation. But when it comes to "operating" land, to use his word, he sees a diversity of informed farmers or foresters to be much more beneficial than a governmental agency. In the end, such individuals are more likely to be motivated by love and an intimate knowledge, as opposed to the "ruthless utilitarianism" that so easily dominates public policy; Leopold remarks that a "tendency to create *monotypes*, to block up huge regions to a single land-use, is visible in many other states. It is the result of delegating conservation to government. Government cannot own and operate small parcels of land, and it cannot own and operate good land at all."[17]

As Marsh does, Leopold ultimately affirms the necessity of both public and private stewardship. Each of these authors also comes to view the two forms of conservation as mirroring complementary needs within a healthy *democracy*—for both wise government and individual responsibility. Public stewardship, as of wilderness areas and other natural treasures at a regional, national, or global level, protects aspects of the environment that are beyond the means, the life span, or the limited self-interest of any individual or family. Further, those natural values being preserved are fundamental to all, just as our society of laws and our institution of universal public education are. That's why we must preserve them from infringement by the local competitiveness of the marketplace. Private stewardship, on the other hand, functions like the diversity of niches in a healthy ecosystem—providing both variety and redundancy and thus bringing stability to an environment that would become too easily stressed as a "monotype." Leopold the ecologist finds in private stewardship the answer to the need for "interspersion," preventing clear-cuts on either the ecological, the ideological, or the cultural level.

How shall we use forests to protect vulnerable hillsides and riverbanks from erosion when the bulk of the timber is up north on the sands where there is no erosion? To shelter wildlife when all the food is in one county and the cover in another? To break the wind when the forest country has no wind, the farm country nothing but wind? For recreation when it takes a week, rather than an hour, to get under a pine tree? Doesn't conservation imply a certain interspersion of land-uses, a certain pepper-and-salt pattern in the warp and woof of the land-use fabric? If so, can government alone do the weaving? I think not.[18]

From its inception, this prophetic tradition in conservation thought has been democratic in emphasis. Not only did Marsh address ecological and agricultural challenges facing the young American republic, but he also involved himself in improving the fisheries and agricultural policies of his native Vermont and spoke directly to farmers, as in his important Address to the Rutland Agricultural Society. At a time when Vermont was seeing many of its young people emigrate to the newly opened farmlands of the Midwest, Marsh proposed cultivation and husbandry as ways to develop a more enduring sense of place. Though the language here is more florid than Wendell Berry's, the connections proposed anticipate Berry's modern agrarian vision:

A youth will not readily abandon the orchard he has dressed, the flowering shrubs which he has aided his sisters to rear, the fruit or shade tree planted on the day of his birth, and whose thrifty growth he has regarded with as much pride as his own increase of stature and who that has been taught to gaze with admiring eye on the unrivalled landscapes unfolded from our every hill, where lake, and island, and mountain and rock, and well-tilled field, and evergreen wood, and purling brook, and cheerful home of man are presented at due distance and in fairest proportion, would exchange such scenes as these, for the mirey sloughs, the puny groves, the slimy streams, which alone diversify the dead uniformity of Wisconsin and Illinois![19]

Leopold, though much more appreciative of Wisconsin, especially its waterfowl, nonetheless builds directly on Marsh's sense of an affinity between agriculture and civic pride. He discusses how integrated, biological pest control, preservation of wildlife habitat, and the pleasures of native wildflowers could all contribute to a farmer's quality of life on the land. Rachel Carson addresses her fellow citizens even more inclusively, speaking not just to the dwindling segment of the population who are farmers but to all Americans—in our capacity as consumers of agriculture's products and coholders with the farmers of our nation's soil and water. To that extent, she is the most radically democratic writer of the three. But by the same token, her emphasis inevitably circles around to the public sphere. Only legislation at the congressional level can restrain pesticide use promoted, despite a woeful lack of research, by such influential institutions as universities, public agencies, and the chemical corporations that provide so much funding to them.

. . .

The problems Carson faced as a writer had to do with the vastness and diversity of her audience. While Marsh's book was an immediate success and Leopold's *Sand County Almanac* has become a staple in environmental studies courses across America, of the three only Carson was a bestselling author (first for such books as *The Sea around Us* and then for *Silent Spring*) in her own lifetime. Part of this achievement came from her extraordinary skills as a teacher. Building on Leopold's success in explaining the value of both predators and wetlands, she, more than any other scientifically oriented writer, introduced the sciences of ecology and evolution to a broad, worldwide audience. Carson did so in *Silent Spring* in the most thoroughgoing way, explaining how matter was transformed into energy through "the endlessly turning wheels of oxidation within the mitochondria" and about the related "charging of the battery, in which ADP and a free phosphate group are combined to restore ATP."[20] Her mastery of such technical exposition is essential to showing the dangers of chlorinated hydrocarbons like DDT in "uncoupling" this process, and thus destroying the energy on which all life, including human life, depends. It is hard to imagine a more compelling description of basic science than that which frames her critique of our careless use of agricultural pesticides.

Rachel Carson's remarkable clarity about these matters is accompanied by a voice that is so reasonable and so sharply focused as to be majestic. Such a voice served her well when the inevitable assaults on her book came from industry and its university representatives, showing their attempts to call her motives or information into question as themselves biased and unresponsive to her pointed questions. Within Carson's general tone of reasoned analysis, however, there are a couple of other characteristics of her writing in *Silent Spring* that gave readers a sense of her urgency. One of these is her amazement at the carelessness with which our nation had been persuaded to use poisons. Marsh and Leopold have their own capacity for sarcasm in the face of misguided policies. But Carson's discussion frequently adopts a posture of incredulity, as in her aptly titled chapter II, "Beyond the Dreams of the Borgias."

> If we are troubled by mosquitoes, chiggers, or other insect pests on our persons we have a choice of innumerable lotions, creams, and sprays for application to clothing or skin. Although we are warned that some of these will dissolve varnish, paint, and synthetic fabrics, we are presumably to infer that the human skin is impervious to chemicals. To make certain that we shall at all times be prepared to repel insects, an exclusive New York store advertises a pocket-sized insecticide dispenser, suitable for the purse or for beach, golf, or fishing gear.
>
> We can polish our floors with a wax guaranteed to kill any insect that walks over it.[21]

In this passage, Carson addresses not only her fellow citizens but, more specifically, her fellow consumers. In arguing against the deceptions offered by "the soft sell and the hidden persuader,"[22] she introduces a new chapter in environmental discourse, one that continues to the present day: the argument that in a society as affluent as our own, our choices as consumers have far-reaching environmental and ethical implications.

In an earlier discussion, on the widespread use of the pesticide Malathion, Carson had drawn an analogy to the poisoned robe presented by Medea to Jason's new bride. Anyone who put it on would die horribly. Carson writes, "This death-by-indirection now finds its counterpart in what are known as 'systematic insecticides.' These are chemicals with extraordinary properties which are used to convert plants or animals into a sort of Medea's robe by making them actually poisonous. This is done with the purpose of killing insects that may come in contact with them, especially by sucking their juices or blood."[23] This image is characteristic of Carson's approach, both in its emphasis on the urgency of our present situation and in its literary resonance. Indeed, *Silent Spring* abounds with literary references, from her epigraph drawn from Keats's "La Belle Dame Sans Merci" and her chapter title ("And No Birds Sing") from the same poem to her reference to Robert Frost in the concluding chapter, "The Other Road." Her comprehensive perspective conveys the sense of the ecological crisis as being also a cultural one, and as a danger calling for discerning, energetic response from the fullest range of scientific and artistic resources. As her references to Keats and Frost—and my discussion of Wordsworth in the next chapter—reflect, the conservation movement is ultimately an outgrowth of Romanticism, with its own revolt against mechanistic domination.

Finally, Carson is writing not just on behalf of a particular technological correction but also in advocacy of a far-reaching process of cultural evolution. In this, she is closely aligned with her predecessors Marsh and Leopold. They believe, as she does, that the mistakes of the present may be either the beginning of the end for our society or the prologue to a wiser and more balanced approach. One reason for the inclusion of literary references may be to recognize the vital role of imagination in envisioning another perspective from the one prevailing today. Marsh's archaeological researches invite his readers to adopt a more expansive view of history. Carson's extrapolation of current agricultural trends similarly calls for envisioning their long-term effects. "Future historians may well be amazed by our distorted sense of proportion. How could intelligent beings seek to control a few unwanted species by a method that contaminated the entire environment and brought the threat of disease and death even to their own kind? Yet this is precisely what we have done."[24] If we can only step outside received opinion about the use of pesticides, evading the commercially motivated arguments of "the soft sell and the hidden persuader," we may be able to see how *primitive* such an agricultural approach is. The dangers for Carson don't originate in the fact that our science and technology are so advanced but rather in the fact that they are so unbelievably crude. Rachel Carson is a scientist who wants not to rebel against the fruits of research but to refine them. Indeed, we have no choice. As she writes in her final chapter, summing up the main line of her critique throughout, "The 'control of nature' is a phrase conceived in arrogance, born of the Neanderthal age of biology and philosophy, when it was supposed that nature exists for the convenience of man. The concepts and practices of applied entomology for the most part date from that Stone Age of science. It is our alarming misfortune that so primitive a science has armed itself with the most modern and terrible of weapons, and that in turning them against the insects it has also turned them against the earth."[25]

I have argued that this prophetic lineage in conservation thought is both a continuous tradition and a progressive one. Like Marsh, Leopold and Carson start by describing disasters to which most of their fellow citizens may not have been alert, then turn to considering how society might change its ways. Leopold introduces a personal narrative voice that integrates Marsh's insights with the genre of nature writing, bringing much greater literary impact to his arguments. Carson extends this prophetic tradition in two particular ways. On the one hand, she relates the problems caused by careless use of pesticides to our own choices as consumers and to our own physical health. On the other, she insists that the environmental crisis of our day is also a cultural and personal one; that we are ethically implicated in technology's impact on nature and that we register its damage in our own bodies at the cellular level.

It is important to acknowledge that both these authors regretted the necessity for their prophetic calling. They thus stand in the line of Jonah, as well as in that of Jeremiah and Isaiah. In the original foreword submitted in 1947 with the manuscript that would become *A Sand County Almanac*, Leopold follows his "litany" of ecological losses with a striking paragraph: "One of the penalties of an ecological education is that one lives alone in a world of wounds. Much of the damage inflicted on land is quite invisible to laymen. An ecologist must either harden his shell and make believe that the consequences of science are none of his business, or he must be the doctor who sees the marks of death in a community that believes itself well, and does not want to be told otherwise."[26] In February of 1958, as she was marshaling her forces to write *Silent Spring*, Carson similarly wrote to Dorothy Freeman that she had reluctantly given up her belief "that the stream of life would flow on through time in whatever course that God had appointed for it—without interference by one of the drops of the stream—man." She continued, "These beliefs have almost been part of me for as long as I have thought about such things. To have them even vaguely threatened was so shocking that, as I have said, I shut my mind—refused to acknowledge what I couldn't help seeing. But that does no good, and I have now opened my eyes and my mind. I may not like what I see, but it does no good to ignore it." And so she proceeded with her research for what, at this stage, she referred to simply as "the poison book."[27]

While much of Carson's power as a writer comes, as Marsh's does, from her compelling historical perspective, she also reframes the context. While he emphasizes the impact of deforestation occurring over many generations, and thus invisible to people at any one moment in history, she emphasizes the suddenness of change in the post–World War II era. Marsh helps us understand the effects of deforestation by relating practices in the Woodstock of 1810 to thousands of years of land use around the Mediterranean. Carson illuminates the dangers of pesticides by showing that they were products of an accelerating and untested technology in the years immediately following the war's conclusion. "Over the past decade these problems have cast long shadows, but we have been slow to recognize them."[28] Hers is a wake-up call—not to change long-established practices, but to understand the dangers of sudden changes in our attitudes which developed in the postwar euphoria. "Our attitude toward poisons has undergone a subtle change. Once they were kept in containers marked with a skull and crossbones; the infrequent occasions of their use were marked with the utmost care that they could come in contact with the target and nothing else. With the development of the new organic pesticides and the abundance of surplus planes after the Second World War, all this was forgotten."[29]

With the sequence from Marsh through Leopold to Carson, the outlines have been drawn for a critique of environmental carelessness that continues and accelerates in our own day. Problems are identified, within social practices that most of their fellow citizens might not have found problematic; the nature and degree of the problem are explained with reference to data and insights from science; and a historical context is offered through which readers can understand both the necessity of and the possibility for resolving the problem. I believe that this sort of critique has in fact been a major resource for social correction and environmental improvement—not protection per se, since the mistakes precede the analysis. It is a chastened tradition, which continues to draw its creative power from the dialogue between errors and insights. I would like to close this discussion by glancing at two contemporary writers who extend the tradition in specific, recognizable ways.

Bill McKibben's *The End of Nature*, published in 1989, was originally serialized, like *Silent Spring*, in *The New Yorker.* McKibben's book also resembles Carson's in two other regards. One is that it relates a grave and pervasive environmental problem to the daily choices made by American citizens. For example, it documents the impact of one ton of carbon, released into the atmosphere annually by the average American car, on global climate change. Like Rachel Carson's, McKibben's task is to make visible the effects of mundane practices—in this case, of something as routine as driving to work—to draw attention to the alarming aspects of technology, about which we have been lulled by the suave voice of advertising. Second, as Carson does, he approaches this necessary reversal of attitudes by insisting that environmental disasters can come very fast, though their impact can be all too long-lasting. McKibben begins his book with the sentence, "Nature, we believe, takes forever."[30] His purpose is to demonstrate how sudden the impact of technology can be, and in particular how drastic a change has already been caused by the deposition of carbon into the atmosphere within our own life span. "[T]his is not something that has been happening for a long time. It is not a marathon or the twenty-four hours of Le Mans. It's a hundred-yard dash, a drag race, getting faster all the time."[31] From *The End of Nature* through *Enough,* his book on biogenetic engineering, McKibben admonishes his readers in the spirit of George Perkins Marsh. But he also speaks to the spaciousness—psychological, cultural, and spiritual—that can emerge once we become more mindful of a world beyond our power and designs.

Another contemporary who perpetuates and extends the prophetic tradition of conservation is Stephanie Mills. While her interest in land-use history recalls Marsh's and her attention to biological systems builds on Carson's, she is closest in her personal narrative approach to Leopold. Indeed, as a person who has settled in the upper Midwest, she continually cites him as an inspiration. Her book *In Service of the Wild: Restoring and Reinhabiting Damaged Land* combines visits to restoration projects around the world with accounts of her own healing from a serious car accident and of her efforts to bring back native hardwoods on her thirty-five-acre homestead in Michigan. I have been personally inspired, as our family seeks to identify more closely with the Vermont landscape, by her ability to connect these elements into a single narrative of wholeness. Her summation speaks to the entire lineage flowing out of Marsh's book, while also registering a continuing shift toward nature as the force behind restoration and the human role as participating in rather than directing that process:

> We have come to a moment in time when a wounded but willing humanity may look to healing itself in the land. In the individual, as well as in the ecological community, restoration begins with recapitulating the history in order to heal the land in the light of truth. Whatever sort of self we bring to the meeting with the wounded land, we may gain heart as we witness the Earth's response to care. The process is not solely in our hands; we have a part to play, but the power to restore belongs to Nature. We can only be abettors, not inventors in this endeavor; ours to defer to the greater art. Ecosystems are the greatest teachers.[32]

Looking at the tradition as a whole, we can recognize that responding decisively to environmental disasters is frequently akin to grief work. It can only happen by overcoming denial; it may begin in anger, but it must move to identifying a larger process of loss with the immediate circumstances and choices of our own lives and to undertaking constructive measures. The goal of grief is ultimately neither lamentation nor obsession with the past. It is an honest assessment of painful realities, the better to allow for a vital future.[33] Such a reorientation may be most readily accomplished when individual losses can be related to the larger patterns that connect and to the resources that foster our lives together on this beautiful earth.

8

THE BROKEN
SHEEPFOLD

We live in a day when love of the earth can feel like a long grieving. One sometimes wants to shut the door on grief, through the denial or the anger that are so often adopted by the newly bereft. Even if avoiding the distractions of travel, possessions, and the other comforts that are offered so lavishly by our consumer society (and few of us middle-class Americans avoid them to a very significant extent), devotees of nature can easily fall into another form of evasion. Our moments of serenity in lovely natural settings can sedate us against the dreadful damage done to the fabric of nature just beyond our ken.

When Edward Abbey died in 1989, Edward Hoagland praised him in a *New York Review of Books* eulogy for his clamorous outrage at the environmental holocaust of our time. We need such anger in our writers, Hoagland wrote, rather than "mystical transcendentalists" engaging in "Emersonian optimism." "Emerson would be roaring with heartbreak and Thoreau would be raging with grief in the 1980's. *Where were you when the world burned? Get mad, for a change, for heaven's sake!*"[1] But such anger, while necessary, must ultimately be transmuted into an effort of creative grieving. It must commit itself to achieving, as Marsh did in *Man and Nature* and Abbey himself did in *Desert Solitude*, a whole vision that begins with but also looks beyond the fact of loss. Such creative grieving aims at an integrated perspective on cultural and ecological health, acknowledging that there is no environmental crisis separate from our own daily choices. The basic question facing citizens today is how we can more respectfully and hopefully inhabit a beautiful, shadowed landscape—our home on this ridge between watersheds and centuries.

. . .

Reading *Man and Nature* during our meandering months in Europe helped me to connect disparate writers I had already loved within a larger, testimonial vision. Marsh clarified the presence of certain strands of feeling and fidelity, angles of vision, or patterns of resistance to the presumption of human dominance connecting poetry from the English Romantic era, Japan's haiku legacy, and contemporary poetry with the current achievements of American nature essays. Though not a tradition in any continuous, linear way, these authors coalesce for readers in our own time because of their shared sensitivity to an ecology of poetry and the earth. They define for me the larger literary landscape in which Marsh and the prophetic tradition he inaugurated gain their fullest relevance. Furthermore, just as we in the West encounter an author like Bashō within a context provided by the Romantics, Marsh too can be directly related to the Romantic movement and the American Renaissance. It's important to remember that Wordsworth was the dominant poetic influence on the English-speaking world when Marsh was growing up. George's cousin James Marsh, who became president of the University of Vermont, was a prominent early scholar of the German philosophy so important to Wordsworth and Emerson alike. David Lowenthal writes, "In the late 1820s, Kant and Coleridge, as glossed by James Marsh, became the philosophic linchpins of American Transcendentalism under Emerson's guidance."[2] Through such connections we can understand the modern conservation movement as an outgrowth of the organic, antihierarchical thought associated with Germany and England in the late eighteenth and early nineteenth centuries. Culture, like the life of a forest, becomes an interwoven network of root hairs when one looks beneath the separations of the surface.

. . .

Investigating the literary context for the environmental movement, I have been particularly struck by certain instances in which Wordsworth, Bashō, and Leslie Marmon Silko focus on images of *stones* in their meditations about the wholeness of nature and culture. These passages evoke for me the rugged landscape around Vallombrosa, with its Masso del Diavolo and Masso di San Giovanni Gualberto. Stones, like stories and poems, can be both receptacles for memory and prompts to imaginative sympathy with specific places on earth. Though much more long-lasting than many natural forms, stones too are finally impermanent —like every other physical object and like the great globe itself. By transcending our short human span while still remaining transient, stones offer us an image both for our anxieties concerning loss and death and for what may still be achieved in our passage through this world of flickering forms. A remarkable passage on the place of transcendent beauty and value in an always vulnerable world comes near the beginning of Book 5 in Wordsworth's *Prelude*. Wordsworth's title for this section of his autobiographical masterpiece is "Books." The question he ponders in it is why the divine beauty of literature can only be conveyed from age to age by the easily lost or destroyed medium of printed volumes.

> Oh! Why hath not the Mind
> Some element to stamp her image on
> In nature somewhat nearer to her own?
> Why, gifted with such powers to send abroad
> Her spirit, must it lodge in shrines so frail?[3]

In the following 95 lines, the poem's speaker relates a vision that once came to him in a dream. He had fallen asleep while reading *Don Quixote* in the suggestive setting of a seaside cave. He "passed into a dream" where, "amid a boundless plain / Of sandy wilderness, all black and void," he encountered

> . . . an Arab of the Bedouin tribes:
> A lance he bore, and underneath one arm
> A stone, and in the opposite hand, a shell
> Of a surpassing brightness. . . .

In the course of the dream, the speaker shows himself standing and gazing, then following the Arab on foot as that mysterious figure rides off on his dromedary. But only the Bedouin speaks in this encounter, explaining the meaning of the objects he is carrying in a way that is finally beyond the narrator's power to convey with any precision.

> . . . the Arab told me that the stone
> (To give it the language of the dream)

Was "Euclid's Elements"; and "This," said he,
"Is something of more worth"; and at the word
Stretched forth the shell, so beautiful in shape,
In colour so resplendent, with command
That I should hold it to my ear. I did so,
And heard that instant in an unknown tongue,
Which yet I understood, articulate sounds,
A loud prophetic blast of harmony:
An Ode, in passion uttered, which foretold
Destruction to the children of the earth
By deluge, now at hand. . . .

Wordsworth's speaker, although looking steadfastly at the stone and shell, "Nor doubted once but that they both were books." He followed after that gaunt figure until the rider began to grow agitated and glanced repeatedly over his shoulder:

And, looking backwards when he looked, mine eyes
Saw, over half the wilderness diffused,
A bed of glittering night: I asked the cause:
"It is," said he, "the waters of the deep
Gathering upon us"; quickening then the pace
Of the unwieldy creature he bestrode,
He left me: I called after him aloud;
He heeded not; but, with his twofold charge
Still in his grasp, before me, full in view
Went hurrying o'er the illimitable waste,
With the fleet waters of a drowning world
In chase of him; whereat I wakened in terror,
And saw the sea before me, and the book,
In which I had been reading, at my side.[4]

On one level this unforgettable dream expresses the longing for immortality, so prominent also in Wordsworth's Romantic successors Shelley and Keats. There seems a painful gap between the transcendent beauty of mathematics and poetry and their transmission through the decaying objects of a physical world. The stone and the shell, though objects and thus subject to the laws of physics and eventual destruction, have a potential for enduring far longer than any book—not to mention lasting so much longer than the span of a human life as to seem practically eternal. The fact that, as the Bedouin rider confides to the speaker, "he himself /

was going there to bury those two books" promises further protection against violence that might crack the stone or shatter the shell. Beneath the dry sands of the desert, even the shell might last for eons.

The real nightmare image is still to come, though, and relates to the disappearance of the physical world itself. It is like the fading of the green fire that Leopold saw in the eyes of the dying wolf. As is so often the case with images of remoteness and safety, the desert is also an emblem of impoverishment. It is a scoured landscape, "all black and void," inhabited only by the speaker, the rider, and the "unwieldy steed." It is featureless and flat, so "boundless" as to make traveling a kind of free fall, without friction, purchase, or points of reference. In this sense, the Arab's quest is a flight from the world or, putting it another way, a loss of the world. So that when "the illimitable waste" is finally overwhelmed by "the fleet waters of a drowning world," it can be seen as the culmination of his errand as well as its defeat. The flight to save the mystic stone and shell from the perils of the physical creation turns out in fact to be a headlong gallop toward destruction. Nature and the glories of the human imagination are finally inextricable; you cannot abandon the one and retain the other.

The rider's mission to bury the two "books" recalls the Parable of the Talents in chapter 25 of the Gospel according to Matthew. The master in that narrative distributes his wealth to three servants during his absence, five silver talents to one, two to another, and a single talent to the last. The first two stewards, having invested and doubled the talents they received, are richly rewarded and commended as "good and faithful" servants. "But he that had received one went and digged in the earth, and hid his lord's money." When receiving the single, unearthed talent back, the lord condemns this steward's caution. "For unto every one that hath shall be given, and he shall have abundance: but from him that hath not shall be taken away even that which he hath. And cast ye the unprofitable servant into outer darkness: there shall be weeping and gnashing of teeth."[5] This is one of the most challenging of the Parables of the Kingdom, and clearly speaks to much more than the blessedness of the stock exchange. With all its sharp edges, though, one way it can be read is as a lesson about stewardship, specifically about the need for a good steward to take risks. There is no safe place to bury our treasures when the world, the treasure to which all others refer, is itself subject to inundation.

Many readers have noted the affinities between the parables of Jesus and Zen koans, those mysterious utterances urging their listeners to go beyond "attachment" to their possessions and ideas and to transcend worldly standards of success. The publication of the Gnostic Gospels has provided an even firmer bridge between these cryptic, challenging traditions. The environmental writer and activist Peter Forbes has suggested applying the Buddhist teaching of nonattachment specifically to the conservation movement in this country. He suggests that conservation in general and the wilderness movement in particular might be seen as attempts to cling to beautiful landscapes, preserving them against the social and physical flux swirling around us on all sides. In reference to the dream of the Arab and the stone, one might view such conservation efforts as attempts to cross the desert and bury the "books." But even the biggest western wilderness area is not sufficient to maintain genetic vitality in its herds of bison or its populations of bears. Hence, The Wildlands Project's interest in developing "corridors" that would connect Quebec and the Adirondacks or link the parks along the crest of the northern Rockies, and in fostering "stewardship zones" to buffer these cores of wilderness. Neither the products of human genius nor the beautiful landscapes we so prize can be safely buried anywhere out of harm's way. But they can be *planted* in the world, setting their roots and stretching their branches as they accomplish the alchemy of water, soil, and sun. Neither the world nor we ourselves are stones that may be safely buried. The writings of Gary Snyder and the commitments of the Italian farmer Giuseppe Moretti both remind us of a fundamental truth. There can be no sustainability, either physically or spiritually, in lives separate from the larger flow.

In this regard the actual stones in the world are not symbols of permanence so much as they are temporary landmarks or bookmarks. They are reminders of an ongoing dialogue between humanity and the natural world, a lineage of landscapes that have found responsive hearts. A quieter, but also a more hopeful, poem by Wordsworth is "Michael." It is a simple "domestic tale" of the shepherd Michael, his wife Isabel, and Luke, the child of their old age. Before Luke departs to work in a distant city, and to make the money that would clear a debt lodged against their ancestral land, he and his father labor to build a circular stone sheepfold. It is intended both to offer protection for their flocks against winter storms and to mark "a covenant" of trust and connection between parents and son, family and land. But the promise of Luke's errand fails, and he never returns; nor is the stone sheepfold ever completed. Despite (or because of) the incompleteness of that circle, however, another circle can be inscribed within the poem: that of an inclusive sympathy rooted in the land. "Michael" is a poem that moves through loss and grief to a deeper sense of identification with the brokenness of the natural and human world. It offers failure as the starting point for a more inclusive sympathy that gathers the passing years and generations into a circle of wholeness.

This poem of 482 lines opens with a quiet narrative frame, describing an abandoned landscape that contains a little pile of stones. But the speaker then redirects the reader within this landscape, past what might have seemed a dead end.

> If from the public way you turn your steps
> Up the tumultuous brook of Green-head Gill,
> You will suppose that with an upright path
> Your feet must struggle; in such bold ascent
> The pastoral mountains front you, face to face.
> But, courage! for around that boisterous brook
> The mountains have all opened out themselves,
> And made a hidden valley of their own.
> No habitation can be seen; but they
> Who journey thither find themselves alone
> With a few sheep, with rocks and stones, and kites
> That overhead are sailing in the sky.
> It is in truth an utter solitude;
> Nor should I have made mention of this Dell
> But for one object which you might pass by,
> Might see and notice not. Beside the brook
> Appears a straggling heap of unhewn stones!
> And to that simple object appertains
> A story. . . .

Just as the story "appertains" to the stones, they too are part of the story and its landscape. Such a pattern of mutual enclosure corrects the impulse to retreat and burial that were found in the dream of the Arab. It indicates the organic wholeness of a world in which, though forms decay and ways of life disappear, living connections can be sustained. Life is perpetuated not through separation but through the openness that comes from being broken. At the poem's conclusion, after both Michael and Isabel have died, we read that their

> . . . cottage which was named the EVENING STAR
> Is gone—the ploughshare has been through the ground
> On which it stood; great changes have been wrought
> In all the neighborhood:—yet the oak is left
> That grew beside their door; and the remains
> Of that unfinished sheepfold may be seen
> Beside the boisterous brook of Green-head Gill.[6]

This is from one perspective a scene of defeat and abandonment. Not only has a family line failed in the land but an entire pastoral culture has also been eradicated. The plow that turned the soil where this shepherd's cottage once stood marks the introduction of large-scale commercial agriculture.[7] But the brook remains, with its sentinel oak and the "straggling heap" of stones that was to have been a sheepfold. Though relics of loss, these are also sufficient ingredients for an act of revitalizing sympathy.

Returning to the Parable of the Talents, from this brief reflection on the stones framing and framed by "Michael," reminds us that actively "investing" our resources in the world is no more proof against loss than burying them for safekeeping turned out to be. Stewardship, no less than preservation, confronts a current that will eventually (and maybe soon) sweep us all away. The only question is what to make of our brokenness—how to return our energies most creatively and effectively to the fund of life. Our ideals must be continuously reanimated in the world. It is noteworthy that soon after describing the stone the Arab calls attention to the shell, as "something of more worth." It is an object that, though wholly calcified, still seems filled with life. A shell is, looked at from a certain perspective, a hollow stone. Its lack of solidity makes it at once more breakable and more hospitable to life. When the speaker puts his ear to the stone, as directed by the Arab, he hears the rushing oceans that will soon appear in the poem. But the shell also produces, in its "unknown tongue," "articulate sounds, / A loud prophetic blast of harmony; / An ode in passion. . . ." Unlike the stone, the shell can speak; its eloquence encompasses prophecy and passion, not just the elegance of Euclid's diagrams and equations. Throughout the poetic lineage of stones, there is a similar compound process. Wanderers encounter landmarks that help them connect their spiritual and emotional experiences with the physical world. But then they turn back to the larger landscape of life. Marker stones help us take our bearings, so that we may then move on.

. . .

Although Matsuo Bashō lived and wrote over a century before Wordsworth, I come to him after and in the context of the English poet. There is no question of direct influence. Wordsworth would never have heard of the Japanese poet; the dream of the Arab and the stone is as close as he got to "Orientalism." Nevertheless, the affinities between Wordsworth and Bashō are striking and significant. Chief among these are that the two poets find in nature a repository of wisdom about the shape and meaning of a human life, and that both are also prodigious walkers. In *The Prelude*, Wordsworth walks from the Lake District to London, as well as across revolutionary France and up into the Alps. Bashō, who lived from 1644 to 1694, undertook a series of journeys on foot around Japan during the last decade of his life. These trips were eventually turned into prose narratives interspersed with haiku. Although Wordsworth's *Prelude* is both a much longer work and written in blank verse, it is often surprisingly similar in tone and impact to Bashō's masterpiece *The Narrow Road to the Interior* (*Oku no Hosomichi*). Wordworth's poem is an extensive and discursive narrative, but many passages within it (especially in Books 1, 5, 6, 12, and 14) are as distilled and reverberant as haiku.

Bashō describes one encounter with a stone that evokes the dream of the Arab; it also occurs, as did Wordsworth's passage, near the center of the whole work. Not far from the coastal city of Sendai, the poet visits an ancient stone marker. "The monument was about six feet tall and three feet wide, and the engraved letters were still visible on its surface through thick layers of moss." He transcribes the inscription that relates the stone to an earlier castle on the same site, identifies the two generals who built and remodeled that vanished edifice, and specifies that the stone itself was placed there during the reign of the emperor Shomu (701–56). Bashō's emotional response to the massive stone, which has been standing in that remote northern spot for nine centuries by the time he comes upon it, surprises and overwhelms him: "In this ever-changing world where mountains crumble, rivers change their courses, roads are deserted, rocks are buried, and old trees yield to young shoots, it was nothing short of a miracle that this monument had survived the battering of a thousand years to be the living memory of the ancients. I felt as if I were in the presence of the ancients themselves, and forgetting all the troubles I had suffered on the road, rejoiced in the utter happiness of this joyful moment, not without tears in my eyes."[8]

This at first seems an odd moment for such an outburst. The inscription on the rock is a matter-of-fact one and there's little sense on Bashō's part of either preparation for the encounter or reflection about it after the fact. The two paragraphs of description are slotted into the narrative, without any explicit transition, between an account of visiting a painter named Kaemon and a little excursion to an old temple and cemetery in a pinewood. Finally, though, despite the lack of a direct connection, Bashō's response to the stone monument of Tsubo-no-ishibumi is consistent with his central concerns throughout the narrative, namely, with his obsession with the passage of time. *The Narrow Road* begins with this famous paragraph: "Days and months are travelers of eternity. So are the years that pass by. Those who steer a boat across the sea, or drive a horse over the earth till they succumb to the weight of years, spend every minute of their lives travelling. There are a great number of ancients, too, who died on the road. I myself have been tempted for a long time by the cloud-moving wind—filled with a strong desire to wander." At first glance, his opening statement seems to give this poetic wanderer a motivation precisely opposite to that of Wordsworth's Bedouin rider: a desire to race *toward* the all-devouring wave of temporality. Thus it might at first seem even more surprising for Bashō to find the unwavering persistence of the ancient, mossy, inscribed stone so moving. But both the "cloud-moving wind" and the stone marker give him the same enhanced sense, not exactly of his own mortality, but more specifically of his aged vulnerability. On the first day of his journey, he writes, "I walked all through that day, ever wishing to return after seeing the strange sights of the far north, but not really believing in the possibility, for I knew that departing like this in the second year of Genroku [1689], I should only accumulate more frosty hairs on my head as I approached the colder regions."[9]

. . .

Bashō's is a journey into age, and his frequent and anxious references to the likelihood of inclement weather make it plain that he considers illness and death a likely outcome of this challenging itinerary. Even so, his excursion is a pilgrimage, and an escape too: a pilgrimage to places like the stone monument where earlier generations had recorded their own poetic responses, and a passage, step-by-step, into the glorious and tragic history of Japan. An escape from the anxieties of aging by turning his face directly to the circumstances he might most be expected to fear. There's also an implication in *Oku no Hosomichi* of a self-sacrificial undertaking for the general good. Indeed, despite his self-depiction as a frail figure on a punishing road, Bashō achieved both a literary and a spiritual revolution in Japanese culture. More than any of his predecessors in the practice of haiku, he combined sharply focused impressions with a sense of their ethical implications. Bashō's eye for humble phenomena in telling juxtaposition conveys a deep faith that every detail in the world, if attended to clearly enough, contains all that we need to lead a rich, happy, and giving life. The problem is that we generally *don't* notice the world around us with such vividness, and thus we get stuck in a conventional, unnourishing, and isolating mind-set.

Bashō's combination of a travel narrative and a haiku sequence in *Oku no Hosomichi* is much more artfully strategic than any generalized "worship of nature." It also involves a reaction to a specific, deplorable historical context. He, like George Perkins Marsh in his ambassadorial years, like Wordsworth, and like us, lived through an era of postwar indulgence. When affluence leads to a loss of restraint, its ecological impact can be as disastrous as that of deforestation or any other questionable practice. Marsh saw his native country during the Gilded Age as "a morass of materialist greed."[10] Similarly, Bashō's radical aesthetic of simplicity both looked back to classical expressions in Chinese and Japanese poetry and spirituality and responded to notable excesses in his own day. Centuries of conflict had preceded the establishment of Japan's Tokugawa shogunate in 1603. One result of the new stability was a great flowering of the arts, in part because so many people of samurai heritage, like Bashō, reinvented themselves as writers, calligraphers, musicians, and masters of Go. But in the culture as a whole, the traditional samurai contempt for money was replaced by a new hunger for making fortunes and for extravagant display; this was true both among the previously despised merchant class and among the hereditary daimyo, including succeeding generations of the Tokagawas themselves. The pursuit of haiku, like the practices of the tea ceremony and Shodo, or brush calligraphy, had originally grown from the simple forms, textures, pat-

terns of nature. But in Bashō's time they, like the monastic practice of
Zen Buddhism in which he was also schooled, had become the bailiwick
of wealthy connoisseurs. Rustic tea implements used by famous masters
and wealthy amateurs were, despite their rough appearance, priceless
objects, famous in their own right; low, wooden tea huts were built by
the finest craftsmen and could cost as much as a palace.

Bashō's career was dedicated to carrying haiku and the cult of nature
back out under the sky. He turned away from the refined enclosures of
the formal garden or moon-viewing pavilion, forging into increasingly
provincial districts until he finally reconnected with Japan's rural traditions. Though he wrote a century before Wordsworth, and in what
essentially remained a feudal society for most of the following two centuries, Bashō anticipated the English poet in his effort to free poetry from
the elegant artificiality of an urban elite. Wordsworth's declaration in
his 1800 preface to the *Lyrical Ballads* speaks to the motivation of both
poets:

> The principal object, then, proposed in these poems was to choose incidents
> and situations from common life, and to relate or describe them, through-
> out, as far as was possible in a selection of language really used by men, and,
> at the same time, to throw over them a curtain colouring of imagination,
> whereby ordinary things should be presented to the mind in an unusual as-
> pect; and, further, and above all, to make these incidents and situations in-
> teresting by tracing in them, truly though not ostentatiously, the primary
> laws of our nature: chiefly, as far as regards the manner in which we associ-
> ate ideas in a sense of excitement. Humble and native life was generally cho-
> sen, because, in that condition, the essential passions of the heart find a bet-
> ter soil in which they can attain their maturity, are less under restraint, and
> speak a plainer and more emphatic language; because in that condition of
> life our elementary feelings co-exist in a sense of greater simplicity, and,
> consequently, may be more accurately contemplated, and more forcibly
> communicated; because the manners of moral life germinate from those el-
> ementary feelings, and from the necessary character of rural occupations,
> are more easily comprehended, and are more durable; and, lastly, because in
> that condition the passions of men are incorporated with the beautiful and
> permanent forms of nature.[11]

"Common," "primary," "humble," "native," "essential," "plainer," "ele-
mentary," "necessary," "rural," "durable," and "permanent" define the
quality of experience Wordsworth and Bashō seek. By stripping away the

false elaboration of fashion and wealth, both poets find that passions and the unifying charge of imagination are magnified.[12]

A number of Bashō's haiku celebrate meetings with country people and reflect the "more emphatic language" of those in "rural occupations." In the town of Sukagawa he composes a poem based on some women he saw in the fields as he crossed the Shirakawa Barrier into northern Japan: "The beginning of art— / a rice-planting song / in the backcountry."[13] But the chief value of "humble and rustic life" for Bashō is not so much the beauty of its setting as the degree to which it is "durable," incorporated as it is with "the beautiful and permanent forms of nature."

The core of Bashō's poetic vision on this final haiku journey is close to the integrated vision of loss and endurance that encloses Wordsworth's "Michael." Ruins, relics, vestiges of battle and defeat, all serve to represent both transience and endurance for Bashō. After his visit to Zuiganji Temple, the poet sets off for Hiraizumi and a landscape marked by the ruins of old mansions and the sites of celebrated wars.

Here three generations of the Fujiwara clan passed as though in a dream. The great outer gates lay in ruins. Where Hidehira's manor stood, rice fields grew. Only Mount Kinkei remained. I climbed the hill where Yoshitsune died; I saw the Kitakami, a broad stream flowing down through the Nambu Plain, the Koromo River circling Izumi Castle below the hill before joining the Kitakami. The ancient ruins of Yasuhira—from the end of the Golden Era—lie out beyond the Koromo Barrier, where they stood guard against the Ainu people. The faithful elite remained bound to the castle—for all their valor, reduced to ordinary grass. Tu Fu wrote:

> The whole country devastated
> Only mountains and rivers remain.
> In springtime, at the ruined castle,
> The grass is always green.

We sat a while, our hats for a seat, seeing it all through tears.

> Summer grasses:
> all that remains of great soldiers'
> imperial dreams.[14]

The grass growing on the ruin is in one sense the final defeat for those ancient warriors—displacing their mortal grandeur and effacing the signs of their regime. It is, as the poet says later in the passage, "the all-devouring grass." But it is also an affirmation something stronger than military prowess: the annual return of greenness to the world over five hundred summers. Bashō's quiet allusion to the classical Chinese poet Tu Fu reinforces this sense that nature is at once the source and the final repository of human glory. A contemporary Chinese poet has bitterly rewritten Tu Fu for our own day when unprecedented prosperity and industrialization pollute the skies of China, poison the soil, and drown the revered landscapes of the Three Gorges: "Though the mountains and rivers perish / the capital remains."[15] Even had the Arab managed to bury the stone and the shell, those two "books" of human glory, it would have availed nothing in the face of a drowning world. Nature is the gauge by which our own transience may be registered and understood. Our own transformations through nature's seasons and cycles may allow us to identify with and participate in a process larger than our little lives; larger too than our institutions and our history.

"All that remains" reverberates with the final, ambiguous line of Robert Frost's poem "The Most of It": "And that was all." Frost's speaker in that poem, intent on eliciting from nature some "counter-voice, original response," instead "only" saw a buck swim across a mountain lake and clamber onto the shore "pouring like a waterfall." It fell short of whatever startling or supernatural revelation he thought he wanted. But by the same token, as a manifestation of nature's vitality and autonomy, it was all he could have longed for, and more.[16] So, too, the grass bending under a summer's breeze was a monument to those vanished warriors both more lasting and more beautiful than the ancient stone parapets near which it grew. Soldiers advanced into the splendor of the grass, each blade of which was more arresting for Bashō than the tall battle pennons that once flapped above those hills.

An echo of this transformation of historical grandeur by nature's homely persistence comes to Bashō some days later, when he visits a shrine in Kanazawa. Having inspected the ornate battle helmet of Lord Sanemori, one of the samurai leaders who fell in the storied battles between the Minamoto and the Taira, he writes the following haiku: "Pitifully—under / a great soldier's empty helmet, / a cricket sings."[17] The juxtaposition of helmet and cricket might seem at first to mock the proud old warrior who wore that helmet in his final battle. But the insect's song also both reanimates the helmet and amplifies the natural sound within its echo chamber. Like the shell in Wordsworth's Book 5, it is a hollowed-out relic, bereft of the former life that filled it. But its emptiness lifts up the passing wind into "articulate sounds / A loud prophetic blast of harmony." An abandoned helmet, like a shell, is the record of a life subsiding into the realm of sand and stones. A haiku, too, is a kind of shell—a scouring away of life into the austere balance of a constellation. The sadness of Bashō's poetry comes from the way in which each new experience of meaning in the natural world feels like both a greeting and a good-bye. We give up our own campaigns for dominance, even our strategies for endurance, not because we surrender to a *permanent* natural order, but rather because we find in the world a sensual rhythm of arrival and departure, to which we belong and to which we can assent. The "beautiful and permanent forms" of nature are not stone landscapes that escape decay. They are swirls in the water through which new water flows until those swirls dissipate and similar ones, animated by other water, appear. The broken sheepfold and the empty helmet are opportunities for compassionate identification with vanished lives.

. . .

George Perkins Marsh was the first modern conservation writer to demonstrate that the fabric of our living planet, too, is impermanent. He showed that human heedlessness can disrupt the stability of natural processes—diminishing the fertility of the soil, the abundance of the water, and the temperateness of the weather, and ushering all to an untimely end. Marsh observed that when vegetation was stripped from the surface of the earth it became "less able to protect itself by weaving a new network of roots to bind its particles together, a new carpeting of turf to shield it from wind and sun and scouring rain. Gradually it becomes altogether barren . . . and thus the earth is rendered no longer fit for the inhabitation of man."[18] In *Man and Nature*, he argued that such destructiveness is both inimical to human survival and unworthy of the "higher" character of the human spirit. The recognition of nature's vulnerability, to which his writing contributed so significantly, has marked a watershed in our perceptions of human rootedness in nature. In our present era of global climate change, anticipated so strikingly in Marsh's writing, even the grasses and the insects are endangered as the weather shifts faster than the evolutionary adaptability of our established ecosystems.

We live in an era akin in certain ways to Wordsworth's dream of the stone and the shell. In a "black and void" desert, with no crickets and no grass, we can still listen to the shell. But to one in flight from temporality, it will always foretell "Destruction to the children of the earth / by deluge, now at hand." Riding through the desert, attempting to make our individual escape from a history of desecration, we will find no future but a flood. The alternative is to stop and make a stand amid the waste of our own destructiveness. In a sense, Marsh and the environmental writers who have succeeded him have taught us to see our modern era as a desert—or, in Aldo Leopold's words, a "Sand County." What has been lost is also what we may now begin to see. We can finally recognize that natural systems, like the familial line and pastoral community of "Michael," may be reduced through greed and carelessness to the disarray of "a straggling heap of stones." The environmental stewardship to which we are called is a matter of cultivating both gratitude and compassion for this shattered landscape where we read the consequences of our own oblivion. We pledge ourselves to love the world, in a covenant of loss.

Wordsworth and Bashō view nature as both a gauge against which human transience may be registered and the field of change, decay, and new growth in which our lives find their wholeness. Those two poets from such different cultural contexts adopted strikingly parallel strategies of venturing out into the countryside, where simple scenes of natural beauty, rustic people, and old stories could enrich their lives far more than the sophistication and artifice of the capitals. Leslie Marmon Silko, from yet a third, highly distinctive tradition, is another author who takes stones as the landmarks of her explorations of meaning and continuity in the land. Raised on the Laguna Pueblo of northern New Mexico, Silko is best known for her fiction, especially for the novel *Ceremony*. But I have always been especially grateful for an essay she published in 1986, called "Landscape, History, and the Pueblo Imagination," in which she describes her people's interpretation of their local landscape as a "story-map." This essay is an incisive response from the Native American tradition to the western wilderness movement. Silko stresses that when indigenous people look at the sublime western landscape, they see *stories;* "wilderness" is, from her point of view, a newcomers' word for terrain that is to them still blank. Such an orientation to stories may be especially helpful now, as we attempt to bring the monolithic claims of the wilderness movement into a conversation in which the voices of history and stewardship may also be heard. Native American stories in the land emphasize human transience and vulnerability in a way that is compatible with the insights of Wordsworth and Bashō. It is opposed to that Western sense of imperial entitlement to which the wilderness movement is also, in its own way, a rebuke. In this sense, the two poets, the Native American stories, and the wilderness ethic may be seen as balanced constellations—bright stones cast together in the sky, admonishing us against falsely elevating our sense of human prerogatives in this world.

Silko explains that the Pueblo people developed a sense of history closely accommodated to the details of their landscape and perpetuated through a constantly expanded and refined oral narrative. "Whatever the event or the subject, the ancient people perceived the world and themselves within that world as part of an ancient continuous story composed of innumerable bundles of other stories."[19] The section of her essay in which she makes this statement is called "Through the Stories We Hear Who We Are." At its center are two particular stories which she tells and reflects on, and which suggest a couple of important but also quite distinct levels on which such grounding narratives work. The first story bears on figures from the Pueblo creation myths, while the second is an event in the living memory of her own family. Yet there is an interesting similarity in the ways these two contrasting narratives begin. One starts like this: "There is a giant sandstone boulder about a mile north of old Laguna, on the road of Paguate." The other like this: "A high dark mesa rises dramatically from a grassy plain fifteen miles southeast of Laguna, in an area known as Swanee."[20] Neither of these narratives, though the first will look back through the mists of creation and the other takes place 140 years ago, begins with any equivalent of "Once upon a time." Rather, because of their specific topographic references, they are resolutely framed in the present moment. Thus, though the events they describe may be old, they are not remote. Both narrative frames not only refer to a particular landform but in fact give the exact mileage from Laguna. Any reader of the essay could find the boulder and the mesa by traveling in one direction for a mile or in the other for fifteen miles. One can to this day go and stand before these objects—as before the illustrations in a book—as a way of entering into the stories.

The boulder is a reminder of the time Kochininako, Yellow Woman, was chased by the monster Estrucuyo, who nearly caught and ate her before the Twin Hero Brothers came to the rescue. "After killing the Estrucuyo with their bows and arrows, the Twin Hero Brothers slit open the Estrucuyo and cut out its heart. They threw the heart as far as they could. The monster's heart landed there, beside the old trail to Paguate Village, where the sandstone boulder rests now."[21] It's fitting that this mystic story should circle back to the boulder in the present moment, just where it began. I'm reminded of Wordsworth's narrative framework in "Michael." He too begins in the present, ushering the reader up into a hidden valley and pointing out a "straggling heap" of stones, the significance of which one might easily overlook except for his statement "And to that simple object appertains / A story." Similarly to Silko, Wordsworth concludes his past-tense narrative by returning to the present landscape of his poem's frame, where "the remains / Of that unfinished sheep-fold may be seen / Beside the boisterous brook of Green-head Gill."

Silko makes a subtle distinction at the conclusion of her first story, one that applies equally to the giant sandstone boulder and to the tumbled remains of Michael's efforts. "It may be argued that the existence of the boulder precipitated the creation of a story to explain it. But sandstone boulders and sandstone formations of strange shapes abound in the Laguna Pueblo area. Yet most of them do not have stories. Often the crucial element in a narrative is the terrain—some specific detail of the setting."[22] Though for her, as for Wordsworth, stories are mapped and illustrated by "some specific detail of the setting," such associations are neither universal in the land nor arbitrary. A "story-map" is not a random fantasy but a deep affinity, a lived truth essential to the intimate relationship between the human community and the land. From such a perspective, a story is less an act of individual creativity than an experience devised by "the beautiful and permanent forms" of nature and guarded in memory across the generations. While enhancing each person's sense of the landscape, such a "bundle" of stories also has the experimental and pragmatic quality of what scientists might call a longitudinal study.

The second of Silko's stories concerns a September afternoon when "my great-grandmother's uncle and his brother-in-law" were slain by Apache raiders, who ambushed them and took their sheep. The Pueblo herdsmen were not alert enough, on this occasion, to the way the mesa at Swanee blocked their views across the plains as they came closer to it. "Using the mesa to obscure their approach, the raiders swept around from both ends of the mesa. My great-grandmother's relatives were killed and the herd lost." The main point of this story, as Silko tells it, is not one of enmity or vengeance, despite the two murders. Rather, by insisting on such a central role for a landform that her audience might see for themselves today, Silko places her own emphasis on the importance of sensitivity to the landscape, and on the absolute dependence of her people's culture on such awareness:

> Survival in any landscape comes down to making the best use of all available resources. On that particular September afternoon, the raiders made better use of the Swanee terrain than my poor ancestors did. Thus, the high dark mesa and the story of the two lost Laguna herders became inextricably linked. The memory of them and their story resides in part with the high dark mesa. For as long as the mesa stands, people within the family and the clan will be reminded of the story of that afternoon long ago. Thus the continuity and accuracy of the oral narratives are reinforced by the landscape—and the Pueblo interpretation of that landscape is *maintained*.[23]

By returning over and over to the boulders and mesas of her home landscape, Silko finds, as Bashō and Wordsworth did, that cultural and imaginative values, too, become more "durable."

While Silko's story of the Estrucuyo grounds the Pueblo creation story in the local terrain and perpetuates the vividness and coherence of their spiritual vision, the story of the mesa raid also emphasizes the qualities of mindfulness that will help their community survive into the future. Two phrases from the latter account refine our sense of these dynamics. "For as long as the mesa stands" is one of them. The life of a geological formation like this one is so much longer than the life span of either a person or a community as to make it seem eternal. But Silko's language insists that it too has had a beginning and will have an end. The light and dark strata of its flanks speak to its origination through sedimentation and uplift, while the deep runnels down those stone surfaces record the process of erosion that also constantly reworks this giant sandstone boulder. The sciences of geology and paleontology aren't necessary to confirm the life and death of desert stones. The gravel sifted through arroyos and the sand drifting up against the mesa's skirts tell the same story. A dynamic landscape accommodates and sustains a dynamic culture. Silko's phrase "the Pueblo interpretation of that landscape" in effect defines the core of such a culture. Interpretation is an act of integrating data into a pattern. It is a constantly reiterated process of gathering together the stones with which significant experiences have been associated—not gathering them into some new place on earth, but rather gathering them into the mind, in the renewing coalescence of a walk through the landscape of home. Passing through storied terrain like this, we follow what Aboriginal Australians know as the "song lines." Such stories are reexperienced throughout a lifetime. Their deepening harmony has its nearest equivalent, for me, in the northern New England landscape where my family and I are rooted—in the colors that suffuse our mountains every fall, the peepers whose ludicrous, magnificent choruses rise up from the wet margins of roads and meadows every spring.

Images such as these speak to both the psychological wholeness of an individual's life and the vitality of a land-based culture. But the austere character of Silko's arid landscape also raises the question of physical survival. At one point in her essay, she describes how a deer-hunting story, for instance, may also become a "map" because of the care with which it described "key landmarks and locations of fresh water." "Lost travelers, and lost piñon-nut gatherers, have been saved by sighting a rock formation they recognize only because they once heard a hunting story describing such a rock formation." Stories thus become essential to the kind of mindfulness required by a world of extreme temperatures and scarce resources. Just as the Pueblo stories about the Estrucuyo and the Apache raiders root the exercise of memory and alertness in episodes of danger and loss, the people's hope for sustaining their community is similarly framed and enhanced by what might seem their challenging environment. Within such a cultural landscape, the shadowed beauty of the name Vallombrosa retains its pertinence to a tragic vision of stewardship. Marsh's insights emerged from his ability to read a smaller story of carelessness as part of a much bigger chronicle of loss. As he wrote at the end of *Man and Nature*, "[I]n the vocabulary of nature, little and great are terms of comparison only; she knows no trifles, and her laws are as inflexible in dealing with an atom as with a continent or a planet."[24] To follow the consequences of our daily practices was equivalent for Marsh to observing the constellations of Orion and Scorpio facing each other across the Aegean sky. Only if chastened by the shadows of our human destructiveness might we gain the imagination and commitment to protect our forests. Only with reference to all that has been lost may we achieve a firm hope for social sustainability and for the dignified relationship with the natural world that Peter Forbes identifies with the term "forbearance."

In our own day, the dangers and losses are even more disturbing and widespread than in Marsh's. In addition to clear-cutting our forests and eroding our soils, we have gone far toward scraping bare the living bed of the sea, and toward disrupting the climatic patterns with which life on earth is so closely coordinated. But this dark moment, too, offers the possibility for an increase of maturity and forbearance in our human sense of purpose. Specifically, our shadowed context may promote a true dialogue between the wilderness and stewardship traditions in American conservation thought. So often, the "preservation"-"conservation" split has prevented us from achieving an integrated vision in which culture and landscape are regarded as at once whole and inextricable. The problem with stewardship has been too arrogant a sense of its own prerogatives, too complacent an assumption that technological fixes will solve our current imbalances, and too abstract, limited, and economic an understanding of "cultural resources." The wilderness ethic has been a vital corrective to such utilitarianism, but without always adopting a sufficiently complex historical perspective. Human land use, indigenous and settlement history alike, has done much to shape the landscape. In our own day, as the skies above the vastest wilderness areas are streaked with vapor trails and rattled by sonic booms, the interwoven reality of human and natural systems has become clearer than ever. In such an era, both stewardship and wilderness become chastened values. This is a time to acknowledge the faults and partial vision not only of these conservation values but also of the broader political, religious, and educational institutions from which they draw their energy. The adolescent assumption of unlimited opportunities will no longer work for a nation as large and prosperous as ours. Through increased awareness of our own errors and vulnerability, we may gain an enhanced sense of our responsibility. We may also discover an opportunity for participation in a more comprehensive community of life.

Silko connects the barrenness of her people's desert landscape with the sense of reverence and community that have made her culture a sustainable part of it:

> The bare vastness of the Hopi Landscape emphasizes the visual impact of every plant, every rock, every arroyo. Nothing is overlooked or taken for granted. Each ant, each lizard, each lark is imbued with great value simply because the creature is there, seemingly because the creature is alive in a place where any life at all is precious. Stand on the mesa edge at Walpai and

look west over the bare distances toward the pale blue outlines of the San Francisco peaks where the ka'tsina spirits reside. So little lies between you and the sky. So little lies between you and the earth. One look and you know that simply to survive is a great triumph, that every possible resource is needed, every possible ally—even the most humble insect or reptile. You realize you will be speaking with all of them if you intend to last out the year. Thus it is that the Hopi elders are grateful to the landscape for aiding them in their quest as spiritual people.[25]

Our era is as challenging, its landmarks as stark and eroded, as the bare distances surrounding Walpai. But the ecological losses in our time, and the dangers of further devastation, also hold out the possibility for a closer and more mindful relationship with the earth. Marsh's contribution was telling the human story in a way that attributed to us both a greater power for destruction than had been recognized and an enhanced possibility for stewardship. *Man and Nature* too is thus a stone witness, one that helps us to remember the consequences of our errors. These losses, like the starkness of Wordsworth's and Silko's deserts, imbue everything that remains with great value; they bring the humble details of nature into focus. A prophetic lineage of stones can map a pilgrimage to wholeness and renewal. It can initiate a new capacity for hopeful action within a landscape of chastened memory.

9
MOWING

Following the footsteps of George Perkins Marsh into the landscape and culture of Europe places the conservation movement in an enriched historical and cultural context. Such an enhancement allows us to understand stewardship not as a rejection of our tradition but rather as a way of interpreting, activating, perpetuating, and reforming it. The attainment of practical mindfulness requires both perceptiveness and discipline. As Aldo Leopold writes in *For the Health of the Land,* "Conservation . . . is a positive exercise of skill and insight, not merely a negative exercise of abstinence or caution."[1] It is a schooled manner of living, pursued under the instruction of scientists, poets, and saints and informed by the practical wisdom surviving in our own rural lifeways. If conservation were, instead of such a distillation, nothing but a cry of protest within the wash and hype of contemporary politics, the outlook for environmental reform would be far bleaker than I believe it to be. Marsh's journey should not suggest that the destiny of American environmentalists is to adopt a more European perspective, however, any more than the present book would suggest that Vermonters go to Italy and, as he did, stay there. His insights germinated in Vermont, were cultivated in Europe, and are now dispersed throughout the world. But nowhere have they taken firmer root than in America. Despite recent and deplorable retreats at the level of governmental policy, our country remains a leader of conservation in general, and of national parks and wilderness preservation in particular. My goal in writing *Pilgrimage to Vallombrosa* has been to circle outward, the better to return.

I have also found *Man and Nature* to be highly compatible with current stewardship initiatives in Marsh's native Vermont. This last connection has made my reflection on his life and thought, as well as my journeys through his landscapes, much more than an intellectual project. Marsh's insights directly inspire our family's participation in Vermont's sustainable-forestry movement, as we work on tending our land and pursue a dialogue with other landowners in our area. Central to my sense of vocation as a teacher of literature has always been the experience that certain books can both enliven our sense of community and shape our fidelity to home. Marsh helps me find a whole-landscape vision of Vermont through relating our state's environmental history of woundedness and recovery to our daily, practical choices and by illuminating the assumptions underlying them. I have been similarly helped by the writing of Robert Frost. Frost's life (from 1874 to 1963) bridged the gap between Marsh's writing and the Vermont where our family has settled. More important, his poetry conveys a special acuteness about the history and feel of postagricultural northern New England. Frost registers both the losses and the persistence within such an era, and the fact that human labor continues to be a significant part of the shifting ecology. To live in a landscape where a great poet worked is always a special gift for one trying to cultivate a deepened sense of place. When such a writer focuses as often as Frost does on natural history and is also versed in the practical aspects of agriculture, the significance of one's terrain is enhanced in a special way. Just as I have followed Marsh along the route of his Italian pilgrimage, I have tried to pay special attention, here at home, to Frost's human figures in the landscape.

Frost provides a crucial hinge between the Romantic legacy and our family's Green Mountain landscape. Like Wordsworth, he acknowledges the ways in which social and personal failures may be openings to a closer sense of affiliation with nature. With all the attention paid by recent critics to the destructive energies in Frost's poetry, several other aspects of the work are in danger of being overlooked. One of these is his continuity with Wordsworth's quest for spiritual meaning in nature. While Frost is much less likely than Wordsworth to see Providence at work in the abandoned farmland and third-growth woods of Vermont, he never stops exploring the possibility for sustaining values, even if they must be defined through absences. But one way in which Frost's experience of the landscape is much more robust than his English predecessor's is that he also writes as a farmer. Wordsworth watches the Solitary Reaper from afar. "Alone she cuts and binds the grain, / And sings a melancholy strain. . . ." But as he listens, "motionless and still," to the melody of her song, the meaning of its Gaelic verses elude him: "Will no one tell me what she sings?"[2] Rather than observing from a distant hillside, Frost enters the field with his own scythe. The refrain which this implement whispers in its back-and-forth over the stubble, while always mysterious, is a sound with which he is intimately familiar. Frost's poetry holds a place for physical labor in a brushy landscape of recovering forests. In discussing Frost as well as in "Ottauquechee," the third and final section of this book, I explore stewardship as a model for direct, multigenerational participation in the larger balance of nature, and within the narrative of culture. We pursue such efforts in Vermont under the aegis of a great poet who brought home and localized both the topography of literature and the mountains of home.

. . .

"Go to grass. You have eaten hay long enough. The spring has come with its green crop."[3] So Thoreau exhorts us in "Walking." Both our institutions and we ourselves always require the refreshment of nature's present moment. Revelation subsides into theology and insight ossifies into a curriculum as surely as the newly gathered grass turns into hay. High time, once more, to walk back out into the mysterious, unmown field.

Over the past decade, many teachers and scholars have been trying to reconnect the study of literature with the living earth. As with the environmental movement as a whole, however, the terminology associated with such an effort is continuously being reformulated. The evolution of this field of study may be tracked by looking at certain terms that have dominated the conversation at different stages. The term "nature writing" arose to describe a lineage running from Gilbert White and Thoreau up through contemporary authors like Edward Abbey, Barry Lopez, and Terry Tempest Williams. By calling attention to the deeply rooted history as well as to the continuing power of the genre, this term has helped literary studies go beyond the conventional categories of poetry, fiction, and drama. It has celebrated a rich American tradition of reflective nonfiction, grounded in appreciation of the natural world yet also open to creation's spiritual significance. The example of nature writing has also established a firmer connection between literature and the natural sciences, bridging the "two cultures" and fostering the development of interdisciplinary environmental studies programs in our colleges.

Nature writing continues to flourish, both as a form of writing and as a rewarding field of study. This is not as comprehensive a genre as the name itself might suggest, though. It refers to just one variety of the personal essay rather than to the whole range of imaginative writing about the earth. In addition, for reasons suggested by the social history in Lawrence Buell's book *The Environmental Imagination*, it is a form that has been practiced largely by white writers. By using the more inclusive term "environmental literature," a number of scholars have sought to broaden the conversation. This has allowed for connections between Thoreauvian nature writing and treatments of nature in other genres. In addition, it has called attention to many authors of color—including Zora Neale Hurston, Langston Hughes, Rudolfo Anaya, and Leslie Marmon Silko—who powerfully depict and reflect on nature in their novels and poems.

Another reward of this greater inclusiveness has been a fresh look at canonical literature in English. Increasingly, critics are investigating the place of landscape and natural history for such mainstays of English literature as Shakespeare, Milton, Wordsworth, Tennyson, and Woolf, as well as in the work of Americans like Melville, Whitman, Dickinson, and Fitzgerald. The term "ecocriticism" has recently been adopted by some of these scholars, in preference to "environmental literature." It avoids any implication that "environmentalism," in the current American sense, was a concern for writers before the twentieth century. It also initiates a dialogue between literature and the science of ecology that offers critics a fresh perspective on such topics as metaphor and narrative form.

The progression in our language, as outlined above, reflects both the ambition and the healthy self-criticism of this burgeoning scholarly field. It does leave out something crucial, though: the role of natural experience in the study of literature. Such experience has not itself been lacking. Many of us who teach nature writing delight in outings with our classes in order to ground our discussions in observations like those the writers themselves made. We have arrived at a point, however, where we need to begin integrating this experiential dimension of teaching and scholarship in a more strategic way. The increasing refinement of our critical terminology can be complemented now by an equally deliberate pedagogy. It may well be that the study of poetry, as the most distilled form of literature, will provide the best context for this next stage of development.

An emphasis on experience may protect against one danger in ecocriticism's emergence as a form of literary theory. Contemporary theory has certainly proved to be a valuable source of insight into literature.[4] But it can sometimes suffer from jargon, self-referentiality, and a narrow professionalism that are the opposite of nature writing's original, liberating impulse. This is why scholars and teachers must now undertake a determined, unceasing effort to ground criticism and teaching alike in the natural experience from which so much of the world's great literature has emerged. Authors like Thoreau or Mary Oliver can inspire us to ventilate and invigorate the merely academic world. Carrying our reading, reflection, teaching, and writing out under the sky can remind us that this scholarly adventure is not about competing with other academic specialties and critical schools. I found that walking across Europe with Rita, then hiking around the forest of Vallombrosa together, brought Marsh's references alive and helped me hear the urgency of his voice. In the same way, relating literature to the specific landscapes of its composition can assist us in the project of renewing literary education and enhancing the vitality of our culture. Just as the experience of rereading *Man and Nature* in Tuscany sent me back in thought to sites like Conques, harvesting olives with Janet and Stefano reminded me how exposure to mowing grass with a scythe can illuminate both the poetry of Robert Frost and the environmental history of Vermont.

. . .

We gather just after sunrise on a morning in July, beside a dewy field of timothy in Craftsbury, Vermont. This introduction to hand mowing is the opening session of Sterling College's Robert Frost Day. It has been organized by Sterling faculty member Ross Morgan in order to offer participants a personal experience of this traditional mode of labor that figures in several of Frost's poems. Our instructors are Roger Shattuck, a noted literary scholar and critic from Lincoln, Vermont, and his son Marc, a welder from Richmond, Vermont, who is a champion mower in annual contests around the state. Roger became interested in hand mowing over thirty years ago when he was looking for a way to keep down the tall grass around his family's cabin. He bought a scythe and became acquainted with the local community that preserved and passed along the art of using such a tool. He also discovered that he had both an aptitude and an appetite for this rhythmic, physically rigorous, and surprisingly effective way of shearing off ripe stems of grass and grains.

The Shattucks demonstrate to our group how to cut a swath. Plant your feet so that you are facing directly toward the row to be mown, then advance in a slow shuffle. The blade passes through an arc that leaves a cleanly mown edge a foot or more to your right and gathers each stroke's sheared grass into a windrow about the same distance to your left. Skilled scythers achieve a surface as close and smooth as any push mower or power mower could achieve. And while mechanical mowers do their best work when the grass is totally dry, it has always been the practice of hand mowers to go out after a rain or, as we are doing now, just after dawn when there is a heavy dew. The wet stalks are heavier and less likely to bend before the scythe's sweep. Our teachers pronounce three watchwords as the rest of us pick up our scythes and try to imitate what we have just observed: "polish," "slice," and "pivot."

Both the point and the heel of the blade are always held in contact with the ground, with no tilt and no lift for a backswing. This continuous motion burnishes the blade's bottom surface and sends a vibration up through your arms as you move forward. The grass is sliced, not chopped, with the blade sliding through the stems at an angle, from point to heel, rather than meeting them squarely edge on. Then it rustles back over the stubble at exactly the same height in preparation for the next slice. This dialogue with the grass makes a rhythmic, sibilant sound that is one of the distinct pleasures of hand mowing.

"Pivot" refers to another sensuous attraction of such work. The power comes not from the movement of your arms but from twisting back and forth at the waist. Turning your torso smoothly left and right, you shuffle forward with knees springy and slightly bent, leaving two dark, shiny tracks in the shorn grass between windrows. This is the whole dance, with the work always out in front, the harvest collecting to your left, and the scythe's whisper music pulling you farther and farther into the mystery of the grass. After we have been practicing for a while, a few of us line up side by side, though slightly staggered to give safe clearance to our blades. We advance together like Vermont contra dancers, leveling a smooth floor in the field. Such coordinated progress is reminiscent of

Tuscan olive pickers, stripping the fruit from tree after laden tree in a rhythm that collects the produce of yet another season.

In the discussion that followed our morning mowing, several of Frost's poems were considered, including "The Tuft of Flowers." But the poem that was most enriched for me by the experience of handling a scythe in the dewy grass was "Mowing," from his 1913 volume *A Boy's Will.*

> There was never a sound in the wood but one,
> And that was my long scythe whispering to the ground.
> What was it it whispered? I knew not well myself;
> Perhaps it was something about the heat of the sun,
> Something, perhaps, about the lack of sound—
> And that was why it whispered and did not speak.
> It was no dream of the gift of idle hours,
> Or easy gold at the hand of fay or elf:
> Anything more than the truth would have seemed too weak
> To the earnest love that laid the swale in rows,
> Not without feeble-pointed spikes of flowers
> (Pale orchises) and scared a bright green snake.
> The fact is the sweetest dream that labor knows.
> My long scythe whispered and left the hay to make.[5]

Though I had long loved this poem, the experience of mowing the hayfield in Craftsbury helped me to enter into it and appreciate it in a new way. As we learned to keep the blades of our scythes down, we advanced from the percussiveness of swinging and chopping to a continuous, beautiful rustling. That subtle sound was in fact the surest guide to effective technique. The words "whispering" and "whispered," which Frost employs in the second, third, sixth, and fourteenth lines of his sonnet, are arguably the most important in the poem. Most readers surely feel their mystery, their suggestion of meanings just out of earshot that the poet, with his chosen stance of "enigmatic reserve," will never make wholly plain. But the experience of working with a scythe helped me to relate that mystery to the subtle pulse of a keen blade sliding along the ground.

In the 1987 *Voices and Visions* documentary on Frost, Seamus Heaney expresses his admiration for the whispering scythe of "Mowing": "It's not the writing-school proficiency of mimicking the movement of a mower by the line breaks. It's the deeper rhythm of labor . . . , the slightly lulling, consoling rhythm of a repeated motion." "What was it it whispered?" evokes with a special precision the mower's experience of pivot and reverse, with its shift of syntax and direction between the word "it" and its reiteration. Heaney singles out this question in Frost's third line for special appreciation, commenting, "It's colloquial. It does have the spring of spoken English about it."[6] Heaney's connection here between the rhythm of mowing and the spring of language reflects the fact that he, like Frost, is a poet who knows the countryside through physical labor as well as through language. But his eloquent formulation penetrates even more deeply as I begin to bring my own physical experience to bear—remembering mowing in the glow of my back and arms, and in the throbbing pulse that echoed an hour spent wading through those subtle waves of sound.

The notable emphasis on sound in this poem is of course set up by the first line: "There was never a sound beside the wood but one." This line also highlights the solitary state of the mower. When Frost was farming in the early years of the twentieth century, haying in the main fields would already have been carried out by a cutting machine pulled behind a team of horses. By the 1920s and 1930s, such a cutter would more frequently have been pulled behind a tractor. Wet ground, low ground, uneven ground, and little strips of meadow between the woods and a road would have been relegated to an individual worker with a scythe. Working away from the clash of machinery and the roar of motors allows the solitary speaker of "Mowing" to *hear* the whispering and to reflect on the significance of this dialogue between scythe and ground. Such an experience is rare for most of Frost's readers today. Our own work out of doors often involves the noise of engines, and our experience of solitude in nature is, conversely, more often associated with recreation than with work.

The urgent physicality of labor powered by muscles, not gasoline, is implied in the fourth line, "Perhaps it was something about the heat of the sun." The day is already far enough advanced for the sun to be warming the scene. In part, though, this remark about the heat may be a token of the muscular effort associated with the speaker's "long scythe whispering to the ground," as he bends over, holding the handle away from his body and pivoting back and forth from the waist. It is also a reminder that the haying must be done before the grass is too dry to shear off cleanly, and so that the windrows will still be able to bake in the sun when the mower leaves "the hay to make."

After that morning in Craftsbury, I was incautious enough to mention to one Frost scholar that the experience of mowing opened up new dimensions of the poem for me. His rejoinder was, "The scythe in that poem means one thing and one thing only." And of course it is true that Frost is always alert to shadows of mortality. Whenever I hear the phrase "Et in Arcadia ego"—death's warning not to be lulled into a carefree state by the beauty of a pastoral landscape—it is always in that poet's dry Yankee accents. But the facts remain that a scythe is a tool as well as a symbol, that it was used by the poet himself in hand mowing, and that its sound and technique inform both the music and the emotional tone of the poem.

There is a tricky balance to observe here. In that same *Voices and Visions* documentary about Frost, William Pritchard calls attention to the period that decisively separates the sonnet's last two lines: "The fact is the sweetest dream that labor knows. / My long scythe whispered and left the hay to make." The poem transcends the experience of labor, as Pritchard insists: "The scythe is just going on, just making its sound, finishing its task. . . . It's really the poet who makes poetry. Not nature, not scythes." My purpose in the present reading is certainly not to reduce the poetry to its germinating instance. Rather, it is to suggest the value of cultivating, in our own physical experience, an appreciation of the soil from which the art has sprung. William Meredith, who is also interviewed in the documentary, refers to Frost's characterization of poetry as "the transition from delight to wisdom."[7] This is a helpful way of formulating a never resolved yet intimate relationship between a finished poem, with its tempered complexity, and the surges of impulse and experience that inspired it and that are perpetuated within it.

Frost's line "The fact is the sweetest dream that labor knows," with its Shakespearean resonance, sums up the importance placed on work itself in "Mowing." Neither the lure of idle hours nor a fantasy of fairies would be satisfying to "the earnest love that laid the swale in rows." Frost understands the erotics of work—exertion passing forward to culmination. Satisfaction lies—and lays—in finishing the job at hand, not escaping it into a pastoral illusion. Any reading of Frost's poetry that reduces the physicality of the landscape or the labor of farmers to nothing more than intellectual argument or abstract music is itself a fantasy in this sense—an escape from the textured solidity of fact. Both work and na-

ture are more than tropes for this poet. They are the world, in which poetry is grounded and by which it is inspired. Through the music and
mystery of poetry we are enabled to reenter nature with renewed senses
and with a heightened capacity for wonder.

Once the experience of hand mowing enhanced the sonnet's meaning
by placing me in the wet field at dawn, I found that the specific ecology of
that New England scene also emerged with comparable concreteness.
Frost is one of the most gifted and precise naturalists among our poets in
English. Over the past thirty-three years of living and teaching in Vermont, I have come increasingly to rely on him as a guide to our state's
geology, forest history, and agricultural history, and to what Linnaeus
would call our "floral calendar." An allusion in his poetry to a flower is
never merely decorative or incidental, despite what many critics seem to
assume. It tells an ecological story and evokes a particular living community.

An example comes in the lines "Not without feeble-pointed spikes of
flowers, / (Pale orchises) and scared a bright green snake." I looked up
pale orchises in my *Newcomb's Wildflower Guide*, since it was not a plant
with which I was familiar. I found that the Tubercled, or Pale Green,
Orchis (*Habenaria flava*) raises a slender flower spike above a couple of
well-developed basal leaves, and that it grows in moist meadows during
late spring and summer. "Swale" is the older, more poetic name for a wet
meadow or low ground. It describes both the sort of terrain that would
have called for a solitary hand mower during Frost's early years as a
farmer in northern New England and the environment in which just this
flower, with its "feeble," sinuously slender stem, would have grown. The
"bright green snake" is a similarly precise and telling reference. Vermont
has relatively few reptiles—and no native lizards at all. The green snake
(*Opheodrys vernalis*) was a fairly common sight until the latter part of the
nineteenth century—often spotted by scythe-wielding mowers as it
slithered ahead of them into the still-uncut grass. With the advent of
mowing machines, green snakes have become much rarer. They are not
fast enough to elude those mechanical blades with the same success
they had in staying ahead of a shuffling, deliberate human laborer.

Pale orchises and bright green snakes are the "facts" that Frost labors
to encompass in his verse, along with the ecosystem and the agricultural
economy in which they would likely be encountered. Marianne Moore

described poems as imaginary gardens with real toads in them. But Frost's swale, snake, and orchis are at once concrete, closely observed, and precisely related to the human labor proceeding around them and in their midst. Because his poetic landscapes resolutely avoid "anything more than the truth," they can balance and sustain the ambiguity, and ambivalence, about spiritual meaning that are so central to his poetry.

. . .

A single morning's workshop on scything could never make anyone a competent mower. But a brief exposure of this sort can still do much to illuminate a poem like "Mowing." One implication may be that those of us who teach writers as sensitive to the living landscape as Frost was should systematically integrate field trips and other outdoor experiences into our courses. This could simply be an occasional outing with our students to experience some phenomenon that figures in the literature we are reading. Excursions of several days would be better, though hard for most teachers to manage during the regular academic term. Regardless of the length of a class's time outside, however, the goal would be the same: to experience personally the images and rhythms we meet again on the page. We dwell in a poem so that the world, with all its other poems, may be renewed. Just so, we can return to poetry with fresh appreciation once we are regrounded in the earth. As John Dewey insisted, the most vital education grows out of the "play of mental demand and material supply."[8] A field trip into the landscape of poetry, like any other pilgrimage, gets our ideas up on their feet.

Such play (in Dewey's sense of the word) becomes especially striking when Frost couples his close observation of the New England countryside with pointed allusions to the English poets. Robert Faggen suggests, for example, that there is a connection between the imagery in "Mowing" and a line in Coleridge's "Christabel": "When lo! I saw a bright green snake."[9] Frost's line is enriched both by the poetic echo and by the precise and appropriate placement of this snake in the unmown grass of a New England swale. A similar effect of compounding can enhance the experience of readers as well. Just as natural phenomena can reground a poem's language for us, so too can poetry mediate and heighten our awareness of the living earth.

An even more intriguing connection arises between the fourth line of "Mowing" and the first stanza of a song from *Cymbeline:*

Fear no more the heat o' the sun,
  Nor the furious winter's rages;
Thou thy worldly task hast done,
  Home art gone, and ta'en thy wages;
Golden lads and girls all must
As chimney-sweepers, come to dust.[10]

As Anne Ferry has discussed, Frost was particularly devoted to Palgrave's *Golden Treasury*, often imitating, responding to, or alluding to
lyrics in that collection. The fact that this selection from Shakespeare
was included in Palgrave's anthology (under the title "Fidele") heightens
the possibility that Frost intended such an echo in his poem.[11] I take special interest in this association because of a story Hugh Kenner relates to
that same stanza from *Cymbeline*. After celebrating the song's evocation
of golden youth and its passing, Kenner goes on to tell that

> in the mid-20th century a visitor to Shakespeare's Warwickshire met a
> country man blowing the grey head off a dandelion: "We call these golden
> boys chimney sweepers when they go to seed." And all is clear? They are
> shaped like a chimney-sweeper's broom. They come to dust when the wind
> disintegrates them. And as "golden lads," nodding their golden heads in the
> meadows around Stratford, the homely dandelions that wilt in the heat of
> the sun and would have no chance against the furious winter's rages, but
> need never confront winter because they turn to chimney-sweepers and
> come to dust, would have offered Shakespeare exactly what he needed to es-
> tablish Fidele's death in *Cymbeline* as an easy, assimilable instance of na-
> ture's custom.[12]

In reading Shakespeare's verse today, as in reading Frost's, most of us
run the risk of missing an entire range of concrete references because of
our separation from the seasonal rhythms and tasks that informed the
poets' own lives. When we do experience these things for ourselves, however, we discover even in poems we have lived with for years that the
metaphors become more satisfyingly extended, the descriptions more
sharply focused and arresting.

The importance of natural experience within the total meaning of a
poem is shown especially clearly by Frost's "The Need of Being Versed in
Country Things." The best-known lines in that poem come at its charac-
teristically roundabout ending: "One had to be versed in country things /
Not to believe the phoebe wept."[13] The poem as a whole is as sly and irre-

ducible as any by this supremely cagey poet, being at once a meditation on the emotional meaning of nature and a stringent insistence that such meaning reflects our basic ignorance of nature. Standing beside an abandoned house—so naturally associated for us with the sadness of loss, separation, and departure—we too easily hear in birdsong the weeping of former inhabitants or the sighing of visitors like ourselves. We project a human presence on the otherness of nature. But conventional academic readings of Frost, which delight in the poet's sardonic debunking of the pathetic fallacy, too often stop there.

Frost's art recognizes both the essential unknowability of the world and the perpetual suggestiveness of natural phenomena. Appreciation of this quality of suspension within his poetry depends on registering his natural details in their concrete particularity. As far as the standard, reductive reasoning goes, the word "phoebe" could as well be replaced by "birdy." "Robin" or "starling" would also do, if rhythm were all. But the fact is that those other birds would not do. Here is where a late-spring or summer field trip to one of the sugarhouses, hunting camps, or abandoned farmhouses that dot the New England woods might enhance students' experience of the poem.

Frost places the phoebe (*Sayornis phoebe*), like the orchis and the green snake of "Mowing," in exactly the habitat where it belongs. It likes to nest under the eaves of buildings far from the road and close to the woods. Phoebes are easy to observe, and students will note their nervous habit of wagging their tails, their frequent shifting from perch to perch, and the constant, plaintive up-and-down of their songs. The phoebe in an unostentatious bird. The feathers of its head, back, and wings are brown with an olive cast and those of its breast are creamy. A robin may have a name that would satisfy a critic looking for no more than a trochee in that line of verse. But its vivid red breast makes it much more of a visual presence, and its full-throated, melodious song could never be mistaken for weeping, no matter how melancholy the human observer or the scene.

The nondescript phoebe, in contrast, has a reedy repetitiveness that can sound heartsick, or even desperate, to a susceptible human. Being "versed in country things" can help us remember that this call is most likely a territorial assertion—translating to something like "I am here now." Without having heard the phoebe's distinctive song, though, a reader might miss the poem's emotional tension and subside into the equally "unversed" sentimentality of hearing no bird beyond the one on the page. Just as our projections onto nature are invariably skewed, so too are our readings abstracted from nature impoverished. Frost offers us the experience of particular natural environments as provocations to our own perpetually personal utterances. With his beloved Virgil, Frost finds in the world "the tears of things, mortal affairs that touch the mind." He knows that the tears may have less to do with nature than with the particular human stories that surround the onlooker—as is also true in the *Aeneid*. But the mortality, and the manifold individuality, of the natural creation are much more than projections.

Frost is piqued by the distinction between a suggestion of weeping in the bird's call and the otherness of the bird's life, just as he is by the insistent but untranslatable conversation between the scythe and the ground. Robert Penn Warren declared that to be a poet was to stand in the rain every day, in the knowledge that sometimes lightning would strike. Frost's poems include both the lightning strike and its afterimages against retina and optic nerve. To be alert and receptive readers of his poetry, we too need to venture out under the sky, into rain and sun. We need to hear the specific calls of particular birds, to startle and be startled by snakes appearing at our feet. To confine our readings and reflections to the library or classroom—as if we had neither arms to swing a scythe nor legs to step forward into the mystery of dewy, snake-braided grass—would be an impoverishment. It would be like the diminishment of weeping in a world where no phoebes nest. Just as my brief exposure to scything did not leave me a skilled mower, so too our walk across England and France and our travels around Tuscany left me with little of George Perkins Marsh's insight into history, geography, and forestry. But such excursions can nonetheless do much to burnish the experience of reading—whether of a long-familiar literary text or of the landscape of home. They neither complete a proposition nor resolve any question of importance; their gift is to complicate and enrich the field of one's awareness.

Thoreau adds the following remark to his celebration, cited earlier, of the spring's "green crop": "The very cows are driven to their country pastures before the end of May; though I have heard of one unnatural farmer who kept his cow in the barn and fed her hay all the year round."[14] Grand enclosures against the weather are an essential part of the agricultural, and the educational, year. But no barn should confine us from enjoying our country pastures. Students and teachers, house-holders and conservationists, must all remember, from time to time, to go to grass.

10

DUST OF SNOW

When I think of literature's power to redirect attention and renew alertness, I remember another outing, when a small group of students from Middlebury College and I were walking in the winter woods with the tracker Sue Morse. Our eyes were fixed on the ground as we searched for more of the bobcat prints we had just traced around the base of a cliff. When Sue called to us, we figured she must have picked up the trail. But instead, when our small group had gathered around her, she pulled back the bough of an overhanging hemlock and released it over our heads like a plucked bowstring. We looked up, startled, as the snow that had been packed on the branch swirled around our warm cheeks and spangled against the sky. As we stood there transfixed, she recited Robert Frost's short poem "Dust of Snow":

> The way a crow
> Shook down on me
> The dust of snow
> From a hemlock tree
>
> Has given my heart
> A change of mood
> And saved some part
> Of a day I had rued.[1]

Nine years later, the gift of this poem still comes back to me when snow-shoeing through a forested landscape, where drifts hang in the trees around my head as well as lying under foot. I'll sometimes push on a branch with my ski pole then look up into the enlivening microsquall that follows. Such moments remind me of the wildness behind all this white serenity and release me for a moment from whatever map or agenda I may just have been following.

One occasion to remember Frost's "change of mood" came while skiing with my friend Peter Forbes on the hilly trails that wind around Craftsbury, Vermont. On this particular outing I never did stop to dislodge snow from an overhanging bough. The truth is that I could barely keep up with my swift companion, even when he tactfully slowed down or called my attention to a scenic outlook that seemed to require a long, reflective pause. But our intermittent conversation included one remark on Peter's part that widened my eyes and shifted my perspective like a wintry spritz in the face. We had been talking about the relationship between Buddhist practice and the environmental movement when Peter asked whether the concept of conservation might not be, on one level, just another form of attachment. It certainly involved a powerful effort of clinging to something precious, he pointed out, with all the personal and social suffering implied by such attempts in a world of transience. We needed to rethink our approach to caring for the natural creation in order to find a more balanced and participatory model.

This was a startling challenge to a core value the two of us shared. In our professions, our memberships, our writing, and our daily choices, we both had long identified ourselves as conservationists. Letting go of the word felt like a kind of free fall. In fact, though, the received vocabulary of environmentalism has also been taking a lot of other hits. In William Cronon's essay "The Trouble with Wilderness," he argues that the term "wilderness" expresses a particular social and intellectual history more than an objective reality in nature. Cronon suggests that such language can actually reflect alienation from the land rather than intimacy with it. Wendell Berry has similarly taken aim at the word "environment" itself. By implicitly separating human beings from what is "around" us, he writes, the word is "a typical product of the old dualism that is at the root of most of our ecological destructiveness."[2]

Rethinking these words, and others like them, need not lessen anyone's commitment to protecting wild habitat and endangered species, to practicing stewardship of natural resources, or to changing the practices that lead to global climate change. But there is something to be said for a spirit of detachment from the *language* with which we surround such projects. We need, even amid the deep snows, to stay light on our feet.

If the word "wilderness" has become a serious point of contention, it's worth exploring different language with which to affirm the value of roadless areas and of unbroken canopies for certain species of wildlife. Such an affirmation certainly does not cover all the important elements of the wilderness ethic—an environmental philosophy for which I continue to feel a strong personal affinity. Still, a provisional shift in our way of talking may allow us to move forward with individuals and groups from whom we previously felt divided. Similarly, if the word "environmental" and its variants seem to be obstructing certain conversations, we might sometimes want to reclaim the language of *citizenship* as we consider our society's place in the larger community of life.

Thoreau's "Walking," with its insistence on "sauntering," helps me to affirm the meandering of our terminology as well as to understand my method in this book. It encourages Thoreau's readers not to follow a predetermined course (like one of those smooth cement walkways that fan out like rays across a college green), but rather to turn and turn with the shifting landforms of our history. Our expeditions away from routine are not for the purpose of discovering wildness in the world outside ourselves but rather for recovering it within us. We also read, on the deepest level, to escape from mechanical repetition and find ourselves again within what D. H. Lawrence called "the Bright Book of Life." Near the end of "Walking," Thoreau writes, "When in doleful dumps, breaking the awful stillness of our wooden sidewalk on a Sunday, or, perchance, a watcher in the house of mourning, I hear a cockerel crow far or near, I think to myself, 'There is one of us well, at any rate,'—and with a sudden gush return to my senses."[3]

We don't need to abandon the lexicon of conservation forever; I won't be able to do without such terminology even until the end of the present chapter. But we could still use a break from time to time. As far as that goes, newer terminology like "sustainability" and "sense of place" will doubtless seem problematic soon enough. That's good. The collapse of accustomed ways of thinking and speaking can let us fall back into a bracing presentness. Which recalls that word "conservation." Distraught as many of us are about heedless development in our home landscapes, not to mention about the dismantling of earth's living systems and the diminishment of biodiversity, it is understandable for a certain clenched and trembling quality to come into our thinking. Our own little efforts feel so inadequate in the face of present destruction and impending dangers. At such a time, it is possible to fall into despair about stemming the tide of harmful changes, or to become bitterly alienated from what seem to be the culture of consumerism and the politics of vested interests. I speak from experience. But these emotions ultimately make us rigid, and slower to adapt to changing circumstances and opportunities. Further, they can dampen our joyful awareness of wild beauty—the wellspring of our most vigorous environmental activism. This is when we need to be shaken up by flurried arrivals and a splash of unanticipated weather. Such refreshing openings to what David Abram calls the "more-than-human world" can restore the elasticity of our spirit and allow us to return to our civic and environmental commitments with new resolution.

Any sudden loss of bearings, within our multitasking, overcommitted lives, can leave us breathless and insecure for a moment. But it is also an exhilarating relief to tumble through the prefab words and concepts and to enter the always-welcome reality of what's happening. Loss of certainty can be as arresting as the northern lights, when the overhanging bough of darkness pulses into life and stops us in our tracks. Surely many of us feel, in such a moment of astonishment, "Yes, I remember now!" Koan study, too, can feel like bushwhacking home through winter woods. So many handfuls of snow, sometimes whapping us in the face, sometimes sliding slyly down the backs of our necks. Look out. Look in. Wake up. For environmentalists (that word again, what can I say?) this can also mean recollecting what Gary Snyder calls our 50,000-year *Homo sapiens* history. From such a vast perspective, the institutions and technology of post–World War II society no longer seem so inescapable. Bearing the millennia in mind may help us cultivate a spirit of vibrant celebration within our communities, and to feel that, rather than running against the tide, we are (quoting Snyder yet again) "in line with the Main Flow." A refreshing rhythm of turning away from our effortful agendas may help us return with new vigor and pleasure to the work of conservation.

Frost's poem and my friend's question were both koans—surprising, momentum-reversing words that continue to reverberate. Haiku, as R. H. Blyth and Robert Aitken have both so memorably discussed, can serve in a similar way. In their pithiness, they strip away the familiarity that so often muffles our perception; in their surprising juxtapositions, they sharpen our awareness of seasonal tides drawing through what might have seemed homely details. When our family was living in Kyoto, we visited the Bashō-An, a simple hut on the forested slope behind Kompukuji Monastery. Bashō lived here in 1670, as did his great successor in haiku Buson, almost a century later. Slender rectangles of wood, not much thicker than a piece of paper, dangle from trees on some of the surrounding paths. Onto them have been brushed haiku by the two poets or occasionally by their present-day admirers. At first, these small placards, shifting in the breezes after the autumn leaves had fallen, felt superfluous to me. But eventually I came to feel that although I wouldn't want to brush past poems on *every* hike, these tokens of appreciation for poetry were touching and meaningful in their own right. They clarified that falling back into a presentness unaligned with our expectations need not imply turning away from other human hearts, any more than the love of wilderness must mean eradication of our social bonds.

We sometimes assume that art is the expression of an original, isolated imagination, amplified by a spirit of estrangement. But there is a great tradition in poetry, running through poets like Bashō, Wordsworth, Rilke, and Frost, and extended by contemporaries like Mary Oliver, that celebrates moments of refreshment and consolation in the larger natural world. This is not a linear, continuous tradition. Wordsworth and Rilke would never have read Bashō, for instance. But this landscape of kindred perceptions and revelations has become available to us today, just as the study and practice of Buddhism flourish here in New England in ways that our ancestor Frost could never have anticipated. Those poems spangling in the trees around the Bashō-An, like "Dust of Snow," can continue to gust and swing in our minds. They remind us how others, too, have found moments of release into the presentness on which we depend every day of our lives. Within every community of effort there is a community needing to awaken, over and over again, to the world beyond our projects and expectations.

A poem can serve both as door into a more spacious world of natural beauty, and as a reminder of the long history of human sensitivity to it. Master Hakuin's Zazen Wasan ("Chant in Praise of Zazen") contains the lines

How near the truth yet how far we seek,
like one in water crying "I thirst!"
Like a child of rich birth
wand'ring poor on this earth,
we endlessly circle the six worlds.[4]

Within the landscape of poetry we find both a prompt to immediate sen-
sation and the reminder of a larger story to which we belong. The dust of
snow shaken down from a hemlock tree removes us neither from history
nor from the human community. It reminds us that those realities exist
within an interwoven world, in which isolation is always an illusion and
a misdirection of our efforts.

Frost's poem echoes not just with Vermont's winter landscape but also
with a particular haiku by Bashō. Here it is in kanji, in a transliteration
of the spoken Japanese, and in a literal English translation.

かれ朶に烏のとまりけり秋の暮

kare eda ni
karasu no tomarikeri
aki no kure

On a bare branch
a crow alights—
autumn's end.[5]

This branch releases no snow, but it does bounce under the weight of
a large bird settling brusquely onto it. The Japanese word *tomarikeri*
includes both the root of the verb "to stop, stay, or settle" and two sylla-
bles, *keri,* added not for any grammatical reason but just to signal the
branch's springy up-and-down on the level of sound. Startled, we look
up into a honed world—black silhouettes of tree and crow sharpening
the edge of a season. One can see the dramatic outline of that hemlock
in the haiku's first kanji, *eda,* which is formed from the radicals for "tree"
and "limb."

I appreciate Peter Milward's translation of the last line ("aki no kure")
as "the fall of autumn," an acknowledgment of the seasons within seasons so essential to a Zen perception of nature. Something is always ending, something always beginning. Here in Vermont, too, autumn has its
spring, when the maple leaves first turn yellow and red and the sumacs
flame up; its summer, when the maples' crimson and orange flood the

mountains, with russet contributed by the oaks and gold by the larches; and the hush of its fall, when branches are bare but the snow has not yet arrived. In that moment of suspension before the next big event, a crow flexes a leafless branch, reminding us that life continues on its way, unregulated by our calendar of human expectations.

How fortunate we are—conservationists, environmentalists, lovers of wilderness, earnest citizens—for moments in which we forget our language, our projects, and even our names. Soon enough, we will turn back to our lifetime projects and our daily work. But it's always good to remember that our path is leading home, under branches shimmering with unexpected but familiar life.

"Dust of Snow" conveys the importance of sensory surprise in freeing the mind from its besetting "mood." Such freshness allows for a return to feeling at home on the earth and is the foundation for stewardship as participation, not dominance or attachment. In "Building Dwelling Thinking," from his late collection *Poetry, Language, Thought,* Heidegger writes of such openness and recovery, "To dwell, to be set at peace, means to remain at peace within the free, the preserve, the free sphere that safeguards each thing in its nature. *The fundamental character of dwelling is this sparing and preserving.*"[6] Conservation, education, and family life prosper within such a "free sphere," fostered by that modest, celebratory sense of our human roles Peter Forbes describes with the word "forbearance." One of the reasons I have been drawn to the idea of pilgrimage in exploring the landscape of stewardship is that it clarifies the relationship between "dwelling" and *departure.* We may make ourselves at home within global cycles of wholeness through our own readiness to awaken and to move. Stanley Cavell helps me put this thought together in the following passage from "Thinking Like Emerson": "The substantive disagreement with Heidegger, shared by Emerson and Thoreau, is that the achievement of the human requires not inhabitation and settlement but abandonment, leaving. Then everything depends upon your realization of abandonment. For the significance of leaving lies in its discovery that you have settled something, that you have felt enthusiastically what there is to abandon yourself to, that you can treat the others there are as those to whom the inhabitation of the world can now be left."[7] Reading too can be an act of leaving. Within the texts to which we abandon ourselves we can also rediscover ourselves in the little figure of a traveler. Turning the pages, we step forward to dwell in the story like pilgrims.

PART III
OTTAUQUECHEE

11

INHERITING
MOUNT TOM

The path up Mount Tom starts from Prosper Road in West Woodstock. It climbs east around a little secondary summit, then veers south to touch the shore of a high pond called the Pogue. My walks through the woods of Vermont often converge with long-abandoned skidder trails. But this one follows a broad carriage road, designed with great care near the close of the last century. The Pogue, while previously existing, was further landscaped in the same era. Both landmarks are artifacts that continue to exist only because of regular maintenance—grading and graveling, dredging and reinforcement. They are features of a remarkable estate including barns, a greenhouse, a summerhouse, and other outbuildings that radiate from a mansion holding a distinguished collection of nineteenth-century American art. No one would call this tract a wilderness.

Returning from Italy meant that we had to draw a new map of Vermont that incorporated the landmarks of our year away. Woodstock and its environs were especially interesting as George Perkins Marsh's birthplace—the other bookend, with Vallombrosa, for his long, productive life. This corner of the state is also notable for the ways in which Marsh's legacy has been recognized and extended here. While far from the rugged grandeur of Glacier, the Tetons, Yosemite, Yellowstone, and our other famous western parks, the thoroughly cultivated landscape around Mount Tom has nonetheless been designated as Vermont's first national park.

Marsh-Billings-Rockefeller National Historical Park was established by legislation signed by President Bush in 1992. Its name honors George Perkins Marsh, who was born on this farm in 1801, and Frederick Billings, who pursued his own vision of stewardship here after he purchased the property in the last third of that century. The land eventually passed to Mary F. Rockefeller, Billings's granddaughter, and her husband, Laurance Rockefeller. Having committed themselves to follow the farming and forestry practices they inherited along with the estate in 1954, the Rockefellers bequeathed the property to the nation and relinquished their tenancy in 1999, shortly before Mary's death. The 555 acres of the estate itself are now managed in cooperation with the adjacent Billings Farm and Museum, a part of the original estate owned by the Woodstock Foundation. A surrounding patchwork of protected lands includes a municipal park at the very summit of Mount Tom (presented to the town of Woodstock by Mrs. Rockefeller's family in 1953) and the adjacent King Farm, owned by the Vermont Land Trust.

The new park's mission statement declared that this would be "the first unit of the National Park System to focus on the history of American conservation and the evolving contribution of stewardship." Although the acknowledgment that environmental thinking and practices continue to evolve is apt, such a progression has been anything but a smooth, steady one. Some biologists now characterize the process of natural selection as one of "punctuated equilibrium." By this they mean that species and ecosystems may remain relatively stable for long periods, then adapt with startling speed when climatic or other environmental changes so dictate. The two centuries since George Perkins Marsh was born in Woodstock represent such a dramatic punctuation in both the ecological and the cultural narratives. While the conservation movement may be seen, from one distanced perspective, as a continuous unfolding, it has also been stimulated by jagged shifts in outward circumstances, including the disruption of major natural systems.

Returning to Marsh's birthplace in the watershed of the Ottauquechee River offers one gauge for our culture's progress on the pilgrimage to stewardship. Both the dramatic reversals of Vermont's environmental history and the range of creative conservation initiatives in this wounded and recovering landscape illustrate broader changes. With the new national park in Woodstock, a lineage of private stewardship here has flowed into a public trust. It has confirmed that, in the civic realm as in the familial one, inheritance is above all a matter of reciprocity and relationship. It is an active process rather than a commodity to be received—an imaginative connection, conceived in history, with those who went before and those who will come after. Beyond the importance of inheritance to me as a historical and literary theme, it bears on our own family's attempt, just up the ridge of the Green Mountains from Woodstock, to become more rooted in the Vermont land. Our projects in sustainable forestry and sugaring are efforts to enter into a living rural tradition, as well as to provide for our successors in this fragile, beautiful community of life we know as home. Though Woodstock, and all of Vermont, are pleasant backwaters when compared with the nearby world of highways and metropolises, they are by that same token places to measure the progress of events and the evolution of conservation thought on national and global scales. It is interesting to note in this connection that Ottauquechee, the name of the lovely river winding around and through Woodstock, is a Natick word that can be construed as a place with "cattails or rushes near a swift current."[1]

. . .

From 1791 through the War of 1812, Vermont was the fastest growing state in the Union. Woods were cut down with a swiftness that had less to do with farmers' need to clear fields than with their desire to produce the charcoal and potash that brought them valuable cash supplements. Flocks of merino sheep were then pastured across Vermont in a boom lasting for just a couple of decades and sometimes referred to as "merino madness."[2] Growing up in Woodstock at a time when Mount Tom was effectively denuded, George Perkins Marsh watched the profile of the mountain erode from year to year. He remembered these effects years later when serving as the U.S. minister to Turkey and Italy, and drew a connection to the damaged productivity of the soil in ancient nations around the Mediterranean. One might propose a sort of equation, in fact, in which the direct experience of Vermont's environmental degradation plus the Old World's millennial narrative equaled the comprehensive vision of *Man and Nature.* Marsh lived through the most drastic era of deforestation and erosion around Woodstock, and he found the long-term implications of such processes recorded in the desertification and social collapse of the classical landscape. Such a combination of personal, historical, and international information reverberates through

Marsh's environmental analysis and critique, with its refrain "and thus the earth is rendered no longer fit for the habitation of man."

As the title of Marsh's book reflects, his was a more human-oriented vision than has recently prevailed in the environmental movement. Marsh always emphasized the necessity for human action to restore the environmental balance on which human society depends. David Lowenthal characterizes Marsh's attitude in this way: "Although man was selfish and short-sighted, he was not irrational. Reform might follow understanding. . . . If he could ruin nature, he might also mend it."[3] In the early conservationist's own terms, "man" must now "become a co-worker with nature. . . . He must aid her in reclothing the mountain slopes with forests and vegetable mould."[4] The founding of our state's first national park reinforces Marsh's broad vision by relocalizing it in the place where it originated. The park announces, in effect, that Vermont has a word of its own to say, one that will complement the western voices in America's environmental discourse. The stories of this long-settled landscape may help us imagine a more inclusive paradigm for American conservation. In the syntax of these mountains, "loss" and "recovery," "wilderness" and "stewardship" may all be spoken, and connected.

. . .

We always enter the story of a place through the narrative of our individual lives. I have to say it feels as if I have been on my way to Mount Tom for over thirty years, and as if this personal passage has tracked along with an evolution of environmental thinking in America over the same period. I grew up in northern California, nurtured in the bosom of the Sierra Club. When I graduated from college in 1969, the civil rights movement, the anti–Vietnam War movement, the women's movement, and the wilderness movement all felt like elements of one sublime and liberating vision. For me, as for many young people of my generation, the grandeur of the Sierra Nevada was the fitting backdrop to this cultural drama.

Coming east to attend graduate school seemed in some ways a falling off—a departure from the western mountains that seemed to ratify all these visionary movements, as well as perhaps a turning toward a professional landscape from the terrain of adventure and youth. I still remember my first hike in the Connecticut woods, and how put off I was by the leaf litter and underbrush. The ground seemed so messy after the cathedral floor of Muir Woods near my Mill Valley home. The landforms also felt too close together to allow a clear look at the horizon. Over the intervening years, however, I've come to love these deciduous woods and to claim them as my familial landscape. "They must go down," Robert Frost writes of the leaves in his hardwood groves, and so they must. First blotched and perforated, then reduced to skeletons, then rolled into a fine moist meal, they sift downward through the strata over four seasons before arriving at their destiny in the sweet, black soil. Vermont may not offer the West's magnificent expanse of sky. But my vision has been drawn downward to what soil scientists call the O-horizon. This is the layer of decomposing organic material, containing so much of a forest's nutrients that the largest trees send fine root filaments *up* to interweave in a mat just below the top two inches of the forest floor.

The way the seasons here are always being processed underfoot has helped me to identify more closely with these Green Mountains, where the members of our family have found themselves, where we lead our lives together, and where, in time, our bodies will be gathered back into the larger fund of life. Perhaps this is always the way it goes, with home ground as an inheritance that we receive and into which we then have an opportunity to enter more deeply. "The Gift Outright," recited by Robert Frost at John F. Kennedy's inauguration began, "The land was ours before we were the land's." With the wind ruffling his white hair and making it impossible for him to read his typescript, the poet of Vermont looked inward and spoke on. He intoned, "Something we were withholding made us weak / Until we found out that it was ourselves / We were withholding from our land of living. . . ."[5]

We must conceive of stewardship not simply as one individual's practice but rather as the mutual and intimate relationship, extending across generations, between a human community and its place on earth. We must recognize that, like the bonds of family, stewardship grows from error, misapprehension, repentance, forgiveness, and hope and cannot simply be the implementation of a policy or master plan. Insofar as a balance between humanity and nature has emerged in Vermont, it is the product of a tragically exploitive history and a providential recovery. Such a landscape offers its own ironic, yet hopeful perspective to the environmental discourse of our day.

Our language about wilderness has often been associated with an impulse toward transcendence—an escape from our lives' dailiness through climbing remote mountains that bear us up to the sky. When environmental historians like William Cronon ask us to rethink the notion of wilderness, they point to complex and dynamic patterns of land use that have not generally been recognized by wilderness legislation.

> The more one knows its peculiar history, the more one realizes that wilderness is not quite what it seems. Far from being the one place on earth that stands apart from humanity, it is quite profoundly a human creation—indeed, the creation of very particular human cultures at very particular moments in human history. It is not a pristine sanctuary where the last remnant of an untouched, endangered, but still transcendent nature can for at least a little while longer be encountered without the contaminating taint of civilization. Indeed, it is a product of that civilization, and could hardly be contaminated by the very stuff of which it is made.[6]

The most fundamental way to call the question is to ask what human history has to do with natural history. The wilderness ethic has emphasized the need to restrict human activity in order to protect natural areas that are, in the words of the 1964 Wilderness Act, "vast," "untrammeled," and "pristine." This philosophy was a vital advance over narrowly extractive or utilitarian approaches to nature. It still represents one of America's enduring contributions to human culture. An awareness has also grown up in the environmental community over the past two decades or so, however, that more direct connections must now be drawn between wilderness and urban America, between environmental preservation and values of social justice. What, we begin to ask ourselves, is the deeper connection between the Gates of the Arctic National Park in Alaska and inner-city Philadelphia?

In attempting to answer this question, we must come back to the idea of stewardship addressed in the new park's mission statement. Vermont might seem at first an unlikely landscape in which to pursue a more inclusive environmental vision. Because of its refreshing contrast to the more urban areas surrounding it, the state is often perceived as a sort of pleasant green blur. It can seem a pastoral vestige, a part of the Northeast that has been spared the congestion and pollution of the Boston-to-Washington corridor. I once saw a T-shirt in Middlebury's Ben Franklin department store on which was printed VERMONT IS THE WAY AMERICA USED TO BE. But our state's mystique, while appealing, is ultimately less nourishing than its true history—of early industry and deforestation followed by a dramatic return of the forests. In many cases, the reforestation has been an unintended effect of agricultural abandonment. More recently, at a site like Marsh-Billings-Rockefeller Park, it has been the result of efforts in which forestry, agriculture, and social health were pursued over the decades as coordinated and consistent goals. Vermont's history of losses, its relics of past eras, and the persistence of certain ideals in this landscape all make it another good terrain in which to pursue a pilgrimage to stewardship.

The first two lines of Frost's "Directive" ("Back out of all this now too much for us, / Back in a time made simple by the loss of detail. . . .")[7] acknowledge both the attraction and the limitations of pastoral nostalgia in northern New England. Such nostalgia can be a form of sentimentality—a mental condition memorably defined as loving something more than God does. Paying attention to the details is important because it prevents such disproportion. Remembering the particular story of a particular place on earth bequeaths a future with creative choices. Stewardship is the story of faithfulness and practicality which can be read along the carriage road to Mount Tom.

In Woodstock this is the story not just of Marsh but also of Frederick Billings, who owned this estate in the latter part of the nineteenth century. The encouraging lesson here is not that one great thinker grew up in this mountain village; it is that a lineage of creative conservation can be traced here from the beginning of the nineteenth century to the beginning of the twenty-first. Billings had lived in Woodstock as a boy but made his fortune in the West as a lawyer during the gold rush and as a partner in the Northern Pacific Railroad. He returned to his hometown and purchased the property where the park is now located in 1869. Five years earlier he had read *Man and Nature*. This book was to have a lifelong effect on Billings, and made it even more significant to him that the farm he had just purchased was the one on which Marsh was born in 1801. While living in California, Billings had often visited Yosemite and became an advocate of preserving the stupendous geology and redwood groves of that region. But reading Marsh's book also convinced him of the importance of stewardship that would preserve the common, working landscapes on which our collective human welfare depended.

Until his death in 1890, Frederick Billings tried to become such an efficient coworker. He wanted his estate to provide a demonstration of the most up-to-date and scientific approach to farming and forestry. In developing both his herd of Jersey cows and his forest park, he was motivated by values that we associate today with the term "sustainability." He believed that, in contrast to the erosive methods of early Vermont agriculture, he could show a long-term profit while also managing a farm and a forest that grew more productive and valuable with each new year. His social purpose was equally ambitious. The carriage road winding past the Pogue was one of his proudest achievements. It related to Billing's goal of elevating his local community through exposing his neighbors to a beautiful and productive working landscape. The *Vermont Standard* of September 1, 1887, reported that

> Mr. Billings' drive to the summit of Mt. Tom is nearly completed, and is a surprise to everybody by reason of its easy grade. From the point where it leaves the "Pogue Hole" road, in the field a little way above the woods, to the summit a team may trot every rod, and a portion of the way one passing over it seems almost suspended in air. The outlook is grand. The road is so broad that teams may pass each other at any point and it is to be graveled and made first-class. Only think what an attraction this is to be to Woodstock! Though a private enterprise, the public are permitted to enjoy it freely.[8]

One challenging dimension of the Marsh-Billings-Rockefeller legacy is its obvious connection with wealth and privilege. For me, though, this is also one of the new national park's advantages. It makes overt and inescapable an issue always inherent in American conservation whether we want to recognize it or not. Private wealth has played a crucial role in the formation of many of our most celebrated parks. Beyond the connections of particular parks with such fortunes, many other aspects of political power and social privilege have been intertwined with our National Park System from the day of the Harrimans and Stanfords to the present. Congressman Phil Burton's remarkable Omnibus Bill of 1978, authorizing new parks, expanding the allocations for land acquisition, and promoting new wilderness areas within existing parks, was described by its critics as "Park Barrel." I celebrate what this legislation accomplished, but feel that the derogatory phrase also pointed out the inescapable connection of enormous conservation projects with patronage and electoral strategy. A political issue of a different sort is that visitors to the parks, like the memberships of major environmental organizations, still show far less economic or racial diversity than America at large. When our family took the ritual tour of Western parks several years ago, we were struck by how few people of color were represented among our fellow visitors.

In contemplating the privileged origins and limited clientele of many national parks, I think about Middlebury College, where I have been on the faculty for over thirty years. Such richly endowed, liberal arts institutions are like the parks in being founded and sustained by private wealth, as well as patronized by a significant percentage of students whose parents can readily afford the high tariff. Such facts might lead one who is inclined to discount the parks because of their elite associations also to reject the college's social legitimacy. But I want to argue against both of these possible rejections. For one thing, I feel personally grateful to the Rockefellers for the gift of Marsh-Billings, just as I do for their extended family's role in establishing the Acadia, Great Smokey Mountains, and Teton national parks, among others. For me, as a child of the middle-middle, it's been wonderful to walk and sleep and reflect among scenes of such beauty. Similarly, I am thankful for the community, the traditions, and the facilities of private colleges like the one that I attended and the one where I now teach.

In order for either these parks or these colleges to continue meriting their special protected status, however, their stewards must now concentrate on making them more accessible to American society as a whole. There are in fact many leaders in the worlds of conservation and education at present dedicating themselves to this task. Current efforts to cultivate more diverse student bodies, through aggressive recruitment and generous financial aid, will determine whether private colleges survive as significant American institutions. Programs sending representatives of the parks to inner-city classrooms, inviting out and guiding groups who might not otherwise get into the parks, and establishing new parks closer to urban areas are parallel efforts that may help ensure the National Park System's long-term vitality. In education and conservation alike, we must pursue stewardship not simply as the maintenance of valuable resources but also as a way of fostering a broader experience of democracy and community. While pilgrimage may be pursued by individuals or small groups, one of its most important functions is a revitalization of the entire culture. This means, in the case of America's conservation movement, that excursions into the mountains continually return to an ongoing civic dialogue. We separate ourselves from the daily routine in order to explore how we may live more sustainably together in the landscape of home.

. . .

Walking toward the Pogue, I pass beautifully tended groves of red pines, hemlocks, and mixed hardwoods, including a few rare species such as brown ash. On the southeastern side of the water, the carriage road continues south and then bends east again toward the summit of Mount Tom, passing three plantations established by Billings in 1887. In addition to lovely specimens of red oak, white ash, and sugar maple, these woods include such imported species as Norway spruce, European ash, and European larch. Scientific forestry was at that time far more advanced in Europe, so that Americans like Frederick Billings and Gifford Pinchot often chose to plant old-world species about which greater systematic knowledge was available. Over the decades in which this land has been owned and managed by Billings and his successors, aesthetic considerations and overall forest health have always been taken into account along with commercial factors.

The forest around me today, largely laid out under the tenure of Frederick Billings, has continued to be managed in accordance with his principles since 1954, when it came into the possession of Mary French Rockefeller and Laurance Rockefeller. More than a century of careful planting, thinning, and harvesting have produced a mature forest in which light filters down through a velvety canopy. While the forest floor still lacks the hummocky richness of decomposition and fungal life of a true old-growth woods, it does have something of the spaciousness and stillness I've enjoyed in ancient groves. I love it here.

Growing up in the West, I have long admired John Muir's insistence on the sacredness of wilderness, an experience of nature beyond all questions of economic value. I still prize the photograph of John Muir hanging on my study wall, with his magnificent bearded profile turned toward the camera and his broad-brimmed hat beside him as he sits on a boulder in the Merced River. But I'm no longer so quick to discount the emphasis on resource management and utility articulated by Gifford Pinchot, Muir's sometime antagonist as director of the U.S. Forest Service. Just as I have learned over the intervening years to love the rich decay of Vermont's forest floor, so too exposure to our Yankee neighbors has helped me understand that the words "conservation" and "conservative" are not necessarily opposed. When I was growing up in California, the latter word often seemed to express a desire to extract wealth from the land without either governmental or moral restraint. In the farming culture around me here, in contrast, a conservative impulse reflects long affiliation with a particular landscape. It is associated with a loyalty to the local community, human and nonhuman alike, that makes people want to go slowly with any changes.

In Leopold's "The Land Ethic," which was such a powerful influence on the 1964 wilderness legislation, he describes the broadening of an ethical circle as human society has come to reject slavery and to acknowledge the fundamental rights of women and men alike. His language sums up for me the relationship between error, urgency, and creative possibility in prophetic conservation thought. We have now arrived at a stage in our moral development, Leopold writes, when nonhuman nature must have its own rights recognized: "There is as yet no ethic dealing with man's relation to land and to the animals and plants which grow upon it. . . . The extension of ethics to this third element in human environment is, if I read the evidence correctly, an evolutionary possibility and an ecological necessity."[9] As Leopold's ethical circle continues to expand, we may find that it will, while more fully comprehending nonhuman prerogatives and values, also include more fully the stories of our human participation in the landscape. Both the history of Vermont in general and the new Marsh-Billings-Rockefeller National Historical Park in particular suggest that forestry and agriculture, wilderness and human settlements, may all be affirmed within our vision of stewardship. I believe that the contradiction some perceive between wilderness and environmental justice is really an inability to achieve a broad enough perspective. In Seamus Heaney's volume of selections from Wordsworth's poetry, he includes a couple of suggestive extracts from that poet's *Alfoxden Notebooks* that address this need to widen our view:

> Why is it we feel
> So little for each other, but for this,
> That we with nature have no sympathy,
> Or with such things as have no power to hold
> Articulate language?
> . . . .

And never for each other shall we feel
As we may feel, till we have sympathy
With nature in her forms inanimate,
With objects such as have no power to hold
Articulate language. In all forms of things
There is a mind.[10]

I treasure the tentativeness of these two verse entries in which Wordsworth tries to express an idea that we are still working to formulate adequately today.

The value of stewardship and the desire to take issues of environmental justice into account absolutely do not lessen the value of wilderness.
On the contrary. There is no one I admire more than Terry Tempest
Williams, fighting for her southern Utah wilderness, or Rick Bass, standing up for his northern range of the Rockies. Efforts like theirs are neither replaced nor discounted by the search for a wider environmental
paradigm. When growing out of fidelity to particular, diverse communities of life, the preservation of wilderness becomes a concrete commitment rather than an abstract value. To the extent to which such a commitment is inclusive and participatory, it can also help us take our cities
more fully into account, broaden the constituency of the environmental
movement beyond its largely white base, and affirm the distinctive cultures supported by agriculture and forestry.

The word that Vermont has to say in the current national dialogue
about nature and culture comes from a history in which the environmental quality and balance of a long-settled state have improved dramatically over the past century and in which people have testified by their
writing and their actions alike about the desirability of such balance.
Nora Mitchell, director of the Conservation Study Institute, has pointed
out the similarity between the words *conservation* and *conversation*. In
Vermont there has been an illuminating conversation in which the
forests and the farms have both held the floor at different stages. It's been
like a long story with many twists and turns. Leslie Silko describes the inclusive Pueblo vision of the world in which "everything became a story."
The park in Woodstock represents a story, too, and a map. It suggests
how, over the generations, soil may be enriched and forests preserved. It
shows that the example of discerning stewardship may be a gift as valuable in its own way as the balanced, healthy landscape it perpetuates.

. . .

In his entry for February from *A Sand County Almanac*, Leopold offers an image for what it means to read the history of a landscape. As in sawing down a lightning-killed oak, one starts in the present and works backward: "Fragrant little chips of history spewed from the saw cut, and accumulated on the snow before each kneeling sawyer. We sensed that these two piles of sawdust were something more than wood: that they were the integrated transect of a century; that our saw was biting its way, stroke by stroke, decade by decade, into the chronology of a lifetime, written in concentric annual rings of good oak."[11] Working our way back to Marsh's insights and conclusions is a similarly retrospective way to think about conservation, just as his comprehensive vision resulted from studying the medieval and classical histories of land use in the Mediterranean region. But one arrives at certain key ideas or understandings that imply a need to work back toward the present again, and to apply our enhanced understandings in the daily practices of our lives. As Leopold writes, in sawing past the center point of that formidable oak, "We have cut the core. Our saw now reverses its orientation in history; we cut backward across the years, and outward toward the far side of the stump."[12] Such reading backward and forward is stimulated by losses like the lightning that killed the eighty-year-old oak, and it takes labor, as in taking up one handle of a crosscut saw. But the final result is both practical and satisfying—as the reader looks over Leopold's shoulder at a split of good oak glowing on his andirons.

Etymology is one of the ways we read backward, renewing our understanding of the language that describes and in a sense governs our choices in the present. In reading the new National Park's Draft General Management Plan, I discovered that the word "stewardship" derives from the Old Norse *Sti-vardr*, "keeper of the house." The image of a Viking long hall leaped to mind. Guests wearing metal hats with horns banged their tankards on a huge, scarred table and bellowed to each other in Wagnerian cadences while a quick-witted *Sti-vardr* settled quarrels, trimmed torches, and kept the mead coming. This vision of smoky glamour faded into the light of a Vermont morning. But that etymology illuminates the meaning of stewardship within the larger ecology of American environmental thought.

Discussions of environmental policy have often framed an opposition between the terms "conservation" and "preservation." The former word has described a utilitarian approach, associated with Gifford Pinchot and the early history of the Forest Service, while the latter has been connected with John Muir and the wilderness ethic he inspired. For one who assumes such a dichotomy, the word "stewardship" would most likely recall the pole of conservation. A term like "ecology," in contrast, with its nonhierarchical connotations and its link to biodiversity, would be allied with preservationism and wilderness. But it is illuminating, in fact, that the Norse stem *sti* and the Greek word *oikos*—from which "ecology" derives—both mean "house." Down at their roots, these words, and the environmental traditions they represent, are joined.

Recognizing such common ground is particularly important today. Heated disputes too often occupy our environmental discourse—reflecting, perhaps, the tenseness of an era when established paradigms are being challenged. Since the early 1960s, the wilderness ethic has dominated the agendas of our private advocacy organizations, inspired the flourishing field of nature writing, and informed the curricula of our emerging environmental studies programs. In the past decade, many environmental thinkers and activists have begun searching for a more socially inclusive paradigm—looking for ways to broaden the circle beyond the relatively privileged constituency of the wilderness movement, and to address more directly both urban issues and problems of environmental justice. At the same time, scholars in the rapidly growing field of environmental history have criticized the wilderness ethic as insufficiently informed by the human record—especially that of indigenous groups—in the roadless areas of the West. Wilderness advocates have counterattacked that such historians are blinded to the realities of wildness by their own obsession with reducing everything, even wolves, to mere "social constructions." Sometimes these salvos have assumed the coloration of *regionalist* strife—a conflict between eastern and western perspectives.

America's environmental thinking needs to move beyond this polemic standoff. One way to do so is by exploring the connections implicit in the similar derivations of "stewardship" and "ecology." Ecology, the science of our earth household, is a particularly capacious concept. It describes a circuit of energy that includes and sustains the full range of biological diversity. As Aldo Leopold so memorably suggested in his essay "Thinking Like a Mountain," for instance, wolves have always been much more than the "natural enemy" of deer. By controlling the size of a herd, they protect an entire mountain against overgrazing and allow it, in turn, to continue supporting healthy populations of deer and other animals alike. In our environmental thinking no less than in our approach to wildlife, we need to become aware of a broader ecology of relationships. Utilitarian and preservationist impulses that may seem superficially opposed, and landscapes with obviously divergent environmental histories, may in a deeper sense complement one another.

Protecting the biological integrity of even our vastest western wildernesses requires much more, after all, than merely drawing and then guarding their federally designated boundaries. Tracking the migrations of animals with radiotelemetry, to determine the adequacy of their food supplies and study the cycles of their populations, is a painstaking form of scientific stewardship. Negotiating with ranchers and politicians about the fate of bison or wolves that cross into private lands is a challenging form of involvement on the civic and political fronts. Such practical commitments are—to borrow a term more often associated with the vocabulary of conservation than with the wilderness movement—essentially skilled "management." Conversely, any farming or forestry undertaken with a true concern for the ecological well-being of its region pursues practices that would most accurately be described as preservation. Keeping machinery away from heavily sloping land where logging would mean undue erosion, leaving standing snags as habitat for cavity-dwelling birds and animals, and preserving broad, brushy margins between the cultivated fields and the streams that flow through a farm are all examples of a stewardship that eschews a more limited, human-centered conception of utility. When we take a broad view of American environmental thought, we find that conservation and preservation are in fact kindred and continuous values.

Ecologists speak of "edge effect" at the boundary between two ecosystems. Such edges, or "ecotones," contain a greater diversity of species than live in either of the constituent ecosystems, as well as a higher absolute density of organisms. They are fertile but risky environments, and a creature who ventures out from one familiar landscape in search of life more abundant sometimes ends up as a meal for a fellow pioneer from the other side of the zone. Alertness is the key to survival in such an environment, especially since the ecotone itself is typically in flux—as in the tidal world of a rocky shoreline or in the successional phases where an abandoned cornfield or meadow gives itself over to the woods. The concept of stewardship represents just such a dynamic edge in America's environmental thought. It is a word that has been current in English for centuries longer than the language of our contemporary "environmentalism" and thus might seem as old-fashioned as the loosely tied, romantic cravat worn by George Perkins Marsh in his most famous portrait or, for that matter, as outmoded as the high starched collars in photographs of Frederick Billings. Previous generations' vocabulary, like their clothing, can easily strike their successors as impractical, albeit decorative. Similarly, Vermont, with its idyllic villages like Woodstock, set off by agriculture and framed by thickly forested ridges, might be seen as a beautiful, but irrelevant, relic of a bygone, pastoral America. However, ideas and locales that may have seemed marginal from a narrow perspective can turn out to define central, energizing ecotones when the map of our attentiveness expands.

In order to understand why the concept of stewardship, in particular, might offer such edge effect—connecting the ecosystems of conservation and preservation within the ecology of our environmental thought —it is useful to return once more to the root word *Sti-vardr.* We have a tendency to consider stewardship as an abstract value. But it actually begins with, and draws its richest meaning from, the concrete image of an individual steward. By reflecting on the appropriate role for such a person, we may bring the meaning of environmental stewardship into sharper focus. I believe that four qualities are in fact requisite for successful stewardship, and that each of these also forges an essential connection between the vocabularies and concerns of "conservation" and "preservation."

The foremost requirement for environmental stewardship, as for all stewardship, is faithful service. The psalmist and shepherd David was faithful to his God, and the steward of a castle or manor was faithful to the king or master. Clearly, in a democratic and religiously pluralistic society we must reformulate the meaning of faithfulness. Nonetheless, I believe that this quality remains absolutely vital in our contemporary context as well. It both emphasizes human responsibility and guards against an anthropocentric outlook. The point is that stewardship, by definition, must always be on *behalf* of something. From an environmental perspective, this places humanity not above but decisively in the midst of, and in service to, nature. The environmental steward is a servant of the whole *community.* This would certainly include the human community—starting with Woodstock and our other towns and broadening to include the entire republic and, finally, the community of all nations that inhabit our planet. In this context, the concept of stewardship overlaps significantly with that of citizenship. Every citizen of a democracy is called upon to assume the responsibilities of a steward if the commonwealth is to be sustained.

But we must also understand our citizenship, and our stewardship, to be within the larger community of life on earth. Aldo Leopold writes that "a land ethic changes the role of *Homo sapiens* from conqueror of the land-community to a plain member and citizen of it." The Leopold scholar Peter Fritzell has noted the implicit tension between such "plain" citizenship and the need, distinguishing us from all other animals, to restrain our environmental practices with an "ethic." If there is a tension here, however, it is finally less Leopold's problem than a defining ambiguity of the human condition. This is the true context for environmental stewardship. Though we human beings belong indisputably to the animal kingdom, we also seem to be unique both in our unparalleled power for manipulating natural systems through technology and in our impulse and capacity to assume responsibility for our actions. Given this complex reality, environmentalists often discover their deepest motivation through identifying lovingly with the intricate, dynamic, exquisitely adaptive beauty of biodiversity, and through service on its behalf. From an evolutionary perspective, such stewardship may be understood as a form of filial piety.

Effectiveness is the second principle of stewardship I would like to affirm. This is the nitty-gritty of counting and measuring, and could also be expressed with the words acuity and knowledgeability. Each of the four principles being proposed here is tricky—the threading of a particular needle. This one comes perilously near the corrupting influence of mere quantification. Our values-based institutions are always in danger of corruption when they assume that success can be counted. When the Forest Service overemphasizes board feet or the Park System dwells too much on visitor hours, they run the same risks faced by churches obsessed with membership lists and contributions, or by colleges gloating over their endowments and dreaming about their annual rankings in *U.S. News and World Report.* These American institutions' *true* purposes are, respectively, long-term protection of our forests; the refreshment and edification of our citizens; inspiration, guidance, and service; and education and scholarship. But such missions can always and easily be displaced by the simpleminded but clear-cut equations of the market.

Having said all this, though, it remains true that a good steward must be skilled at counting and, in the best sense, calculation. The steward of a manor, or of the religious order that welcomed pilgrims to a site like Conques, needed to have an informed idea about how many bushels of grain are likely to come out of the fields in a given season, as well as a good memory for how many barrels of beer are supposed to be in the cellar. As I have already argued, the attempt to promote biodiversity also, and increasingly, calls upon advocates of wilderness to behave with the care and skill of effective stewards. Their carefully calibrated efforts are motivated by the beauty of ecological stability and aspire toward the balanced complexity that Leopold described as "thinking like a mountain."

Just as a steward's faithfulness must be matched by acumen, both those qualities must be balanced by an awareness of the community's living history. To put this another way, a steward must be a skilled storyteller. This third principle of effective stewardship is particularly important for American environmentalists today. We too easily fall into an apocalyptic and isolated psychology. One of the central missions of the new national park in Woodstock is to insist that we do in fact have ancestors in the land, and vital models in the exercise of stewardship. To return to Silko's essay, we are part of "an ancient continuous story composed of innumerable bundles of other stories." The tradition of responsibility shown for this one beautiful place on earth is one especially heartening bundle of stories within the larger continuity of American environmental thought. Such living examples may also make it easier for us to remember the Iroquois ideal of stewardship—that of evaluating all our actions by their effects on our descendants to the seventh generation. We need to remember that our own individual stories, too, may significantly influence the future character and prospects of the landscapes where we now live. It is up to us to make sure that they contribute to, rather than undermine, the health of our local and planetary communities.

The fourth and final element for effective stewardship is inventiveness, and a willingness to take risks. Our vastest tracts of congressionally protected wilderness are still not large enough to secure the biodiversity within them, or even to maintain the air and water quality at their interior. Merely guarding the boundaries and enforcing the legislated guidelines, like burying a single talent for safekeeping, is not enough. It will be necessary for proponents of wilderness to invest our civic energies and

creative imagination broadly if we are adequately to preserve and to repay the original trust. Here in Vermont, at Marsh-Billings-Rockefeller
National Historical Park, there is an equally bracing mandate—to invent
an entirely new kind of park. It must be one where the human stories
and the natural history are intertwined; where the relatively small
acreage serves as an educational resource for the entire National Park
Service and a seedbed for American environmental thought; and where
the legacy of American conservation and its future enter into dialogue,
advancing the formulation of a new environmental paradigm for our
day.

Insofar as the leadership and community of Marsh-Billings-Rockefeller National Historical Park are successful in their pursuit of such purposes, they will also ensure for themselves a constantly shifting and perpetually challenging situation. To return to the ecological imagery of
edges, they will find themselves in a fertile, dynamic, chancy ecotone—a
highly productive environment, where the last thing one should ever do
is stay still.

· · ·

While my first hike into the new park was in late October, my next visit
was in an early December snow squall. Though the air was thick and
white, only a few inches had accumulated on the ground as I began, so
that I could trudge in without snowshoes or skis. Majestic Norway
spruces, darkly spired, arose momentarily in rifts amid the swirling snow
then, as suddenly, were gone. The snow continued to thicken, though, so
that even those intermittent landmarks disappeared entirely, and my
footing became tricky on the steeper grades. When I reached the Pogue,
I hunkered down beside it to watch the flakes colliding with the water
and melting into a cloudy O-Horizon just below the flat black surface.
Then I turned back toward Prosper Road and my car. A clearer afternoon would come, when I would once again follow the carriage road all
the way to the summit. In the meantime, I had also enjoyed this day's
beautifully broken hike, with its reminder that the story of Mount Tom,
too, was nowhere near the end.

12

FOREVER WILD AGAIN

At the Woodstock Historical Society, I found a print depicting the view from Mount Tom during the last decade of Marsh's lifetime. The slopes of the Green Mountains to the south and east were largely shorn of trees, except for occasional rows of pines and maples separating pastures. In many cases, fields for grazing sheep extended almost all the way to the ridge lines. The Ottauquechee was plainly visible down below, too, as it followed its broad curve around the village. This is the view that would have greeted townsfolk who drove their carriages up Frederick Billings's grand new roads and continued on up around the Pogue. Today, though, when I sit down on a midsummer day to take in the landscape from the same vantage point, the light green of pasturage has been replaced by the dark mass of a northern hardwood forest blanketing the mountains.[1] There are now only a few open fields east of the river, cultivated by the Billings Farm in connection with its livestock and dairy operations. Except where the river occasionally flashes into the sunlight when it meanders beside Route 9, the Ottauquechee has vanished from sight.

A new vision of stewardship must consider not only the long-tended forest of Mount Tom itself, and the values of mindfulness that Marsh conveyed so forcefully to his successor Billings. It must encompass, or give itself to, the thickly encroaching woods. Stewardship in Vermont is not just a recognition of the good choices human beings have made. It is also a modest and receptive appreciation of all that has happened in the world when we weren't looking. Acknowledging this larger process of natural reforestation can be a start to more mindful and modest participation in the community of life on which we humans too depend.

The ridge of the Green Mountains connecting Woodstock with my home in Bristol has largely been overtaken by resurgent woods. This is especially true on the west side of the ridge, where there are generally fewer ski areas. Bristol Cliffs Wilderness Area extends south from our town—a patch of recovering wildness running to the west of the village of Lincoln. Then comes Bread Loaf Wilderness, at 22,000 acres the largest federally designated wilderness in Vermont. It goes all the way down to Route 125 in Ripton, ending only at the lawns and hay fields that surround the Bread Loaf School of English. On the other side of 125 begins another roadless area in the national forest, protected from development by a line of peaks running perpendicular to the main north–south ridge. A new set of wilderness proposals have requested that this area of about 20,000 acres now be established as the Romance Mountain Wilderness. And so it goes, a sequence of wild new forests cresting along the line of the Green Mountains toward Woodstock.

Having stood atop Mount Tom and surveyed the tended beauty around the new national park, I'm taking a different perspective now—from the southern edge of the Bread Loaf Wilderness Area. I want to explore further the relationship between the ethos of stewardship and the wilderness ethic. So on a cool morning in August, I climb the Burnt Hill Trail. It begins from Steam Mill Clearing, on a dirt Forest Service road just west of the Bread Loaf School of English. As the names of the trail and the clearing suggest, these mountains were humming with industry in the nineteenth century. Forges and mills followed the watercourses, and enormous pyramidal kilns for charcoal and potash (made of tightly stacked logs) smoldered and glowed through the nights. But in this state's long history of disappearances and recoveries, such industrial sites were abandoned early. The collapse of the sheep industry followed, after which came the slow dying out of hill farms and the hamlets they supported, chronicled in so many of Robert Frost's poems. Now that early phase of Vermont history endures only in names like these or Potash Brook or Forge Hill. Often, even the features to which they refer, like this clearing beside a dirt road, would no longer exist if not maintained by the Forest Service as a parking spot for hikers taking this branch trail up to the Long Trail—Vermont's "Footpath in the Wilderness" from Massachusetts to Canada.

As I start up the Burnt Hill Trail, I hear in its name an echo of the sort of fire that scoured Mount Tom and left such an impression on George Perkins Marsh.

> Between fifty and sixty years ago, a steep mountain with which I am very familiar, composed of metamorphic rock, and at that time covered with a thick coating of soil and a dense primeval forest, was accidentally burnt over. The fire took place in a very dry season, the slope of the mountain was too rapid to retain much water, and the conflagration was of an extraordinarily fierce character, consuming the wood almost entirely, burning the leaves and combustible portion of the mould, and in many places cracking and disintegrating the rock beneath. The rains of the following autumn carried off much of the remaining soil, and the mountain-side was nearly bare of wood for two or three years afterward. At length, a new crop of trees sprang up and grew vigorously, and the mountain is now thickly covered again. But the depth of mould and earth is too small to allow the trees to reach maturity. When they attain to the diameter of about six inches, they uniformly die, and this they will no doubt continue to do until the decay of leaves and wood on the surface, and the decomposition of the subjacent rock, shall have formed, perhaps hundreds of years hence, a stratum of soil thick enough to support a full-grown forest.[2]

But with the efforts of Frederick Billings, Mount Tom recovered its tended beauty. And on the Burnt Hill Trail, too, a recent surge toward *wildness* can be felt. As I begin this morning's hike, red maples along the creek show where the flatter terrain was logged just a few decades ago. But these will gradually be replaced by sugar maples as the trail tilts upward, beginning a series of switchbacks that will carry me all the way to the ridge.

Amid the red maples there are sunny patches where asters and goldenrod grow thickly. But as I climb, the sugar maple and beech canopy filters out more of the light, until ferns along the creek account for most of the greenery on the forest floor. Fungus of various kinds becomes more abundant now, with the hummocky richness of logs and branches yielding themselves back to the fund of life. And there are occasionally small patches of other plants, like the Indian cucumber, which lifts its two little florets of pointed leaves, one over the other like nested umbrellas. I don't dig any of them up, since this is now a protected wilderness, but know from experience that below the ground they have a slender white tuber with a sweet, nutty crunchiness. If the early settlers in New England had more of an exposure to Chinese restaurants, they might have called this Indian water chestnut. For now, I envision the small white root and taste its crunch in my mind, just as I remember an industrialized and deforested Vermont when reading the names Steam Mill Clearing and Burnt Hill Trail on my topo map.

While Bread Loaf Wilderness may lack the sublimity of vast reserves in the northern Rockies or Alaska, there are aspects of hiking in these cutover woods that I prize more every year. Because this forest is small and near my home, it is one of several that I have now hiked through over and over, and in all seasons, for three decades. This is certainly not yet old growth, but it is by that token a *familiar* wilderness, in whose ongoing process of recovery I feel a personal stake. Some of the lower parts of the Burnt Hill Trail were clear-cut not long before Rita and I moved to Vermont in 1973. Near the beginning of his hike in "Directive," Frost writes,

> As for the woods' excitement over you
> That sends light rustle rushes to their leaves,
> Charge that to upstart inexperience.
> Where were they all not twenty years ago?[3]

The ability to remember when the trees were not there lends a special interest to the recovery of a forest. It relates the successional process of these woods to familial transitions of one's own life. All the hikes one undertakes along a given trail flow into one composite experience; they become part of Silko's "continuous bundle of stories."

Thinking about the return of wilderness to Vermont, I recall another late-summer hike, in a part of the Bread Loaf Wilderness not far from here, with the naturalist Alcott Smith. This was an outing organized by Forest Watch and the Vermont Natural Resources Council in order to celebrate the existing wilderness areas in Vermont and build support for establishing new ones. Smith began by acknowledging that these early-successional woods were far from old growth, which he defined as "a multi-age forest shaped by natural events over several centuries or more." But one of the pleasures of wilderness protection here, he said, was the knowledge that "old growth is already on its way back." When a

logging road is abandoned, yellow birch is one of the first trees to establish itself. This species can't get started very well in the duff of a forest
floor, but with its profuse seed production it can blanket a scarified and
recently abandoned surface like a dirt road. You can usually trace old
logging roads from the air even after the canopy has closed above them,
because of the subtly distinctive greens of the species like yellow birch
and pin cherry that are the first to fill them in.

Hiking with Alcott Smith also made me more aware of the role of
fungi in breaking down and mobilizing the forest's resources. At one
point, he called fungi "the facilitators of the forest." Sometimes we fall
into the assumption that a healthy forest is marked by straight, robust
trunks. But the galls caused by maple borers and the yawning vertical
holes called cobra canker are tokens of the insect and larval activity
that, like fungi, constantly shape and elaborate the bark. In forest ecology, as in cultural history, a breakdown can also be seen as the start of
something new. When a tree is knocked down by the wind or by another
falling tree, it often responds by promoting one of the remaining
branches into, in effect, a new trunk. Once one begins to focus on these
"adventitious branches," they are everywhere in the forest, thickening
and leafing out where something else met its end.

In these lower elevations of the Bread Loaf Wilderness, there are also
plentiful beaked hazelnuts—a special favorite in the late-summer diet of
the black bears who have returned with the thickening woods. Starting
at the end of July, bears will eat as many as 5,000 hazelnuts a day, according to Alcott. They seem to prefer them now, when they're still
green, because of their high nutritional value. That fact reminds me of
Tuscans' preference for oil crushed from olives that are still green, and
bursting with spicy freshness. Human diets, like those of animals, evolve
in distinct, local, and seasonal ways within the larger processes of succession.

In these early-successional woods near the trail's beginning and along
the brook there are numerous jewelweed—both yellow and spotted.
Bears love to eat these too, just as they root up the soil in such places for
the bulbous roots of allium, a fragrant member of the onion family. One
will often spot bear scat in such a place. These are all reminders, like the
songs of the hermit thrush that thread through the August woods, of
the beautiful compounding of wilderness—at the edge of our vision and
out of view as well as beside our chosen trail. The blue cohosh, doll's eye

(white baneberry), and plantain-leaved sedge also growing in nearby patches similarly bring to mind the composition of the soil itself. These plants, which I recognize from our family's sugar bush just to the north of here in Starksboro, require a calcium-rich soil. We guide ourselves into the wilderness along paths and orient ourselves by the succession of the trees, but need then to give ourselves to a proliferation of perceptions before becoming truly "lost enough to find ourselves."

· · ·

But it's time now to forge on up the Burnt Hill Trail, and to track along through two big stories of succession. One is the return of forests after two waves of cutting, and the recovery of biodiversity that has accompanied the trees. This is a wounded and recovering landscape. George Perkins Marsh has taught us to look at the larger effects of ecological change. And small patches of woods like the one I'm hiking through this morning are so widespread throughout northern New England and New York that together they make up what is increasingly called the Northern Forest—one of the most extensive and ecologically significant forests in the world. The second successional gradient I'm climbing through today is the ancient association of certain species with particular elevations. Red maple, sumac, and poplar in the flat terrain near the trailhead soon give way to a community of sugar maples, beech, hop hornbeam, basswood, red oak, white pine, and hemlock in the middle reaches of the trail. But from about 2,000 feet upward, a third and final forest community begins to appear. Paper birches begin to be common, sometimes filling whole bowls beside the trail as if in planted orchards. What appears to be a thick mass of individual trees might better be seen as one organism with many trunks—rising from runners that snake along below the surface. This ability to reproduce clonally lets birch trees grow on the cold ridges where the seeds of other hardwoods would not often find hospitable conditions to germinate. The capacity of their smooth white bark to take in sunlight and supplement the photosynthesis of summer leaves is yet another advantage birches have over trees like the maple. White pines are an additional species that hangs on at the ridge line. They were the dominant species after the first clear-cutting of the Green Mountains, but now rise more often as mighty individuals, lending character to what would otherwise be the mountains' smooth silhouette with their massive, individual boughs, curving upward at the tip. Above 2,200 feet or so, though, the mountains really belong to spruce and fir. Sometimes white spruce appear in boggy areas, but the main species here are black spruce and balsam fir. Their slender, sharply pointed profiles, combined with limber, downward turning branches, allow them to survive well in this high ground of fierce winds and long-lasting, ice-crusted snowpack.

The hiking just before I reach the Long Trail is delightful, with slow winds moving through the shaded world and bearing the sweet scent of the fir. A trail continues on past the Long Trail to Skylight Pond and Skyline Cabin, one of the loveliest spots for through hikers to camp. But I turn right instead, to the south, in order to reach a viewpoint just off the main trail. Less than a hundred yards after this turning I spot a narrow opening, winding through blueberry bushes to the southwest, and a ledge jutting out over Bread Loaf Valley and Middlebury Gap. Delicate mountain ashes, going to berry now, and mountain maples overhang this side trail. They're the main understory species at this elevation. They've marked a succession in the subcanopy, replacing the sumac at the bottom and the hobblebush of the middle elevations, just as hermit thrushes and wood thrushes initially took over from the red-winged blackbird around the trailhead and the tsst-tsst of warblers buzzes the air around us now.

There's a steep drop-off at the lower, western end of the ledge, and I watch my footing carefully before pulling myself up onto the rippled gray table of stone. I take out my water bottle and lean against my sweaty day pack while surveying the 180-degree view. Far below are the lawns and yellow clapboard buildings of the Victorian resort that now houses the Bread Loaf School of English and Bread Loaf Writers' Conference. One of Bread Loaf's mown fields lies directly across Route 125 from the inn. Students read and write in their green Adirondack chairs there or follow a trail across it to the West Fork of the Middlebury River. Gazing down at the campus now, I find the view inseparable from my more than twenty summers of teaching there, and from the writing and drawing workshops I have often led in that field south of the inn. Such a compounding of seasons is like the remembered taste of Indian cucumber whenever I spot those neat little whirls of leaves in the hardwood forest, or like a certain suggestion of smoke in the fresh morning air when I hoist my pack in Steam Mill Clearing. Within the compounding seasons of a familiar wilderness, each new experience can be the seed from which memories germinate. This is the personal equivalent of Marsh's historical insights. In eroded and abandoned regions of the Mediterranean world he could read a story like the scouring of Mount Tom in his boyhood. Such a connection also allowed him to see what the future of his Vermont home would be if present practices were continued. Stewardship is rooted in memory, both the personal memories that make a given place on earth precious and the historical vision that illuminates the ecological and cultural implications of our economic practices. On both the individual and the social levels, such a sense of affiliation allows "this earthly life of ours," in Marsh's words, to be "a school from cradle to grave." The alternative, as he puts it later in *Man and Nature*, is the carelessness and loss that accompanies "this life of incessant flitting."[4]

Beyond the final Bread Loaf meadow roll the forested ridges, uninterrupted as far as I can see, of the Green Mountain National Forest. A little state highway cuts through at Brandon Gap, about thirty miles farther south. But basically this whole central range of Vermont has returned to deep woods in the century and a half since Marsh wrote. Stewardship here will have less to do with management in an active mode than with protecting the providential wilderness that has grown up when we were not paying attention. Sustainable forestry of the sort Marsh advised will be appropriate in the 80 percent of Vermont's woodlands that remain in private hands. But here in the heights there is a core habitat that must be protected for the ecological health and biodiversity of the region as a whole. This is not an alternative to the stewardship practiced at the national park or on private lands. It is a fulfillment and a context for all those efforts of careful management. Wilderness brings stewardship into focus. It offers a criterion for human participation and restraint in other terrains.

. . .

Our six wilderness areas within the Green Mountain National Forest range from less than 4,000 acres in Bristol Cliffs to almost 22,000 at Bread Loaf. Gates of the Arctic they're not. Stone walls break through the ferns and jewelweed of these slopes, broken choker cables lie half-buried beside trails that were logging roads not so long ago, and cellar holes collect and compost leaves in the thick woods far from any trail. These tracts of third-growth forest were not included under the original 1964 Wilderness Act, being neither "primeval" nor "untrammeled."

Only after the passage of the 1975 Eastern Wilderness Act, which Vermont's George Aiken helped move through the Senate, were the lands protected because of their beauty and their biological significance. They were allowed, in effect, as afterthoughts—honorary wildernesses.

Such Vermont woodlands may have seemed marginal when added to the National Wilderness Preservation System in 1975 and in 1983. I believe, however, that they and the other wilderness areas of the Northeast are now emerging as central to our national conversation about nature and culture. I don't mean this in a spirit of regional competitiveness. The great wildernesses of the West and Alaska are incomparably magnificent. I will always be grateful for the protection those holy sites have received and for the opportunity to travel to them on pilgrimage. Glacier National Park and Kodiak Island will always frame my experiences of landscapes, just as the church at Conques and the caves at Pech-Merle will be landmarks of my spiritual life. But we do seem to have arrived at a moment—in our nation's ongoing dialogue about how human society will accommodate wilderness—when a place like Vermont might have a helpful word to say. Our modest wilderness areas here offer an ecotone between landscapes and perspectives that might earlier have seemed to be distinct, or even opposed. Wildernesses like those in Vermont might turn out to be *centrally marginal*. They define a boundary zone where the wilderness ethic may engage with recent developments in the field of environmental history, and where the ideal of preservation transcending a narrow utilitarianism may engage with the tradition of stewardship. We need to move beyond polemic in our discussion of these important matters. Vermont's wilderness offers one promising landscape within which to reframe the conversation.

Like much of northern New England, as well as New York's Adirondack region, Vermont is a landscape in recovery. The first half of the nineteenth century saw deforestation in our region that was as rapid and relentless as anywhere in America. Trees were cleared not only to open fields for crops but also to raise cash for the farmers and other early entrepreneurs of the region. Throughout the Green Mountains, kilns smoldered day and night, producing charcoal and potash for the forges, mills, and factories along the nearby rivers. Between the deforestation and the scantiness of our heavily glaciated topsoil, Vermont went from being the fastest-growing state in the Union after the Revolution to being the slowest-growing one for most of the time between the Civil War and

World War II. Since the middle of the last century, however, this wet land so good at growing trees has also gone from 60–70 percent deforested to being almost 80 percent reforested. Bill McKibben has described our region's resurgence as "an explosion of green." The irony of eastern wilderness is that while it may have seemed to receive that title as a courtesy, the *vector* of wildness may actually be more remarkable here than anywhere in the West. Not just the trees but also the animals have returned to a dramatic extent. Sightings of catamounts are reported with increasing frequency. And current proposals to reintroduce wolves into the Adirondacks and Maine hold out the possibility that we may someday see those predators at least in the northern portions of Vermont as well.

"Recovering wilderness" would perhaps have seemed an oxymoron just a few years ago. But that concept reflects an intriguing convergence between the environmental history of Vermont and the current emphasis on "rewilding" in The Wildlands Project. Corridors, or "connectivity," between relatively undisturbed areas of wild habitat are one main emphasis of the project. The striking resurgence of wildlife in Vermont, even in the absence of large "core reserves," suggests that there are already special possibilities for connectivity within our state's distinctive natural and human situation. I don't just mean corridors connecting and extending protected habitat. I am also referring to the connections between human culture and the wild, as well as to the potential for a more diverse and ecologically inclusive approach to conservation thought in America.

. . .

The thick forests embracing the Bread Loaf campus returned without any human management or, for that matter, protection. This is a providential wilderness and, accordingly, a messy one. The forested heights define a wild corridor running north and south between the towns planted along Route 7 and those following Route 100. There have been credible reports of catamounts near the Bread Loaf building known as the Printer's Cabin—less than a hundred yards west of the main meadow. Those big cats were tracking along in a band of rugged, heavily forested land—one that reaches down this ridge to connect the southern part of our state with the much less interrupted habitat of northeastern Vermont and Canada. But the east–west traffic on Route 125, with its Victorian resort turned writers' conference, also establishes a *human* presence in the midst of *wilderness*. Such a convergence makes this a good place to ponder the ways in which nature and culture have each other surrounded.

Wilderness in Vermont is a fruitful confusion, inseparable from the history of human enterprise and excess, failure and insight, associated with this place. Such a landscape of reversals may help us move beyond the current polarization between advocates of wilderness and their critics among environmental historians. When I follow the sometimes contentious exchanges between representatives of these groups, I am often struck, in fact, by how important the insights are on both sides. On the one hand, I identify strongly with the wilderness movement's testimony about the inherent value, and the sanctity, of wild places. One of the greatest contributions of environmentalism in the tradition of Muir has been its resolute challenge to narrow economic assumptions about the uses and value of land. At the same time, it is important to acknowledge that the wilderness movement itself is a historical phenomenon, inextricable from the social history, religious values, and economic situation of its proponents. Such a recognition does not mean defeat or repudiation of the wilderness ideal. It's simply a reminder that the transcendent values people espouse are always informed by and complicated by their immediate human contexts. I am convinced that the best way to consolidate and extend the wilderness ethic today—and to protect wild habitat —will be to integrate it with a more inclusive social perspective and a more ironic self-awareness.

Cronon's essay "The Trouble with Wilderness" has caused particular consternation among activists with its assertion that "[t]he dualism at the heart of wilderness encourages its advocates to conceive of its protection as a crude conflict between the 'human' and the 'nonhuman'— or, more often, between those who value the nonhuman and those who do not."[5] I believe there is truth in this assertion, if not the whole truth. From John Muir to the present, there has been a religious dimension to the wilderness movement. Not surprisingly, sectarian language has sometimes been the result. One example would be Bill Devall and George Session's influential 1985 book *Deep Ecology*, which provided a valuable service in pulling together many of the sources informing spiritual and ethical aspects of the wilderness movement. But it sometimes slid into an approach of separating the sheep from the goats—to the extent of downgrading a constructive environmental thinker like René Dubos for his "narrow Christian stewardship" or declaring that a writer of

Wendell Berry's stature "falls short of deep ecological awareness."[6] The point I want to make, though, is that our thinking about wilderness continues to evolve. This holds true for subsequent writing by wilderness thinkers, including Sessions and Devall, and is even more dramatically evident in the ambitious innovations of the Wildlands Project. My main reservation about Cronon's essay is finally that it wields too broad a brush, painting the wilderness movement as both more monolithic and more static than it really is. Still, his analysis remains very useful as a spur forward in our thinking about such matters.

The part of Cronon's essay that I find most helpful is his discussion of "wildness."[7] He points out that Thoreau preferred this word, with its more qualitative connotations. In "Walking," Thoreau wrote, "The West of which I speak is but another name for the Wild; and what I have been preparing to say is, that in Wildness is the preservation of the World. Every tree sends its fibres forth in search of the Wild. The cities import it at any price. Men plough and sail for it. From the forest and wilderness come the tonics and barks which brace mankind."[8] Wildness, for Thoreau, has less to do with expanses of roadless terrain than with a certain quality of alertness to our immediate experience. Muir, in contrast, emphasized the expansiveness of "God's wilderness." From my Vermont vantage point, I find both words useful—"wildness" for evoking the exhilarating recovery of our cutover landscape, and "wilderness" for defining the new protectiveness and ambitiousness with which we are beginning to regard our forests. There need be no war between these alternative terms, any more than celebration of Vermont's third growth implies a lessening of support for Oregon's old growth. Whatever the differences in their language, the fact remains that Muir claimed Thoreau as one of his chief inspirations, propping his Concord ancestor's picture on the mantel of his Martinez ranch. The most important task is not to defend a particular vocabulary but rather to protect the land, and the human and nonhuman communities it supports. This distinction might emerge even more clearly from the Cronon essay if its title were slightly altered to read "The Trouble with 'Wilderness.'" Though "wilderness" is an exciting and resonant word, the mysterious web of life to which it points is not captured by *any* language. Our plans and our vocabulary are fine as far as they go, but the world always offers vistas beyond our expression. At this moment in the story of Vermont's landscape it feels helpful to return to the old word stewardship. But that term, too, will eventually need to give way. Relinquishment of our received language is part of the process by which we identify ourselves more fully with the larger cycles of the land.

We need not only to understand ecology as a biological dynamic but also to enact it as a more encompassing, less hierarchical approach in our thinking about conservation and culture. The science of ecology describes a circuit of energy that includes and sustains the full range of biological diversity. While never ceasing to affirm the value of wolves and wilderness, we must also pursue a respectful dialogue with those whose livelihood is on the land and with advocates of healthier cities. Many efforts of this sort are already underway.

One reason to avoid defensiveness about terminology is to keep from getting stuck at an earlier stage in our own thinking. I have already referred to a shift in wilderness thought over the past decade and a half. One aspect of this, as my colleague Chris McGrory Klyza has pointed out to me, has been a move from valuing wilderness primarily in relation to human solitude to focusing on its importance for the protection of endangered species. Similarly, as an initiative like the Wildlands Project moves from the conceptual phase to that of implementation, it places greater emphasis on such concepts as stewardship. An illustration of this evolution comes in a recent Sky Island Alliance document coauthored by Dave Foreman of the Wildlands Project. "Stewardship zones," at both low-use and moderate-use levels, are affirmed as supporting the health and connectivity of core reserves. That discussion focuses on "linkages" or "corridors" at the biological level. But it also reflects an enhanced sense of connectivity within the ecology of our environmental *thought.*

As I argued in the section of this book entitled "Landmarks and Covenants," it is important to place the recent arguments of environmental historians within a larger context. Native American writers like Silko pose trenchant challenges to the wilderness ethic when they argue for the importance of human experience and stories to the character and value of sublime western landscapes. Silko emphasizes that the topographical stories passed down to her people over the centuries are also constantly revised in light of individuals' own experience. In order to receive the wisdom of such narratives, a listener must creatively participate in them. This is why it makes sense to describe Laguna culture as "an ancient continuous story composed of innumerable bundles of other stories." "Bundles," like "ecology," feels like an appropriately inclusive image for our ongoing conversation about wilderness. New perspectives can add to, and sometimes help to correct, our previous insights. There's always room for one more story if it's rooted in attentiveness to the land, or for a new take on one of the beloved old tales.

The wilderness of Vermont adds its own story to the bundle. It offers an antic, and an encouraging, tale in which the wilds surge across and between the roads of history. Such apparent incongruity can be disconcerting, but it can also be an opportunity to tune our ears to new harmonies. When the great New England composer Charles Ives was growing up, his father, George, was a town bandmaster who loved to have two bands march past each other on the town green playing different tunes. Ives compositions like "The Fourth of July" and "Putnam Camp" lovingly re-create such effects. Harmonies grow thicker, discords more jagged, as the bands march closer and closer. It's hard work listening to such massive and playful novelty, just as it is hard trying to negotiate a vocabulary where "wilderness" and "stewardship" can enter into non-antagonistic dialogue with one another. But it's also exciting to begin discerning new harmony where we earlier found only conflict. As the different tunes and vocabularies converge, moments also come when the familiar songs soar up with a new glisten. Then the bands march on, though with new ears, and the music and controversy fade into the quiet of this dusky corridor in the Green Mountains. Now comes evening, and the darkness of a Vermont unrestricted by the history or politics of "Vermont." Now begins the nightly conversation of a wilderness more wary and improvisatory than any lexicon.

. . .

One of the ways in which the wilderness ethic and the ideal of stewardship are converging, after their artificial separation in recent years, has been in their shared emphasis on protecting habitat. Originally, the justification for setting aside vast tracts of wilderness beyond any extractive use was to preserve a realm for solitary adventure and revelation. Amid the unsettled peaks, individuals could restore their souls and pursue their quest for life's meaning. Inspirational books like John Muir's *The Mountains of California* and Sigurd Olsen's *The Singing Wilderness* fostered this aspect of the wilderness ethic. As our human population increased and as a critique of wilderness was formulated as nothing but

the playground of an elite, wilderness advocates turned to a more utilitarian argument. Especially in looking at the tropical rain forests that
were being cut at such an alarming rate, they pointed out how many
species still unknown to science existed in these regions. Their potential
value as pharmaceuticals, perhaps even providing a cure for cancer or
AIDS, might far exceed these forests' worth as saw lumber or as clearings
to fatten cattle for fast-food restaurants. But in the Wildlands Project, especially, there is now an emphasis on biodiversity as the central goal of
conservation, as distinct from (but not opposed to) both preservation of
sublime scenery and careful use of natural resources. We have now
reached the point where we need to understand such habitat, not as an
alternative to sustainable forestry and sustainable agriculture, but
rather as their fulfillment and protection. We need a more capacious and
carefully articulated vision that includes wilderness, farming, villages
protected from sprawl, and the corridors for human and animal travel
that allow us to safely meet our other needs.

Such a vision is fostered through the vivid stories of loss and recovery
in the land with which Marsh fills *Man and Nature*. Beyond his formidable scholarship and his single-mindedness as a researcher, Marsh's most
important gift was his acuteness of physical observation and his ability
to bring all his learning to bear on the lineaments of a particular landscape. He was a looker and a rememberer. Gazing out over a deforested,
eroded landscape in the Mediterranean world, he at once remembered
the ancient civilization that had flourished there before destroying its soil
and silting in its harbor and recalled the careless cutting around his
Woodstock home that had already displaced many farmers and ruined
the fishing. Describing both regions, his intent was to help his readers visualize the inevitable effects of their actions unless they were quickly re-
versed. He was illustrating the story of carelessness and destructiveness,
but also offering images, from such landscapes as the forest at Vallombrosa, for an alternative narrative of stewardship and sustainability.

Marsh's admonitory tales are equivalent in their way to the story of
mighty hunter Orion's desire to demonstrate his prowess by killing all
the animals in the world. And the Greeks' characteristic connection between mythology and constellations in turn parallels the linkage between many Native American narratives and specific, highly recognizable landforms. The cultural anthropologist Keith Basso has written an
essay entitled "'Stalking with Stories': Names, Places, and Moral Narra-

tives among the Western Apache." In it he describes his interviews with members of the Apache community near Cibecue about how that landscape itself serves as "a repository of distilled wisdom." Particular landforms or locations evoke certain morally charged stories. Amid all the distractions of modern life, they bring people back to the roots of their culture and also "discourage forms of socially unacceptable behavior." In this way, Basso writes, "Mountains and arroyos step in symbolically for grandmothers and uncles."[9]

From Marsh's stories, as from the Greek myth and the Apache narratives, emerges the same insight: we human beings *are* the potential catastrophe from which we seek to protect the wildness and diversity of the world. From which we ourselves must be protected. We are the perpetually hungry hunters and the restless loggers. This is the context within which the concept of stewardship needs to be cultivated, as opposed to any sense of moral obligation or of sophisticated approaches to "managing the earth." We need to restrain our own appetites, and can do so only if more or less constantly reminded of the consequences if we do not. If there is a deluge against which we must build and provision the ark of stewardship, we must bear in mind that we are the flood as well as the navigators.

But the medium of story dramatizes the challenge of human responsibility in ways that can also delight and connect. While revising this chapter, I have been rereading the provocative recent essay "The Death of Environmentalism," by Michael Shellenberger and Ted Nordaus. Those authors take as their focus a set of political, economic, and institutional factors quite different from my own emphases on forestry and Marsh, Italy and Vermont. But in rounding off their argument they declare, "Environmentalists need to tap into the creative worlds of myth-making . . . to figure out who we are and who we want to be."[10] It is when our stories are rooted in the land and in the cycles of nature that they can truly gain the resonance of myth. George Perkins Marsh reminds us that even a history of abuse can offer the basis for renewal when we map it carefully and enter into it with both imagination and resolve.

13

INTO THE
WIND

Our Cessna four-seater taxied down the Middlebury Airport's narrow runway, then swung around to the north in preparation for takeoff. The pilot John McNerney checked all the mechanical systems one more time, recalibrating his compasses and shutting off each spark plug in a given cylinder to make sure that the other half of the combustion system functioned independently. Before we started to roll, he explained to his three passengers that we would be taking off directly into the wind. In contrast to what we might have assumed, this was preferable to having a tail wind. The important factor was not ground speed but wind speed around the wings. Surging into resistance, we could more quickly gain the totality of momentum that would pull us aloft in the suction and pressure of the Bernoulli effect.

Our pilot began by flying us through Middlebury Gap. The plane had climbed to about 2,400 feet by the time we reached Ripton and the campus of the Bread Loaf School of English. Traveling so low and sitting in such a small plane gave me a perspective on Vermont quite different from what I had expected. Whenever I'd taken a small commercial plane from Burlington to Boston in recent years, I'd been impressed by how heavily forested the landscape was. Except for the main highways, the expansive farms by Lake Chaplain, and urban areas like greater Burlington, it basically seemed ALL forest. But small as those two-prop planes may have seemed, with their dozen and a half passengers, they flew considerably higher and faster than we were going today. This flight left me much more aware of clearings and habitations in the woods. The forest that swathes Vermont struck me now as an emphatically domestic one.

I was of course expecting the commercial establishments along Route 7—tire stores and self-storage facilities surrounded by their oversize parking lots. Even the expanses of Johnson's and Lathrop's lumberyards did not take me surprise, since I have so often looked down on Lathrop's from the road leading into Bristol. But given the disappearance of most agriculture in the mountains long ago, I was not anticipating all the hayed fields that appeared beneath our plane in the course of the morning—far past the cluster of houses surrounding each town's church and school. In some cases, these fields might have gone with small farms operated by people who also held a job in town. In others they might have been kept open through subsidized haying by people who just wanted some space between them and the crowding trees. Several tennis courts and swimming pools suggested this latter explanation. There were also some long, well-maintained dirt roads winding way up into the mountains, past where I would have thought the Bread Loaf Wilderness Area would have begun. A couple led to tin-roofed hunting camps, a couple of others to what may have been year-round houses. From Addison and Shoreham to the Ripton-Lincoln ridge, there is a continuum from totally cultivated to totally wooded, but cultivation of one kind or another rises much higher up the ridge than I suspected. Rectangular patches of drought-browned hay field or pasture were defined by the dark green of trees. Though there were sometimes conifers marking where clear-cutting had taken place decades earlier, most of the trees seemed to be hardwoods. Toward the ridge, white pines began to poke up above the canopy.

As the last hay fields disappeared, we began to see more and more beaver clearings. Some of the beaver ponds showed one or two intact lodges, but a greater number had already filled in considerably. The process of eutrophication made them a beautiful emerald color—the greenest part of the whole forest. This long string of beaver ponds and meadows reminded us that beavers are one of the major forces shaping the New England woods. They open large clearings that affect everything from forest succession to bird and animal populations. They also do this within the space of decades, in a timescale not so different from that of the human clearings and roads that open and close in the wilderness of this wet, resilient region. If the forested ridge between Middlebury and

Hancock is like a dense green paragraph, the watercourses that divide its valleys are its basic syntax, the roads that sometimes parallel them are a kind of inflection (perhaps with a slight nonnative accent), and the clearings—human and beaver—are punctuation marks. Beaver ponds, always growing or diminishing, are like commas or colons. Human clearings may seem to be periods, or interrupting dashes, given their asphalted surfaces, concreted footings, and engineered intentions. But we've been here long enough by now to recognize that forest succession is really an unending process of revision in which sentences get combined or eliminated despite what a given period might have seemed to assert. If it had been possible for a small plane to take this same trajectory 120 years ago, a passenger seated in it would have seen many more farmsteads, fields, and roads. Eutrophication on a social and economic scale has planted trees in all those vestigial fields.

Accompanied by Pat Berry and Matteo Burani, I was embarked on a flight to explore the Champion lands of northeastern Vermont. This outing had been arranged by Elizabeth Courtney, director of Vermont Natural Resources Council, the organization for which both Pat and Matteo worked. John McNerney had volunteered his time and plane under a program called Northern Wings, "Aviation Services for the Environmental Community." Skilled pilots take up environmentalists, potential funders, politicians, or people checking on easements so that they may get a broader view of the countryside. We were headed up today to inspect a landscape that is of decisive importance to the future of stewardship in our region.

We took off from Middlebury Airport at 9:00 AM and were away for about four hours, including a brief stop at the grassy runway in Island Pond. After crossing Middlebury Gap, we turned north along Route 100, then followed 100B when it split off to the left. From this vantage point we passed directly over the new McMansions in Warren. One was almost incredibly large, surrounded by paddocks like vast putting greens and Kentucky-style white-board fences. It seemed as big as a hotel. Another had new copper roofs, gleaming like gold under our wing. Although we subsequently saw a good assortment of luxury homes around Stowe, none compared to the pod of half a dozen we saw in Warren. That's what goes in the clear-cuts behind our "beauty strips."

When we reached Hardwick, we circled over a dam that the Vermont Natural Resources Council was proposing to have removed. Located on the Black River where Routes 14 and 15 converge, this dam widens the stream out into a shallow expanse that makes the water warm and silty and damages the fisheries. One reason Marsh's writings interest me so strongly is that he so fully anticipated environmental concerns in the present. In 1857 he observed, "Many brooks and rivulets, which once flowed with a clear, gentle, and equable stream through the year, are now dry or nearly so in the summer, but turbid with mud and swollen to the size of a river after heavy rains or sudden thaws . . . [H]uman *improvements* have produced an almost total change in all the external conditions of piscatorial life, whether as respects reproduction, nutriment, or causes of destruction, and we must of course expect that the number of our fish will be greatly affected by these revolutions."[1] Although there were strong ecological arguments favoring removal of the dam, there was significant local opposition, too. It came from people who'd gotten used to things the way they were, or who just didn't like the idea of big organizations, whether nonprofit or governmental, mixing into local environmental choices.

It's not hard to understand why rural Vermonters might be feeling squeezed out by the influx of money and power from more populous and affluent regions. Look at those McMansions. Look at our own town of Bristol, as far as that goes, where it has become increasingly difficult for the children of locals to afford the sort of housing their parents owned with the sort of jobs their parents held. These families are being priced out of their own lives, invited by changing economic circumstances to move somewhere less desirable. Current social changes and disparities in our state often have the effect of inflaming discussions about environmental issues as well. One place such a controversy has been raging is in the Champion Lands of northeastern Vermont, where 132,000 acres have recently been purchased and conserved. I wanted to see this terrain from the air, out of a desire to get the whole picture.

For centuries, Vermont's remote Northeast Kingdom had been dominated, like much of northern New England and the Adirondacks, by vast private timber holdings. Local communities had grown up in relation to the logging industry, and the companies had also made seasonal camps available for nominal leases. Through both connections, many Vermont families developed deep roots in the region—through multiage, seasonal gatherings that might be compared both to the development of an old-growth forest and to the hunting camp evoked at the beginning of

Faulkner's "The Bear." Private land felt like a vast commons, and the companies themselves seemed intent on being stewards of cultural as well as natural resources. But at about the time the St. Regis Company was absorbed by Champion International at the beginning of the 1980s, all this was changing. The wood pulp industry was already shifting to the Southeast of the United States and to South America, where wood regenerates so much faster than in our region. In addition, Champion was one of a series of international conglomerates that took control of the timber industry at this point, companies with no particular bond with any region. Timber was a commodity for them, not part of a sustainable economy, and logging communities were economic factors rather than partners or constituents.

Champion liquidated their stock of trees, preparatory to abandoning their holdings and their mills in the Northeast. They cut way beyond the ability of the forests to regenerate, since they had no intention of doing business here for long. Before the environmentalists came into the picture, local loggers had already become deeply concerned about how the woods were being stripped out. Indeed, from the air we could see some clear-cuts half as big as a mountain, flat areas that looked like velvety bogs until one realized that they were actually places where every last tree had been removed, leaving only a few years of herbaceous growth and seedlings. Having accomplished their extractive and uncivic purposes, the new corporate owners announced that they were putting their entire northeastern holdings on the market. This encompassed several hundred thousand acres in all, including those in the Northeast Kingdom.

The likely outcome of Champion's announcement would have been the purchase of large blocks of land by concerns more interested in real-estate development than sustainable forestry. Shutting off large areas for commercial hunting ventures and the construction of hunting and fishing camps along the shores of remote lakes might well have followed were it not for a coalition put together by the Conservation Fund, in Virginia, and its in-state partners the Vermont Land Trust and the Nature Conservancy of Vermont. Working under considerable time pressure, they assembled a consortium of buyers that included the Silvio Conte Refuge of the National Fish and Wildlife Agency, accounting for 26,000 acres of the total; the State of Vermont, for 22,000 acres of a core ecological reserve around West Mountain; and approximately 84,000 acres of land sold back to Essex Timber, a private landowner committed to sustainable forestry. Development rights for the private land were purchased with a grant from the Vermont Housing and Conservation Board and the Freeman Foundation of Stowe, Vermont, and New York. Easements on the land being resold for sustainable forestry were to be coheld by the Land Trust and Housing and Conservation Board.

This was an amazing outcome, by far the biggest conservation deal the Vermont Land Trust had ever been involved in, and the preservation of an undeveloped area larger than any comparable property in the state. It was also extremely contentious from the start. Wilderness advocates complained that not more of the land was dedicated to wild habitat. They especially regretted one provision of the easement on the Essex acreage, namely, that after forty years had passed, one-half of the increased growth in a given ten-year period should be cut. This was described by some as a "forever logging" provision, because it prevented establishing future protections at a higher level. The Land Trust leadership responded that it was committed to keeping the faith with rural communities and with a state legislature that had often been wary of conservationists' motives. Such constituencies feared that this would be just the first step in phasing out traditional livelihoods in favor of a wilderness-oriented, recreational economy in which local people would be left with seasonal and service-oriented employment. The Land Trust wanted to show that it was a trustworthy partner, not an opportunistic one.

Having been hammered on that side, the Land Trust and its allies then got pummeled from the opposite direction. A coalition of camp owners, sportsmen's groups, and legislators loudly objected to the core ecological reserve on West Mountain. They hated the idea that camp leases would eventually be voided, and distrusted the effects of no-logging policies on certain species. Because deer, partridge, and other game tended to multiply in the browse that succeeded a heavy cut, they wanted to see logging undiminished throughout the area. The Land Trust and its partners answered that the camp owners were being given a much more secure lease under the new provisions than the timber companies had ever offered them, and that any new private owner might well have voided such agreements altogether. The lifetime tenancy plus twenty years that was now being offered meant—with many leases being transferred to grandchildren—that seventy years or more in the camps could be expected. Representatives of the Land Trust and the Nature Conservancy also pointed out that the unlogged woods would eventually foster a more diverse population of wildlife in the region as a whole, including animals like bears that need relative seclusion during denning and neotropical songbirds that rely on unbroken canopies. Even with the core ecological reserve protecting such species, there would still be plenty of "early-successional" conditions nearby for the deer.

While I found the Land Trust's responses in both regards to be clear and direct, I also feel that both the wilderness advocates and the opponents of the core ecological reserve made points that we must continue to bear in mind. It is simply true, for one thing, that Vermont has much less provision for wilderness than is desirable and than many other states have. In order to ensure the larger ecological health of our landscape, we need to have considerably more than the current 1 percent of our landscape receive such a level of protection. The Vermont Wilderness Association's proposals for the Green Mountain National Forest would raise this figure to approximately 2 percent. The same ecological arguments that bolstered the establishment of a core ecological reserve at West Mountain should now lead the Land Trust and others who support the Champion deal to speak up for this modest increase of wilderness in the state as a whole. Wilderness is not an alternative to sustainable forestry but a complement to it.

We also need to think harder about the maintenance of cross-generational familial bonds, and of our traditional rural lifeways in general. For me, those were the deeper issues underlying disputes over hunting, logging, and camps. Such values are threatened not just by the damaged timber economy of northern Vermont but also by influxes of capital that can quickly affect the character of our state. Conservationists will be called upon, not just to conserve agricultural and forestry land, but also to offer meaningful support to communities and individuals who derive their living from such land. It is increasingly clear, for instance, that the purchase of conservation easements by the Land Trust is not simply important for the ways in which those easements protect productive soils from subdivision. They can also do much to facilitate the cross-generational transfer of farm and forest ownership and to encourage dialogue about the future of surrounding towns. A new complexity comes into conservation work from such a perspective, but also a new promise.

I was struck by the fact that the Champion coalition's responses to their stringent critics on both sides echoed one group's arguments in answering the other group. There may be a basis for consensus here. During our break at Island Pond, the three of us who were taking this flight over the Champion Lands sat down with our pilot at a picnic table so that we could spread out several topos. We wanted to figure out how the pieces of the puzzle came together. With our aerial vistas in mind, we could trace how private, state, and federal holdings, each with their different shadings, combined into a larger pattern. Through complementary missions on contiguous parcels, such diverse ownership should be able to protect wild habitat, water quality, and the long-term prospects for a forestry-related economy in the surrounding countryside. If in our discussions about the future of Vermont we can similarly lay a diversity of landscape and cultural values next to each other on such a composite map, we may find that, in such a context too, apparent oppositions resolve into a fabric of ecological wholeness.

. . .

After completing our flight over the beautiful, wounded Champion Lands, we set a course for home. We would follow Route 12 to I-89, then take 100 to the Appalachian Gap. Finally, Route 116 would then lead us back over Monkton and Bristol to Middlebury Airport. All of us were tired from the vibrations of our small craft, and conversation ebbed as we gazed out the windows and gave ourselves to our own thoughts. I was surprised to find that the countryside around Florence came strongly to my mind. Surprised, because that is such a city of stone, whereas Vermont seems, both from the air and on the ground, to be all about forests. Within the built environment, too, Tuscany's tan stucco walls and red ceramic roof tiles seem opposite in effect to our white clapboard villages with houses roofed either in gray slate or in asphalt tiles emulating slate's subdued tones. Still, Florence reveals with special clarity a pattern that also prevails here. The cultivated lands of Tuscany and the city's urban core know and show themselves in relation to each other. In that *L'Unità* article Janet showed us about the loss of olive groves in Impruneta, the journalist reflected that monuments like the Duomo had been conceived against a living texture of pale gray green. The olive-planted hills set off the cathedral's astounding mass of tiles as dramatically as the sky, and were constantly visible behind it for pedestrians and business people going about their tasks. Similarly, from far away, the towers of Florence, and the Duomo in particular, punctuated the rolling Tuscan countryside.

During our time in Italy, Rita and I took the same walk on several Sunday afternoons. We rode a blue municipal bus to Fiesole, followed a network of paths through orchards and vineyards and forests, then came home on a different bus. Often there was just a single farmhouse, monastery, or fortification in the foreground as we walked. But on the horizon we could spot the Duomo again and again over the hours. It was the stone landmark in that terrain to which a variety of stories could be attached: stories of faith, of artistic and scientific genius, of political power that at times affirmed civic pride and at others expressed the most blatant self-assertion of individual and family privilege.

I may have been even more inclined to see the landscape of Tuscany while gazing down at the Green Mountains through the Cessna's window because of two books I had recently read. Both took a broad view of those respective landscapes. *Above and Beyond* is a volume by three planners that uses numerous aerial photographs of Vermont to highlight the effects of incremental changes in rural communities. The authors' emphasis is on giving towns a better way to envision the implications of specific zoning decisions by "remembering the past, imagining the future, and setting up a framework within which a desirable pattern can emerge." By preventing "low-density, scattered development," towns could both preserve their village centers against the blurring effects of sprawl and help to conserve surrounding farms, outdoor recreation, and wildlife.[2] A parallel project, under the auspices of Florence's regional agency for planning and development, was edited and coauthored by Mauro Agnoletti. The resulting volume, *Il paesaggio agro-forestale toscano* (The agro-forestry landscape of Tuscany), uses a variety of GIS maps, historical photographs, and graphs to help readers envision larger patterns of change as traditional agriculture declined. The GIS examples serve like the aerial images in *Above and Beyond* to enrich a reader's perspective. The juxtaposition of historical photos with contemporary ones from the same vantage points evokes a rhythm of deforestation and reforestation strikingly similar to the environmental history of Vermont. Agnoletti concludes the book by affirming that a balance between forests and cultivated lands is essential to both the natural and the cultural health of Tuscany: "The character of the landscape represents, in fact, not just a cultural value but also a strength of our whole system, comprehending within its own equilibrium the environmental and socioeconomic fruit of a positive human-natural rapport."[3]

From the air, we can see that built environments, cultivated land-scapes, and wilderness are engaged in a continuous dialogue with one another. We need to pursue nourishing conversation between these elements, and not to settle for an argument. The steward is a facilitator of such conversations: a translator between different modes of being at home on the earth, and a counselor of tactfulness and restraint. But no one can speak all languages, participate in all conversations, or be conversant with every mountain pass. Perhaps one way to transcend the present controversies about land use and conservation is to acknowledge our need for many stewards, for a definition of citizenship in which each member of the community must help to mediate and cultivate a sustainable conversation—in which both the human realm and the self-willed lands are understood as stories within a larger bundle. We need to approach disagreements between advocates of different landscapes and traditions not as battles between antagonists but rather as vitalizing forms of diversity within the larger ecology of environmentalisms.

This is how I understand the controversies over the Champion Lands. They are opportunities to gain a whole-landscape perspective on conservation. Marsh helped us glimpse the way in which ecological errors, with their distressing consequences, may generate a constructive reaction—a vision of becoming human "coworkers" with nature. The ecological and social losses of the Champion Lands may be like the scarified, mineral-rich soil of an abandoned logging road, or like the exposed mound of soil where a mid-forest tree has gone down under the wind. As the woods converge over such scars, they initiate an early successional state whose end result can be envisioned as the saturated richness of an old-growth forest. Inspecting the scars, and watching the rise of adventitious branches, we may gauge how far we've come. Taking off into a stiff headwind, we may rise quickly if we also put the energy into keeping our ground speed up.

In first discussing the concept of stewardship, I traced it, like ecology, to the image of a house. In order to find the whole-landscape perspective on this role, it's helpful to bring in education as a complementary term. The germ here is the Latin *educere*, "to draw out of." This is very different from the imposition of external models, reinforced by standardized testing, that are often referred to in debates about educational policy. I understand "to draw out" in a positively ambiguous way. On the one hand, it means to draw out the inherent creativity within each human mind, the potential for connection and for identification; on the other, it means to draw people themselves out into the world. We'll be helped not to think of stewards as *presiding* over the house of life if we remember that this is much more than just a human domicile but rather a larger world into which we may *emerge.* A steward is not above, but in nature.

. . .

Drawing closer to Middlebury after this long day in the air, I watched as the town where I work every day slipped into view to the right side of our plane. Its churches, banks, and post office, its lawyers and doctors, theaters, hardware stores, feed stores, and tractor dealerships distill the daily activities of people throughout the landscape. Conversely, the hay fields and cornfields that embrace Middlebury give a seasonal context and character to the town. The agricultural landscape enhances the experience of those who live or do business there. If the farms of Cornwall and Shoreham establish such a dialogue with the seasons on the south and west of Middlebury, the woods and mills of Bristol and Starksboro establish a similar one to the north and east. Logging, sugaring, and hunting take people, individually and in small groups, up into the forests. In a village like Bristol, whose ample clapboard homes make it plain that milling and labor were the real limiting costs, never the lumber per se, we can read the expansiveness of the surrounding woods. The excitement of sugaring and deer hunting that grip the community in March and November, respectively, integrate the daily rhythms of work into the encompassing cycles of the year. In spring and fall, both out over the flat, fertile farmlands along Lake Champlain and here at the edge of the Green Mountains central ridge, Canada geese and snow geese cross overhead in their gathered clans. Central Vermont is only part of their range, but it is as essential to their map of home as their seasonal flights are to human watchers below.

Farther up the slope from Bristol, in the Bristol Cliffs and Bread Loaf Wilderness Areas, comes a zone beyond all narrow economic endeavors but essential to the health of our state. There's no equivalent to it in the countryside surrounding Florence, but Vallombrosa, as a Riserva Naturale, aspires to such a status. The roadless heights sustain a wider range of wildlife, offer opportunities for recreation and solitude, and enhance the air and water quality of towns below. Just as there is a dialogue between the village and its surrounding cultivated lands, so too is there a conversation between farms and forestry and what the Wildlands Project calls "self-willed lands." The Champion Lands are opportunities to gain a whole-landscape perspective on conservation—to view Vermont from the air so that we can come back down to earth with a renewed sense of proportion.

14
MAGGIE BROOK

A road of pale gray cobbles curves up through the abandoned meadow. Goldenrod and sumac crowd in from both sides. On this late-summer morning, black-eyed Susans and chickory intertwine with the taller thickets near the road's edge, while golden seed heads droop with dew in the meadow's central, green-brown tangle of grasses. We'll brush hog this area soon, now that ground-nesting birds like savannah sparrows, song sparrows, goldfinches, and upland sandpipers have had a chance to hatch their young. Along the line where the upper meadow transitions into woods, we expect there are also some yellow throats, yellow and chestnut-sided warblers, and indigo buntings nesting. They like an environment just outside the grasses, an edge of stiffer plants and thicker stalks that is nevertheless defined and maintained by the annual threshing of its buffer zone. The brush hogging will not only hold back the encroaching forest and provide these birds' offspring with a place to nest in future years, but will also make it easier for our own children to cultivate gardens, as well as to have space for the vines, root cellars, or greenhouses that might be part of their plans if any of them ever choose to settle here where the sugar bush lies beside the town road. The lower part of the meadow, where the road that Rita and I are walking on passes over the concrete floor of a long-demolished barn, would be a different kind of ecotone for them.

After a hundred yards or so, the road enters the woods and cobbles give way to a firmly packed dirt surface shaded by sugar maples, paper birches, poplars, and an occasional white pine. Our walking is easier now, and a pleasant breeze stirs beneath the boughs. A brook trickles to our left—a modest seasonal stream that runs several feet below the level of our road in a little gorge edged with mossy stones. As we climb the hill, the road bends gradually in toward the stream. But after it has passed up under the trees it swings strongly to the right, so that Rita and I end up walking straight toward the sugarhouse we built on this property with our sons several years ago. It is a twelve-by-sixteen structure faced with vertical, rough-sawn pine boards, and with narrow battens nailed over the cracks between those boards. The corrugated metal roof includes several panels of translucent plastic in order to let some light into this building so far from any electrical hookup. Centered above the main roof is a smaller one, with louvers on the side that may be lowered when sap is boiling so that the sweet steam can billow out.

This modest sugarhouse continues to inspire improvements. As Rita stands up on the front steps to open the combination lock, we inspect the woodshed that Matthew and I have just added to the north end. It should be big enough to hold six cords and will ensure us of dryer wood than we've had in the previous three years of boiling. The sugarhouse stands more or less at the center of a 142-acre property that the labels on our cans of syrup identify as the Maggie Brook Sugarworks. We've named both the brook and the whole sugaring operation in honor of Rita's mother, Margaret.

This ragged patch of forest, now recovering after at least two episodes of clear-cutting, is where our family is trying to participate in our own modest way in the restoration and conservation of Vermont. Far from pristine, it nonetheless harbors deer, moose, and fishers, whose tracks crisscross the upper slopes in the January snow. Bears forage here, too, as evidenced both by their large tracks on the muddy logging roads of spring and by the fan-shaped patterns of black dots embossed on some of the beech trees near the southeast corner of the land. These scars were left when the bears climbed the trees—either to gather nuts or to tuck their new cubs away temporarily for safekeeping—and dug their curved claws into the smooth gray bark.

In walking this land through the circling seasons, we are beginning to perceive more specifically what Wendell Berry might call "the membership" of this recovering forest. In deciding to develop a sugar bush here, we registered both the prevalence of healthy sugar maples around sixty years old and the presence of plants like blue cohosh and maidenhair fern promising sweet soil and strong future growth of trees. When surveying the arboreal community we also noticed the many handsome paper birch and the straight, dark trunks of the ash. But year by year other trees swim into resolution for us as well. There are the basswoods along an old stone wall on the northwestern line, the red oaks and spruce that form their own little community on the highest ridge, and the hemlocks in colder coves where the brook drops farthest below the level of the surrounding land. Hiking with the ecologist Eric Sorenson in winter conditions, I became more aware, through his eyes, of how common shadbush and maple-leaved viburnum are in these woods. Eric also investigated a woodland seep with me, where water trickles down off the slopes and fans out over hardpan rather than finding any definite channel. Even with snow on the ground, he could identify jewelweed, sensitive fern, cinnamon fern, marsh buttercup, rough-stemmed goldenrod, and golden saxifrage in the area of the seep. He also found some slow-moving water under the snow where there was a tiny white fingernail clam, an indicator that there is commonly water here. Eric subsequently wrote me, "I expect that this seep provides habitat for amphibians (spring, dusky, and northern two-lined salamanders are all species associated with this wetland community type). The seep may also provide spring bear feeding habitat. I would recommend no cutting within 100 meters of the seep."[1]

The more we are able to focus on the specific living communities that inhabit this one undramatic stretch of Vermont woods, the more eager we are to be involved in its ecological restoration and to help protect its long-term future through our own efforts as forest stewards. The damage here was done over more than a generation, and the restoration will require commitment by our family beyond Rita's and my lifetimes. Our family's efforts will thus make most sense within a whole-landscape vision of conservation in Vermont. From such a perspective, privately held forests can surround and buffer the newly established wilderness areas as well as the state's other public lands. They can offer a place to explore and practice the conservation skills for which Marsh called in *Man and Nature*.

Throughout his writing, as I have already noted, Marsh wrestled with the question whether conservation was best promoted by public or private ownership of the land. Toward the beginning, as an independent Vermonter, he was inclined to trust in the enlightened self-interest of individual landowners, but his experience of nation building in Italy and his darkening view of greed and corruption in American history led him to tilt toward public policy as the more promising realm for conservation. In his central chapter, "The Woods," Marsh wrote, "It is a great misfortune to the American Union that the State governments have so generally disposed of their original domain to private citizens."[2] Both the transformation of his family homestead into a national park and the preservation of wilderness areas in the Green Mountain National Forest would thus fulfill Marsh's vision of conservation as a central function of government. But the fact remains that in Vermont, in contrast with places like Wyoming or Alaska, most of the land has been privately held since the state's founding. A whole-landscape vision here must inevitably conceive of public conservation within the context of private stewardship.

Even after the founding of the Green Mountain National Forest and subsequent conservation efforts at federal, state, and local levels, well over 80 percent of Vermont's forest land remains in private hands. This has of course not always been forested terrain. After the failure of most agriculture in the mountains, and the decades when sheep were pastured there, trees have returned to our slopes without human assistance. But farmers struggling to balance the books have cut heavily on their way down and out. A last great wave of clear-cutting on private lands came in the middle of the twentieth century, so that the average age of Vermont's forests today is probably not much more than half a century. At this stage we can just begin to glimpse what a truly mature northern hardwood forest might look like. Even so, this requires looking beyond the life span of our present generation.

Marsh wrote in "The Woods,"

> The growth of arboreal vegetation is so slow that, though he who buries an acorn may hope to see it shoot up to a miniature resemblance of the majestic tree which shall shade his remote descendants, yet the longest life hardly embraces the seedtime and the harvest of a forest. The planter of a wood must be actuated by higher motives than those of an investment the profits of which consist in direct pecuniary gain to himself or even his posterity. . . . But when we consider the immense collateral advantages derived from the presence, the terrible evils necessarily resulting from the destruction of

the forest, both the preservation of existing woods, and the far more costly extension of them where they have been unduly reduced, are among the most obvious of the duties which this age owes to those that come after it.[3]

Such obligation may be easier to feel when a family has been long settled in one region and the effects of their ancestors' stewardship are visible to a particular generation. But in America, as Marsh also points out, social mobility has been more the norm.

. . .

When Rita's mother died five years ago, the portion of her estate that we inherited allowed us to purchase this forested tract of land. Margaret was not a wealthy person. Like Rita and me and like both of my parents, she was an educator—a professor of Romance languages at San Jose State University. Still, our share from the sale of her house was sufficient to buy a parcel of 142 acres that had proven unsuitable for development and was thus on the market at forestry rates. The same amount of money put into our TIAA-CREF retirement fund might have made it possible to retire a year earlier. But we viewed this as a chance to pursue our interest in Vermont's sustainability movement in a direct, personal, and concrete way. It would allow us to participate in the efforts celebrated in the Stewardship Initiative of the Marsh-Billings-Rockefeller National Park and its Conservation Study Institute, and to become more involved in Vermont Family Forests, founded by our Bristol friend and neighbor David Brynn. We could thus enter into the map of Vermont's resurgent forests in a collaborative effort involving not only our neighbors but also our children. Committing ourselves to becoming practitioners of sustainable forestry has taken us far afield from our usual work—just as our pursuit of Marsh's traces in Italy did. And these two explorations have felt like part of a larger process of exploration and consolidation. Perhaps they have to do with our parents' and grandparents' goals in immigrating such vast distances: a family's search for home.

The land we bought, like so much forest land in Vermont, was in certain important ways "out of order"—as Aldo Leopold phrases it in his collection of essays called *For the Health of the Land*. Forests that return after a clear-cut are too close to even age. They arrive at a point where crowded conditions lock in a lower canopy over many years until openings are finally created to let a smaller number of trees surge up to the next level. Cutting some trees in order to foster a mixed-age woods, with both a loftier canopy and a greater abundance of seedlings, is one measure a steward of the forest might take. Another is making sure to leave plenty of "standing snags." These are the large dead trees crucial as habitats for many insects, birds, and mammals. In Vermont, the most important form of forest restoration may simply be closing down old logging roads—throwing logs and brush across them and digging water bars, broad dips that divert water that would otherwise rush straight down those steep old skidder tracks carrying the forest's soil along with them. Water bars should be installed as well in whatever forest roads will remain in use, since protecting the soil and water is the steward's first responsibility.

Our decision to call the stream trickling through the middle of our Starksboro property Maggie Brook, and to give that name also to the sugar bush, expressed the same impulse to honor Rita's mother that made us want to spend a year in Italy. In these woods, as was also true every day of our Florentine sabbatical, we have been continually reminded of the depth of our ignorance. For one thing, we have found ourselves surrounded by new nomenclature. The fact that a water bar was actually a dip in the road rather than some kind of, well, bar took me a surprisingly long time to figure out. And in applying for "current-use" status, whereby the tax rate on our land would be significantly lowered because of its dedication to forestry instead of development, Rita and I had to seek out someone qualified to draw up and file a forest-management plan. Once we were duly registered with the state and had mitigated erosion on the network of old logging roads we'd just bought, we had to start learning how to sugar. Sugaring is a living rural tradition in Vermont, still largely passed on by older relatives to children who hang around the sugarhouses. But we've had to piece this lore together with advice from neighbors and the help of our children. Even after figuring out how to stretch and anchor the sap lines, install the tank and evaporator, and filter, boil, and refilter, we realize we're just getting started. It will be a lifetime effort to refine our technique, through consultation with all the old pros whose land surrounds ours in the mountains.

In the meantime we're working together in the woods and, if way over our heads, at least we're in it together. If tending the forest requires some cutting to open up the canopy and—in the sugar bush's core—to favor certain robust, middle-aged maples, that also implies learning how to use a chain saw with some confidence. I took a couple of workshops in the safety-conscious Scandinavian techniques called The Game of Logging, learning how to plan where a tree would fall and set plastic wedges in the kerf until I was finally ready to cut the last "trigger" and release the tree forward over its "hinge." Firing up my Jonsered saw still makes my heart pound, both because I know how dangerous a tool it can be and because I feel what a serious decision it is to fell a tree that may have been standing on this slope for longer than I have been alive. Still, I believe that cutting trees can be an ethical choice within a larger effort of stewardship. Sitting at my pine desk in our rambling clapboard house, in this room lined with books, it's well to be aware of all the lives that make possible our own family's life. We need to keep the costs soberly in mind.

. . .

In *The Future of Life*, E. O. Wilson sums up the demographic and ecological challenges facing humanity in the twenty-first century: "*Homo sapiens* has become a geophysical force, the first species in the history of the planet to attain that dubious distinction. We have driven atmospheric carbon dioxide to the highest levels in at least two hundred thousand years, unbalanced the nitrogen cycle, and contributed to a global warming that will ultimately be bad news everywhere."[5] The direct line of descent between this statement and the argument of *Man and Nature* is both hopeful and a sobering. The hopefulness comes from the realization that so many creative changes were inspired by Marsh's book, and that learned, imaginative figures like Wilson have continued his prophetic effort. But this time around, as Wilson's language specifies, the catastrophe is on a scale even more far-reaching than the deforestation Marsh chronicled. Changes in the climate of our planet may ultimately be "bad news everywhere," but such changes vary widely by region. Winters in northern New England have been especially affected over the past two and a half decades, with the average winter temperature in Vermont already rising by over 3 degrees Fahrenheit. Since maples germinate at 34 degrees, this change may affect the regeneration of these trees here. And since sap for sugaring flows only when the temperature is above freezing in the daytime and below freezing at night, the temperature change is already beginning to truncate the sugaring season and to shift it toward February from its usual time in March. Some experts predict that sugaring will largely have ended in Vermont within fifty to seventy-five years. We will try to make our forest as healthy as we can through opening up the canopy and preventing erosion. But here in Starksboro we are anything but immune to the global environmental crisis. Our efforts to cultivate a practice of stewardship will be interwoven with the work of grief.

The fact that the name of our sugar bush is a memorial for Rita's mother reflects the kind of stewardship required in our time. The task goes far beyond anything an individual might accomplish. It requires a multigenerational effort to correct a destructive pattern extending over the centuries. This is an opportunity as well as a necessity. Working in these woods together over the past six years has been one of the greatest gifts our family has received. Rita and I frequently go up to the sugar bush on weekends to do a little work on the lines, after which we stray around the woods together in a way that turns tasks into escape—a new pilgrimage beyond routine and into the deep history of the forest. Our son Matthew is a man of few words, but he possesses a strong vision of what he believes and a strenuous drive for excellence. Building a woodshed with him this past summer has been an opportunity for intense collaboration. I carried out the preliminary tasks—buying rough-sawn pine boards from Mike Quinn's nearby mill, having the corrugated roofing and other hardware delivered from Goodro's, cutting three trees to make a space for the shed, and laying out where the posts would go. But Matthew provided most of the strength to get the rocks out and the posts in, as well as the skill to fit the rafters, with the narrow triangles called birds' mouths cut in where they would meet across our four-by-four lintel. To imagine this simple structure rising in the woods beside our sugarhouse, then spend a week of sweat and sawdust bringing it into reality, was a satisfying effort. We hope that our children's children will keep their wood dry under this tall, spacious woodshed as they continue to sugar here in land conserved as forest forever.

Our younger son, Caleb, is a musician. In the recent summer after his graduation from college, he was touring as a fiddler and singer with a bluegrass band. Though Caleb thus didn't get in on the woodshed project, he has a couple of songs on the band's latest CD that express his own devotion to Maggie Brook. Caleb has spent weeks at a time living up here, rolling out his sleeping bag on a tent platform that he and Matthew built together and clamped around a triangle of trees. He typically prefers to walk up to this site from Ruby Brace Road rather than follow the graveled logging road to the sugarhouse. First he crosses the pasture where we let our friend Lindsey pen her sheep and makes his way through the hummocky old meadow with its interspersed copses of poplars. Then he enters a fringe of small trees, mostly sumac and paper birch, that gradually thickens into the maple woods around the sugarhouse. This walk up into the mountain is Caleb's transition and his respite. Where the hermit thrush is the voice of these woods for Rita and me, the barred owls that call in the late-summer and fall twilight express them for him. Under their auspices he follows his own path to wholeness in a complicated world. Here's the chorus of one of his songs:

> Where we are isn't far—
> It's just a short walk through the trees,
> Enough so we don't hear the cars.
> The night is warm enough, my dear,
> That we have time to count the stars.
>
> Oh, my dear, do you hear
> The barred owl calling in the darkness
> And the rivers running clear?
> Hold my hand to let me know
> This is your favorite time of year.

Rachel was already out of college by the year we bought this land and has lived out of state—first in California, then in New York—since then. Though we're sinking family roots more deeply into Vermont than either side of our family has had anywhere in the world for several generations, we are still living in a time with all the challenges, and the blessings, of mobility. Despite our sons' current orientation to this land-based enterprise, there's finally no telling where their other choices in life will lead them. In the meantime, though, we can work together here on developing a sense of the seasons and possibilities of one particular place on earth at the center of our identity as a family. With Rachel this has often necessarily taken the form of letters, e-mail messages, and phone calls, with the annual syrup crop sweetening the season for her and her friends. Now that she is living in New York and just a short train ride away, she can come up to Vermont much more frequently. On a recent visit, we had her out scything in the tall grass along the cobbled logging road. As she drew the blade back then swung it hissing through the brittle stalks, she asked us to take some pictures of her at work in the field so that she could amaze her neighbors in Brooklyn and coworkers in Manhattan with this image of her on home ground.

In this book, and especially in this final chapter, I've grounded my hope for multigenerational stewardship in our own little family. But I mean to propose neither our endeavors nor our landscape in Vermont as norms of any kind. They simply offer the context for conceiving of stewardship that's closest to home for us. With reference to Leopold, I have discussed stewardship as a call for education and skill. It's worth noting that two of the most eloquent writers addressing this multigenerational project of stewardship are explicit about the fact that they have no children of their own. In every aspect of their artistic and environmental vocations, though, Rachel Carson and Terry Tempest Williams illustrate their values through interactions with members of other generations. In Williams's *Refuge*, this means the example of a wise grandmother which continues to strengthen and inspire. Williams recalls traveling out to a bird sanctuary with Mimi and learning about the habits and diets of various species from their tour guide on the bus. But her grandmother took care to balance that scientific information with comments about the emotional and spiritual meaning of the birds: "'When an ibis tucks its head underwing to sleep, it resembles a heart. The ibis knows empathy,' my grandmother said. 'Remember that, alongside the fact it eats worms.'"[6]

A balance of the emotional and the scientific is essential to our personal and familial sustainability as we confront the challenges of a century that E. O. Wilson has called "the bottleneck." It is the equivalent, in our personal ecology, of the way wilderness and cultivated lands complement each other in the health of our state. We also need, as environmentalists, to balance our awareness of specific ecological dangers with pleasure in the world's abiding beauty and mystery. Bruno Bettelheim titled his book about concentration-camp survivors who found the requisite balance of reason and passion to see them through that nightmare *The Informed Heart.* As we face the potential for an environmental holocaust in the twenty-first century, it will be easier to find such balance in the reinforcement of memory, education, and childlike openness. At the heart of stewardship is sympathy, and there is a mutually reinforcing relationship in the sympathy between adults and children and our sympathy with the more-than-human realm.

Just as going back to the roots of terms like stewardship and education can renew our sense of their possibilities, so too the experience of children offers an antidote to the specialization and routines of adults. A wonderful passage from Barry Lopez's essay "Children in the Woods" speaks to the dialogue between mystery and analysis in our experience of nature, and to the connection between children and adults out of doors as an entry into the larger house of life. "In the end," Lopez writes, "you were trying to make sense to children that everything found at the edge of one's senses, the high note of the winter wren, the thick perfume of propolis that drifts down wind from spring willows, the brightness of wood chips scattered by a beaver, that all this fits together. The indestructibility of these associations conveys a sense of permanence that nurtures the heart, that cripples one of the most insidious of human anxieties, the one that says you do not belong here, you are not necessary."[7] Even more essential to stewardship than responsibility and skill is the sense of belonging, as necessary parts, to a community extending far beyond us in both space and time.

Lopez's passage builds directly on an insight of Rachel Carson's. Carson's unique ability to combine science, literature, and activism makes her one of the most inspiring twentieth-century Americans; she is the namesake of our daughter Rachel. Like Williams, Carson had no children of her own. But in her book *The Sense of Wonder* she wrote about her introduction of her great-nephew Roger to nature along her beloved Maine coast. An adult does not need to instruct a child in the specifics of biology or evolution, she wrote, but only to be an interested companion as the child experiences the wonder of creation. Such experiences are the foundation on which structures of knowledge can follow: "If facts are the seeds that later produce knowledge and wisdom, then the emotions and the impressions of the senses are the fertile soil in which the seeds must grow. The years of early childhood are the time to prepare the soil. Once the emotions have been aroused—a sense of the beautiful, the excitement of the new and unknown, a feeling of sympathy, pity, admiration, or love—then we wish for knowledge about the object of our emotional response."[8]

Wonder is the beginning both of knowledge and of the other attribute most necessary for stewards in our day: courage. We are not called upon to manage nature from without or above. We are invited to step back into the house of life with the heart of a child. The environmental crisis of our day is not some plague on nature from without which we need to solve with engineering expertise and a sense of noblesse oblige. It's really not nature's problem at all. The earth has found lots of ways to be, both before there were any people and today. It will continue to change after the human era is over. What we encounter is thus not some melancholy call to altruism—an unavoidable distraction from our true work. It is rather a direct threat to the members of our own household: our mother the earth; our coevolutionary brothers and sisters, the plants and the animals; the sky of our childhoods; and the forest of our dreams. We are now challenged to act on the commitments of our filial piety. And in many cases our strength will come from deep connections of wonder sponsored in our hearts while children by the company of loving and re-spectful adults. Sympathy with nature comes from turning toward, not away from, the life of the human community.

. . .

Rita and I have spent several hours working around the sugarhouse to-day. We've moved the remains of last year's wood supply out to the shed and picked up wire, plastic fittings, and other debris from last year's stringing of a new main line. We've also piled tarps, lanterns, and sap filters into the back of our Toyota truck for a more thorough cleaning at home. But before we drive back down Big Hollow Road to Bristol, we stroll up above the sugarhouse for a last look around. This has become traditional for us at the end of a visit. It's exciting to see the two main lines—gray and dark blue—swooping down the slope toward us, with their pale blue branch lines fanning out to either side. It looks almost like a double-boled tree, its angled branches conducting the surging life of the forest down to the hollow in the woods where the sugarhouse stands. At this hour of the afternoon we can hear the hermit thrushes begin to sing in the more distant branches that rise above our little familial enter-prise: a long tone, followed by a silvery, dying flourish, repeated in a cas-cade of different keys as the light in the forest begins to dim.

To our right and left as we look up along the branch lines are two even more mysterious presences in the forest. These are enormous, dark gray glacial boulders socketed deep into the slope. The one we see to our left, as we walk around the sugarhouse, raises a curved brow of stone that re-sembles a bluff above a strongly meandering river. It's almost the size of the sugarhouse, though inconceivably more massive. Just below it, like a sandbar in a stream, a longer, flatter rock emerges from the ferns and fungus of the hollow. Since the hill rises so steeply around it, we can climb behind the bigger erratic and walk right out onto its top. We some-times sit on that broad stone saddle and regard the sugarhouse below.

Though it's not so far away, the marked difference of elevation makes the structure look like a children's playhouse, or like the memory of an earlier life.

Today, though, we head for the other erratic. This is really a pair of stones, though they used to be one. It looks as if a huge boulder was cloven in two by an ax. Perhaps the frost, finding a purchase in some fissure of the rock, inserted its chisel tip and pried the boulder apart. The edges of division remain sharp to the touch, and the space between the two parts, though rising above my head, is a straight-walled cleft no more than ten inches across. This stone, like the ones we read about in Wordsworth, Bashō, and Silko, is a good mooring for stories—like the story of a glacier that gathered strength in Canada then forged south until, by 18,000 years ago, it overlay a vast portion of what is now the northern United States. When it finally melted out of the Northeast, about 10,000 years ago, it left behind so many tons of stone that the terminal moraine inscribed an arc encompassing all of Long Island and Cape Cod. Throughout the recovering woods of New England we come upon the places where massive boulders were deposited on their long journeys south and settled down to stay. Vermont's glacial erratics came to rest in a landscape devoid of trees. Around them an early arctic community of willows and spruces sprang up, then gradually gave way to the present mixed northern hardwood forest. While deforestation has twice exposed them to the sunlight again, they now once more lie in the ferny shadows. Stone witnesses like these give us a gauge for our human projects in this terrain, and for the larger continuities of climate, seasons, and soil.

The massive presence of these boulders also brings to mind the Abenaki story about Gluskabe's first, unsuccessful attempt to make people. To remember such a story, while looking at this boulder in a forest where ash trees raise their straight trunks and crisply ridged dark bark among the sugar maples, is to experience kinship with a people separated from us in time and culture but nonetheless present with us in this place. And then there are the stories our own family has begun mooring to these remarkable boulders: Memories of sitting on the other, nonsplit boulder or leaning against this one as we took our lunch break. Rita's and my realization that this boulder, at once double and a single whole, might be the place we want our ashes scattered when it's time for our bodies to be returned to the general fund of life. Like the tympanum at

Conques, this boulder offers us a chance to incorporate our individual lives into a larger spectacle of education and familial initiatives. Like Bashō's stone monument at Tsubo-no-ishibumi, it casts our little lives and efforts in the shade. But it also promises that something can endure for long enough amid the flux for our threads of stewardship and inheritance to be attached, for more than a single generation, to the world. The fact that this boulder, too, is on the move, and that another glaciation may return to scour away the woods and sugarhouses and villages of this landscape, helps keep our attempts at stewardship in perspective. Stewardship neither changes the larger story of this slope nor hastens by much the short-term return of the forest. Rather, it is a way of stepping into an encompassing narrative, and of participating in what Gary Snyder has called the Main Flow. Stewardship is a way to affirm the flow of the universe and to make ourselves at home.

NOTES

Prologue

1. Lewis Mumford, *The Brown Decades: A Study of the Arts in America, 1865–1895* (New York: Dover Publications, 1955), 78.

2. Henry David Thoreau, "Walking," in *The Norton Book of Nature Writing*, College Edition, ed. Robert Finch and John Elder (New York: W. W. Norton, 2002), 180.

3. David Lowenthal, *George Perkins Marsh: Prophet of Conservation* (Seattle: University of Washington Press, 2000), 369. I am indebted throughout this project to David Lowenthal—for his masterful study of Marsh, his authoritative edition of *Man and Nature*, his generous conversation, and his help in identifying the principal Marsh archives and collections.

4. George Perkins Marsh, *Man and Nature, Or, Physical Geography as Modified by Human Nature*, ed. David Lowenthal, Weyerhaeuser Environmental Classics (Seattle: University of Washington Press, 2003), 43.

5. Marsh, *Man and Nature*, 279, 280.

6. Wendell Berry, "Conservation Is Good Work," in *Wild Earth: Wild Ideas for a World Out of Balance*, ed. Tom Butler (Minneapolis: Milkweed Editions, 2002), 148.

7. Aldo Leopold, *A Sand County Almanac and Sketches Here and There* (New York: Oxford University Press, 1987), 30.

1. Marrying the Map

1. Joan Chittister, *Heart of Flesh: A Feminist Spirituality for Women and Men* (Grand Rapids, MI: Eerdman's, 1998), 160.

2. Lowenthal, *George Perkins Marsh*, 37.

3. I would like to express my gratitude to Sheila Connor of the Arnold Arboretum for locating this letter, as well as to David Lowenthal for donating the Caroline Crane Marsh papers to the Special Collections at the University of Vermont.

4. Charlene Spretnak, *The Resurgence of the Real: Body, Nature, and Place in a Hypermodern World* (Reading, MA: Addison-Wesley, 1997), 35.

5. Robert Frost, "Directive," in *The Poetry of Robert Frost* (New York: Henry Holt, 1979), 377.

2. Headwaters

1. Zadock Thompson, *Natural History of Vermont* (1853; repr., Rutland, VT: Charles E. Tuttle, 1972).

2. Marsh, *Man and Nature*, 38, 39.

3. Ibid., 39–41, n. 36.

4. William Cronon, foreword to Lowenthal, *George Perkins Marsh*, xi.

5. Mumford, *The Brown Decades*, 72.

6. Marsh, *Man and Nature*, 35.

7. Dante, *The Divine Comedy, Purgatorio*, vol. 1, trans. Charles Singleton (Princeton: Princeton University Press, 1973), 143.

8. Dante Alighieri, *Tutte le opere*, ed. Luigi Blasucci (Florence: Sansoni, 1965), 341 ("florentinus natione non moribus").

9. Lowenthal, *George Perkins Marsh*, 366.

10. Sayers quoted in Mark Musa's introduction to his translation of Dante's *Inferno* (New York: Penguin, 1984), 53.

11. An interesting sidelight on these affinities between the two writers comes from George Perkins Marsh's handwritten list of books in his library. This inventory, now held in the Special Collections of University of Vermont's Bailey-Howe Library, reveals that Marsh owned five different sets of the *Divina commedia* in Italian.

12. Robinson Jeffers, *The Selected Poetry of Robinson Jeffers* (New York: Random House, 1938), 262.

13. The concept of "the middle landscape" is developed in Nora Mitchell and Rolf Diamant's essay "Stewardship and Sustainability: Lessons from the 'Middle Landscape' of Vermont," in *Wilderness Comes Home: Rewilding the Northeast*, ed. Christopher McGrory Klyza (Hanover, NH: University Press of New England for Middlebury College Press, 2001). The authors write,

The long-settled landscape of Mount Tom has been described as the humanized landscape—the ecotone where civilization and wilderness meet. These are lands that have long had a human imprint, areas traditionally used for agriculture and forestry or developed as towns and cities. These areas have been given various names—nonwildlands, cultural landscapes, working landscapes, or protected landscapes. In this chapter, we will use the term "middle landscape." This middle landscape traditionally has not received great attention from the conservation community. Yet the middle landscape provides a vital connection between remote areas of wilderness and the places where most people live and work. In the middle landscape, we have an opportunity to sustain and cultivate knowledge of wildness close to home and to explore the relationship with more remote wilderness. This ecotone landscape is also the place where we can learn to live on the land in a sustainable way. (216)

14. Robert P. McIntosh, *The Background of Ecology: Concept and Theory* (Cambridge: Cambridge University Press, 1985), 2.

15. Marsh, *Man and Nature*, 96.

16. Lowenthal, *George Perkins Marsh*, 239–41.

17. Marsh, *Man and Nature*, 190.

18. Frederick Law Olmsted, "Report on the Management of Yosemite, 1865 or THE YOSEMITE VALLEY AND THE MARIPOSA BIG TREE GROVE," in *America's National Park System: The Critical Documents*, ed. Lary M. Dilsaver, http://www.cr.nps.gov/history (accessed November 30, 2005).

19. Mumford, *The Brown Decades*, 79.

20. Rolf Diamant, conversation with the author, July 2002.

21. Paul Bray, "The Abruzzo and the Adirondack," *Sanctuary* 38, no. 1 (September/October 1998): 14.

22. Mauro Agnoletti, "Monks, Foresters, and Ecology: Silver Fir in Tuscany from XIV to XX Century," in *Le sapin: Enjeux anciens, enjeux actuels*, ed. Andrée Corvol (Paris: L'Harmattan, 2001), 192. My general summary of transformations in the Vallombrosa forest also comes from this survey by Agnoletti.

23. Aldo Leopold, *A Sand County Almanac*, 203.

24. Lowenthal, *George Perkins Marsh*, 366.

25. Lowenthal, *George Perkins Marsh*, 339.

26. Frost, *Poetry*, 379.

3. Compatriots

1. Wendell Berry, *Collected Poems, 1957–1982* (New York: North Point Press, 1994), 151.

2. Antonio Gabrielli, "The Forest before Silviculture," in *The Forest and Man*, ed. Orazio Ciancio (Florence: Accademia Italiana di Scienze Forestal, 1997), 117. In addition to Agnoletti's previously cited essay in *Le sapin*, he, Bronzi, and Gabrielli have all contributed essays on the history of Vallombrosa's forest to *L'Italia Forestale e Montana*, 55, no. 6 (December 2000). Another historical overview is provided by Donald P. Duncan in "Forest Practice at Vallombrosa in Central Italy," *Journal of Forestry* 44 (1946): 347–53.

3. Ernesto Allegri, *Index Plantarum Vallis Umbrosae*, extract from vol. 1 (1970) of *Annali Dell'Istituto Sperimentale per la Selvicoltura Arezzo*, 40.

4. Letter to C. S. Sargent from Vallombrosa, July 20, 1882, as transcribed by Caroline Crane Marsh and read in the Special Collections of University of Vermont's Bailey-Howe Library. Also cited in Lowenthal, *George Perkins Marsh*, 369.

5. Caroline Crane Marsh's Memoir of G. P. Marsh, manuscript in University of Vermont's Bailey-Howe Library. See discussion of watersheds in Lowenthal, *George Perkins Marsh*, 344.

6. William Wordsworth, *Selected Poems and Prefaces*, ed. Jack Stillinger (Boston: Houghton Mifflin, 1965), 346.

7. John Milton, *Paradise Lost*, Book I, lines 300–304, ed. Merritt Y. Hughes (New York: Odyssey Press, 1935), 19.

8. Edward Chaney, "Milton's Visit to Vallombrosa: A Literary Tradition" (1991), in his *The Evolution of the Grand Tour: Anglo-Italian Cultural Relations since the Renaissance* (London: Frank Cass, 1998), 278–313. Cited in Lowenthal, *George Perkins Marsh*, 528, n. 103.

9. Milton, *Paradise Lost*, Book I, lines 286–91.

10. Eva Sanders, Indiana University, e-mail message to author, February 2001.

4. Saint Beech

1. Two of my sources of information about the life and legends of San Giovanni Gualberto were guidebooks purchased at the Abbey: *L'Abbazia di Vallombrosa* (Edizioni Vallombrosa, 1998) and *Conoscere Vallombrosa: Guida alle cappelle* (Edizioni Vallombrosa, 1996). A third was *Alle origini di Vallombrosa: Giovanni Gualberto nella societa dell'XI secolo*, ed. Giovanni Spinelli and Giustino Rossi (Novara: Europia, 1984). This collection of historical essays includes lives of the saint by Andrea di Strumi and an anonymous disciple. In Strumi's narrative, I was interested to find a claim about the holy beech getting its leaves earlier than all the other trees which paralleled Leonardo's statement to us: "A riprova infatti della sua vita veneranda, Dio, creatore di tutte le cose, dal suo primo arrivo fino ai nostri giorni, si degna di mostrare colà un prodigio: una pianta di faggio che domina nelle vicinanze, ogni anno mette le gemme e si reveste di foglie prima di tutte le altre piante" [In fact as a proof of its venerable existence, God, creator of all things, from the beginning to our own day, deigned to show a miracle there: a beech tree that dominates all those in the vicinity and that every year puts out its buds and opens its leaves before all the other trees] (72).

2. Conversations with my Middlebury colleague Christopher McGrory Klyza have helped me to become more aware of such corollaries to the rewilding of Vermont.

3. Antonio Gabrielli discusses a similar contrast between monastic approaches to forests, in this case between the Vallombrosians and the Calmaldoli order in Casentino, in "Le trasformazioni del paesaggio forestale in Toscano: Un tentativo

di sintesi storica," *Annali dell'Accademia Italiana di Scienze Forestali* 46 (1997): 113–17, on 128.

4. The significance of "calvario" paths in Italy was pointed out to us by the environmental historian Marcus Hall, during one of the peripatetic conversations we enjoyed with him in Italy.

5. Gary Nabhan, *Songbirds, Truffles, and Wolves: An American Naturalist in Italy* (New York: Penguin, 1993), chapter 5, "La Verna's Wounds."

6. Leslie Marmon Silko, "Landscape, History, and the Pueblo Imagination," in *The Norton Book of Nature Writing*, ed. Robert Finch and John Elder (New York: W. W. Norton, 2002), 1007.

7. Marsh, *Man and Nature*, 93.

8. Suzanne W. Simard, et al., "Net Transfer of Carbon between Ectomycorrhyzal Tree Species in the Field," *Nature* 388 (August 1997): 579–82. The precis begins, "Different species can be compatible with the same species of mycorrhyzal fungi, and can be connected to one another by a common mycelium."

9. Marsh, *Man and Nature*, 96.

10. J. Donald Hughes, *Pan's Travail: Environmental Problems of the Ancient Greeks and Romans* (Baltimore: Johns Hopkins University Press, 1994), 179.

11. Ibid., 170.

12. Ovid, *Metamorphoses*, trans. Rolfe Humphries (Bloomington: Indiana University Press, 1955), 200–204.

13. John Muir, *Nature Writings* (New York: Library of America, 1997), 473.

14. Gary Nabhan, *Cultures of Habitat* (Washington, D.C.: Counterpoint Press, 1997), 3.

15. Joseph Bruchac, *The Faithful Hunter: Abenaki Stories* (Greenfield Center, NY: Greenfield Review Press, 1988), 9, 10.

5. After Olive Picking

1. Janet Shapiro informed us that it was the Medici "who really introduced the olive into the Tuscan region where the contadini preferred to grow wheat and had to be forced into planting olives at first. This is apparently one of the reasons that they have always been pruned and kept small here so that the wheat could still be seeded underneath."

2. *Gambero Rosso*, no. 6 (1996).

3. The Slow Food Manifesto was adopted in Paris on November 9, 1989, and is reprinted on the organizational Web site at http://www.slowfood.com/principles /manifest.html (accessed November 30, 2005).

4. Simon Schama, *Landscape and Memory* (New York: Vintage, 1995), 119; Jonathan Bate, *The Song of the Earth* (Cambridge, MA: Harvard University Press, 2000), 267.

5. Linda Starke, ed., *State of the World 2002* (New York: W. W. Norton, 2002), 127–30.

6. Gary Snyder, *Turtle Island* (New York: New Directions, 1974), 34.

7. Marsh, *Man and Nature*, 187.

8. Snyder, "Entering the Fiftieth Millennium," in *The Gary Snyder Reader* (Washington, D.C.: Counterpoint, 1999), 394.

9. *L'Unità*, December 15, 1985.

6. Hunter in the Sky

1. A. R. Ammons, *Sphere: The Form of a Motion* (New York: W. W. Norton, 1974), 15.

2. Marsh, *Man and Nature*, 35.

3. Jean-Regis Harmel, *The Tympanum of Conques in Detail*, translated by John O'Callaghan OSB (St. Jean de Vedas: Collection Anais, 1998), 20.

4. Marsh, *Man and Nature*, 43.

5. Wendell Berry, *The Unsettling of America* (New York: Avon Books, 1977), 11.

6. Reflections offered by the guide who led our tour group through the caverns of Pech-Merle.

7. Frost, *Poetry*, 22, 23.

8. Hughes, *Pan's Travail*, 91. A thoughtful complication of Hughes's argument appears in Michael Williams, *Deforesting the Earth: From Prehistory to Global Crisis* (Chicago: University of Chicago Press, 2003), 95–101.

7. Gifts of Prophecy

1. The Brothers Grimm, *The Complete Fairy Tales*, introduction by Padraic Collum (Ware, UK: Wordsworth Editions, 1997), vii.

2. Charles Darwin, *The Illustrated Origin of Species*, ed. Richard Leakey (New York: Hill and Wang, 1979), 223.

3. Marsh, *Man and Nature*, 464, 465. Lowenthal points out, however, that in earlier correspondence Marsh had no difficulty answering his own question about the natural status of human beings:

> The title Marsh had first proposed was "Man the Disturber of Nature's Harmonies." His publisher, Charles Scribner, was dismayed. "*Is* it true? Doesn't man act in harmony with nature? with is laws? is he not part of nature?" "NO," retorted Marsh, "nothing is further from my belief than that man is 'part of nature' or that his action is controlled by what are called the laws of nature; in fact a leading object of the book is to enforce the opposite opinion, and to illustrate that man, so far from being, as Buckle supposes, a soul-less, will-less automaton, is a free moral agent working independently of nature." (*George Perkins Marsh*, 291)

4. Peter Fritzell has explored the complex integrity within Leopold's apparent

paradoxes. See his "Aldo Leopold," in *American Nature Writers*, ed. John Elder (New York: Scribner's, 1996), 541–45.

5. E. O. Wilson, *The Future of Life* (New York: Knopf, 2001), 22–23.

6. Eric Freyfogle, letter to author, December 14, 2001.

7. Leopold, *Sand County*, 129–30.

8. Rachel Carson, *Silent Spring* (Boston: Houghton Mifflin, 1962), 1.

9. Aldo Leopold, *For the Health of the Land*, ed. J. Baird Callicott and Eric Freyfogle (Washington, D.C.: Island Press, 1999), 219, 220.

10. Ibid., 221.

11. Callicott and Freyfogle, introduction to ibid., 7.

12. Mitchell and Diamant, "Stewardship and Sustainability," 217.

13. Marsh, *Man and Nature*, 190. Lowenthal has pointed out to me that Marsh's *Nation* articles against states' rights placed an equally strong emphasis on the need for a strong central state at *home* (e-mail message to author, fall 2003).

14. Callicott and Freyfogle, introduction to *For the Health of the Land*, 5.

15. Leopold, *For the Health of the Land*, 162, 164.

16. Ibid., 171.

17. Ibid., 168.

18. Ibid., 168.

19. George Perkins Marsh, *So Great a Vision: The Conservation Writings of George Perkins Marsh*, ed. Stephen C. Trombulak (Hanover, NH: University Press of New England, 2001), 19.

20. Carson, *Silent Spring*, 202.

21. Ibid., 175.

22. Ibid., 174.

23. Ibid., 32.

24. Ibid., 8, 9.

25. Ibid., 297.

26. Leopold, "1947 Foreword," appendix to Baird Callicott, ed., *Companion to "A Sand County Almanac"* (Madison: University of Wisconsin Press, 1987), 286. This original foreword is placed in context with a brief introduction by Dennis Ribbens. Eric Freyfogle drew my attention to it as a concise expression of Leopold's tragic vision; the use of the word "litany" to describe Leopold's catalogue of losses also comes from Freyfogle.

27. Martha Freeman, ed., *Always, Rachel: The Letters of Rachel Carson and Dorothy Freeman, 1952–1964* (Boston: Beacon Press, 1995), 249, 255.

28. Carson, *Silent Spring*, 258.

29. Ibid., 155.

30. Bill McKibben, *The End of Nature* (New York: Random House, 1989), 3.

31. Ibid., 13.

32. Stephanie Mills, *In Service of the Wild: Restoring and Reinhabiting Damaged Land* (Boston: Beacon Press, 1995), 208.

33. It's interesting to note how Jared Diamond's language evokes grieving's need for active relinquishment when he sums up his "reasons for hope" in the conclusion of *Collapse* (New York: Viking, 2005). After so many striking profiles of societies destroyed by their profligate use of natural resources, as well as of societies that corrected their doomed practices before it was too late, Diamond writes, "The other crucial choice illuminated by the past involves the courage to make painful decisions about values. Which of the values that formerly served a society well can continue to be maintained under new circumstances? Which of those treasured values must instead be jettisoned and replaced with different approaches?" (523).

8. The Broken Sheepfold

1. Edward Hoagland, "Edward Abbey: Standing Tough in the Desert," *New York Times Book Review*, May 7, 1989, 44.

2. Lowenthal, *George Perkins Marsh*, 39.

3. Wordsworth, *Selected Poems and Prefaces*, 203.

4. Ibid., 243, 244.

5. King James Bible, Gospel according to Matthew, chapter 25, verses 29–30.

6. Wordsworth, "Michael," in *Selected Poems and Prefaces*, 146, 156.

7. For a discussion of this process of agricultural transformation, see Raymond Williams, *The Country and the City* (New York: Oxford University Press, 1973), 96–99.

8. Matsuo Bashō, *The Narrow Road to the Deep North and Other Travel Sketches*, trans. Nobuyuki Yuasa (New York: Penguin, 1966), 113.

9. Ibid., 97, 99.

10. Lowenthal, *George Perkins Marsh*, 366.

11. Wordsworth, *Selected Poems and Prefaces*, 446, 447.

12. Lowenthal notes Marsh's own "relish for hard facts" and "zest for homely details" (*George Perkins Marsh*, 311).

13. Robert Hass, ed., *The Essential Haiku* (New York: Ecco Press, 1994), 38.

14. Bashō, *Narrow Road to the Interior and Other Writings*, ed. and trans. Sam Hamill (Boulder, CO: Shambhala, 1998), 19.

15. Reference from Professor Tom Moran, Middlebury College, Department of Chinese.

16. Frost, *Poetry*, 338.

17. Bashō, *Narrow Road to the Interior*, 31.

18. Marsh, *Man and Nature*, 187.

19. Silko, "Landscape, History," 1007.

20. Ibid., 1009.

21. Ibid.

22. Ibid.

23. Ibid., 1010.

24. Marsh, *Man and Nature*, 464.

25. Silko, "Landscape, History," 1014.

9. Mowing

1. Leopold, *For the Health of the Land*, 164.

2. Wordsworth, *Selected Poems*, 368.

3. Thoreau, "Walking," 200.

4. A groundbreaking discussion of the dialogue between conservation and literary theory was SueEllen Campbell's "The Land and Language of Desire: Where Deep Ecology and Post-Structuralism Meet," in *Western American Literature* 24 (1989): 199–211.

5. Frost, *Poetry*, 17.

6. Seamus Heaney, speaking in "Robert Frost," part 1 of *Voices and Visions*, videorecording (New York: New York Center for Visual History; Santa Barbara, CA: Annenberg/CPB Project Intellimation, 1988).

7. William Pritchard and William Meredith, in "Robert Frost," *Voices and Visions*.

8. John Dewey, *Dewey on Education*, ed. Martin S. Dworkin (New York: Teachers College Press, 1959), 107.

9. Robert Faggen, in Robert Frost, *Early Poems*, ed. Faggen (New York: Penguin, 1998), 265.

10. Quoted in Hugh Kenner, *The Pound Era* (Berkeley and Los Angeles: University of California Press, 1971), 121.

11. Anne Ferry, "Frost's 'Land of the Golden Treasury,'" in *Under Criticism: Essays for William H. Pritchard*, ed. David Sofield and Herbert Tucker (Athens: Ohio University Press, 1998), 249–65.

12. Kenner, *The Pound Era*, 122. The "visitor" in question was William Arrowsmith. My attention was drawn to the discussions in Ferry and Kenner by Herbert Tucker.

13. Frost, *Poetry*, 242.

14. Thoreau, "Walking," 127.

10. Dust of Snow

1. Frost, *Poetry*, 221.

2. William Cronon, "The Trouble with Wilderness; or, Getting Back to the Wrong Nature," in *Uncommon Ground: Rethinking the Human Place in Nature* (New York: W. W. Norton, 1996); Wendell Berry, "Conservation Is Good Work," 148.

3. Ibid., 204.

4. Zen Master Hakuin, "Chant in Praise of Zazen," trans. Philip Kapleau, in *Daily Chants and Ceremonies* (Shelburne: Vermont Zen Center), n.p.

5. Bashō, in *Haiku*, by R. H. Blyth (Tokyo: Hokuseido; San Francisco: Heian International, 1981), 1:89. The original characters and the transliteration are from Blyth; the translation is mine.

6. Martin Heidegger, "Building Dwelling Thinking," in *Poetry, Language, Thought*, trans. Albert Hofstadter (New York: Harper and Row, 1971), 149.

7. Stanley Cavell, "Thinking Like Emerson," in *The Senses of Walden* (Chicago: University of Chicago Press, 1992), 138. My attention was drawn to this wonderful passage by a reference in Robert Pogue Harrison's *Forests: The Shadow of Civilization* (Chicago: University of Chicago Press, 1992), 265. Reading it, I also recall Thoreau's second etymology for "sauntering": "Some, however, would derive the word from *sans terre*, without land or home, which, therefore, in the good sense, will mean, having no particular home, but equally at home everywhere" ("Walking," 180).

11. Inheriting Mount Tom

1. Esther Munroe Swift, *Vermont Place-Names: Footprints of History* (Brattleboro, VT: Stephen Greene Press, 1977), 520.

2. See Christopher McGrory Klyza and Stephen C. Trombulak, *The Story of Vermont: A Natural and Cultural History* (Hanover, NH: University Press of New England, 1994), chaps. 4 and 5.

3. Lowenthal, introduction to Marsh, *Man and Nature*, xxv.

4. Marsh, *Man and Nature*, 35.

5. Frost, *Poetry*, 348.

6. Cronon, "The Trouble with Wilderness," 69.

7. Frost, *Poetry*, 377.

8. For an overview of Billings's practice and philosophy, see Mark Madison, *Landscapes of Stewardship*, Report Commissioned by Marsh-Billings-Rockefeller National Historical Park, 1999, 22–52.

9. Leopold, *A Sand County Almanac*, 203.

10. William Wordsworth, *The Essential Wordsworth*, ed. Seamus Heaney (New York: Ecco Press, 1988), 33.

11. Leopold, *A Sand County Almanac*, 9.

12. Ibid., 16.

12. Forever Wild Again

1. It is important to acknowledge that while the forests one sees *from* Mount Tom are composed of native species, the plantation *on* that mountain contains many of the European species favored by Frederick Billings.

2. Marsh, *Man and Nature*, 235 n. 180. Lowenthal appends a note: "This was

Mt. Tom, in Woodstock, Vermont, owned in part by Marsh's father." He goes on to identify it as the site planted with Norwegian spruce, European larch, and white ash in the 1880s by Billings.

3. Frost, *Poetry*, 378.

4. Marsh, *Man and Nature*, 17, 280 n. 250.

5. Cronon, "The Trouble with Wilderness," 85.

6. Bill Devall and George Sessions, *Deep Ecology: Living As If Nature Mattered* (Salt Lake City: Gibbs Smith, 1985), 122.

7. Cronon, "The Trouble with Wilderness," 89.

8. Thoreau, "Walking," 192.

9. Keith Basso, "Stalking with Stories," in *On Nature*, ed. Daniel Halpern (San Francisco: North Point Press, 1987), 114, 113, 112.

10. Michael Shellenberger and Ted Nordhaus, *The Death of Environmentalism: Global Warming Politics in a Post-Environmental World* (New York: Nathan Cummings Foundation, 2004), 34.

13. Into the Wind

1. George Perkins Marsh, "Report, Made under Authority of the Legislature of Vermont, on the Artificial Propagation of Fish," in *So Great a Vision*, 67, 68.

2. Julie Campoli, Elizabeth Humstone, and Alex MacLean, *Above and Beyond: Visualizing Change in Small Towns and Rural Areas* (Chicago and Washington, D.C.: American Planning Association, 2002), xiii.

3. Mauro Agnoletti, ed., *Il paesaggio agro-forestale toscano: Strumenti per l'analisi, la gestione e la conservazione* (Florence: ARSIA [Agenzia Regionale per lo Sviluppo e l'Innovazione nel Settore Agricolo-forestale], 2002), 158. The original reads: "La qualità del paesaggio rappresenta infatti non solo un valore culturale ma un punto di forza del nostro sistema, riasumendo al suo interno equilibri ambientali e socio-economici frutto di un positivo rapporto uomo-natura."

14. Maggie Brook

1. Eric Sorenson, letter to author, December 15, 2002.

2. Marsh, *Man and Nature*, 258.

3. Ibid., 278–80.

4. Leopold, *For the Health of the Land*, 164.

5. Wilson, *The Future of Life*, 23.

6. Terry Tempest Williams, *Refuge: An Unnatural History of Family and Place* (New York: Pantheon, 1991), 18.

7. Barry Lopez, "Children in the Woods," in *Crossing Open Ground* (New York: Vantage, 1989), 149, 150.

8. Rachel Carson, *The Sense of Wonder* (New York: Harper and Row, 1965), 45.

INDEX

farms (*continued*)
on, 205; cross-generational transfer
of ownership of, 232. *See also* agriculture
fast food, American. *See* Slow Food
movement
Ferry, Anne, 177
"Fidele" Shakespeare, 177
field trips: reading environmental literature and, 176; Frost's "Dust of Snow"
and, 181–82
fir trees, 43, 48, 216
Fitzgerald, F. Scott, 169
floods, 84, 87, 88–90, 93, 94. *See also*
arks; disasters, ecological; Noah
Florence, Italy, 33–34, 44, 58–59, 84,
233. *See also* Arno River; olive trees of
Impruneta
footprints, ancient and modern, 116–17
Forbes, Peter, 149, 163, 182, 184, 187
Foreman, Dave, 222
"Forest, The" (Muir), 71
forest of symbols, Baudelaire on, 64–65
Forest Reserves Act (1885), 32
forestry, commitment to wilderness and,
202, 222
forests: cross-generational transfer of
ownership of, 232; as spiritual resources, 113–14; stewardship principles for health of, 134, 242–43. *See
also* forest succession; trees
Forest Service, U.S., 207–8, 212. *See also*
Pinchot, Gifford
forest succession: adventitious branches
as gauge of, 235; along Burnt Hill
Trail, 215–16; compared to revisions
in a text, 228; depicted in Pech-Merle
painted caves, 112; and human and
animal diets, 214; in Vallombrosa, 49;
in Vermont, 50, 133–34
Forest Watch, 213
"For Nothing" (Snyder), 86
For the Health of the Land (Leopold), 130,
131, 166, 242
"Fourth of July, The" (Ives), 223

Foy, Ste., 99–100, 103, 105, 107–8
France: protests against American fast
food in, 80–81; walking across, 5;
walking Grande Randonnée trail in,
15, 21–24. *See also* Conques; Lascaux;
Pech-Merle; *other specific sites*
Francis, Saint, 64
Frantoio olives, 77
Fraternal Tables, of Slow Food movement, 83
Freeman Foundation, 231
frenare, interpretation as self-control, 65
Freud, Sigmund, 26, 117–18, 121
Freyfogle, Eric, 126–27, 130
Fritzell, Peter, 44
FROC (Front de résistance à l'oppression
capitaliste), 80–81
Frost, Robert: affinities with Bashō, 157,
186; affinity with Coleridge, 176–77;
on indirect relationships or connec-
tions, 117; interpretation of poems by,
174; and literary landscape map for
Elder, 10; and nature, 177–79, 185,
195; Palgrave's *Golden Treasury* and,
177; poems citing Vermont history,
211; on postagricultural northern
New England, 167–68; sounds in poems of, 172–73. *See also* "Directive";
"Dust of Snow"; "Mowing"
fungus/fungi: collectors, in Italy, 46; importance in forests, 214; on Mount
Tom, 212
Future of Life, The (Wilson), 124–25, 244

Gabrielli, Antonio, 47, 48, 49
Galileo, 57–58
Gambero Rosso (Italian food and wine
magazine), 79
Garibaldi, Giuseppe, 39–40
Gates of the Arctic National Park, 196
*George Perkins Marsh: Prophet of Conser-
vation* (Lowenthal), 33
Giamatti, Bart, 65
"Gift Outright, The" (Frost), 195
Gilded Age: in Japan during 1600s,

responsibility: and awareness of errors and vulnerability, 164; and environmental stewardship, 207, 208; personal, and global climate change, 55
Resurgence of the Soul, The (Spretnak), 23
revolutions: as human catastrophe, 65. *See also* disasters, ecological
rewilding, in Vermont, 28–29, 63, 219, 256n2
Ricasoli, Bettino, 39
Ricci, Nanni, 82, 83–84, 88, 92
Richard, Thérèse, 2
Rilke, Rainer Maria, 185
Riserva Naturale, Vallombrosa as, 43, 61, 62, 236
risk taking, stewardship and, 208–9
rivers: Arno, 34–35, 38–39, 42–43; history in meandering of, 5–6; meandering, as pilgrimage routes, 39; Ottauqeechee, 10, 38–39, 193, 210. *See also* watersheds
Robbia, Luca della, 76
Roberts, Jeff, 82
Rocamadour, France, pilgrimage church at, 24
Rockefeller, Laurance, 192, 200
Rockefeller, Mary French, 192, 200
Rocque Saint-Christophe, La, 24–25
Romance Mountain Wilderness, Vt., 211
Roman ruins, 21
Romanticism: conservation movement as outgrowth of, 138–39; Frost as hinge between Green Mountain landscape and, 167; Marsh's relationship to, 145
roots: forest floor and, 195; intergrafting at mycorrhizal level of, 68
rural culture: Elders' commitment to, 52; maintenance of, 232

sacred groves, recognition of, 68–69
sacred sites, importance of, 91, 116
Saint Beech (Faggio Santo), 61, 70, 73, 74, 256n1
Saintes, France, pilgrimage church at, 22–23

Sand County Almanac, A (Leopold): commercial success of, 137; on ecological losses, 140, 259n26; on killing a wolf, 127–29, 130–31, 148; on land ethic, 44; on love's importance, 130; on reading history of a landscape, 203. *See also* Leopold, Aldo
Sanj sangend temple, bodhisattvas in, 113
Santiago de Compostela, Spain, pilgrimage church in, 22
Sargent, Charles Sprague, 6, 18, 50
Saul, blindness and recovery of, 129
Sayers, Dorothy, 36
scallop shells, 22–23. *See also* shells
Schama, Simon, 83
science: and balance of emotion, 247; and biodiversity preservation, 98; Carson teaching readers about, 137, 139; Leopold's knowledge of, 131; Marsh on progress and destructive land use using, 29–30; Marsh's vision of, 39; and mystical insights of Leopold and Muir, 129; prophetic conservation writers on future of, 125
Scorpio (constellation), Greek myth on, 119, 163
Scott, Bill, 55
scythes: Frost on whispering sounds of, 172–73; mowing with, 170–72, 246; as tools and symbols, 174
Sea Around Us, The (Carson), 137
seasons: compounding, historical insights and, 216–17; in Green Mountains, 195; and human and animal diets, 214; observation of, 53; rhythms and tasks of, 177, 236; within seasons, haiku and, 186
self-control, human capacity for, 65–66
self-renewal, integrity of native communities and, 130
self-willed lands, Wildlands Project on, 236. *See also* whole-landscape vision
Seneca, 68–69
sense of place, use of term, 183